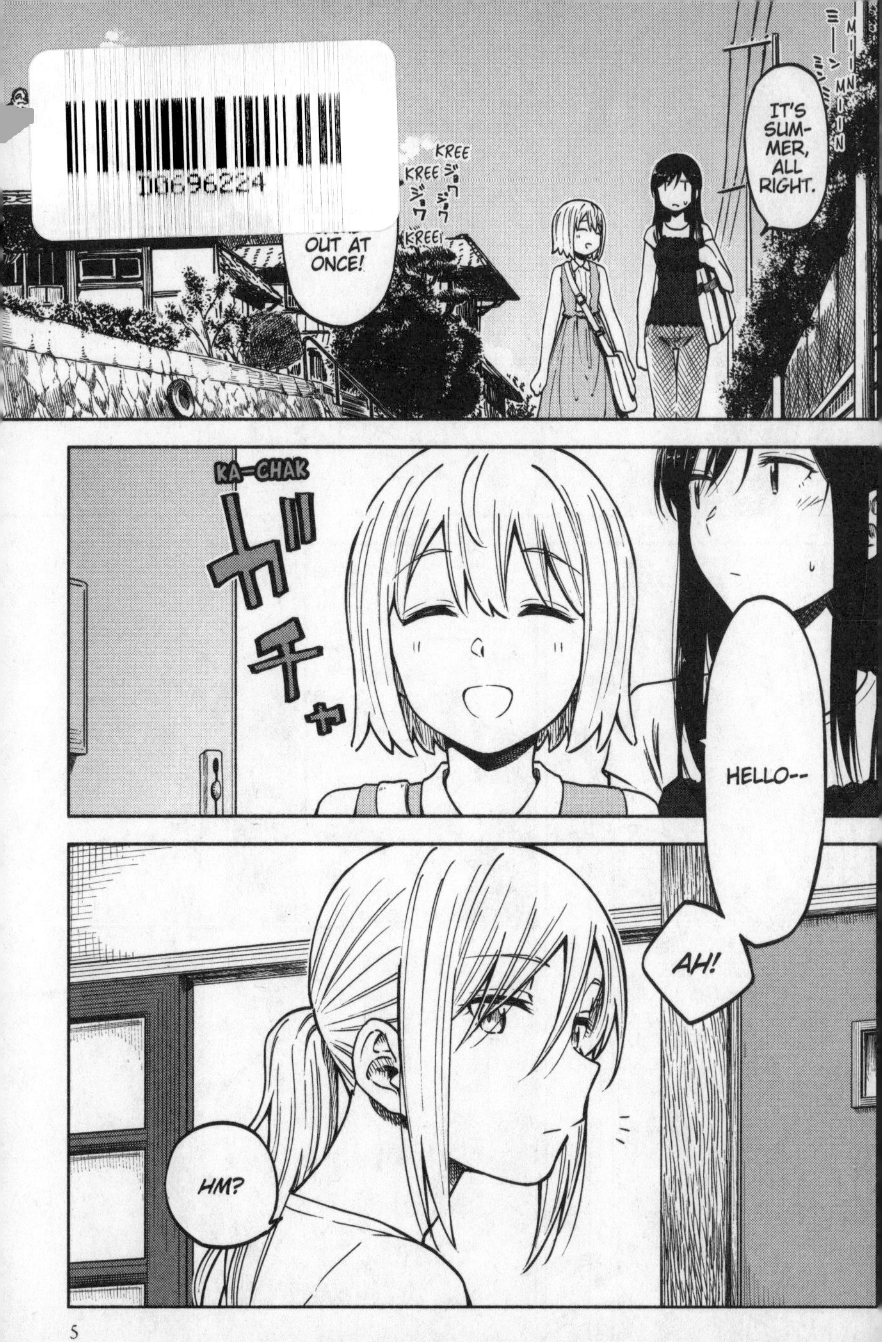
M—I—N
M—I—I—N
IT'S SUMMER, ALL RIGHT.
KREE
KREE
KREE!
OUT AT ONCE!
KA-CHAK
HELLO--
AH!
HM?

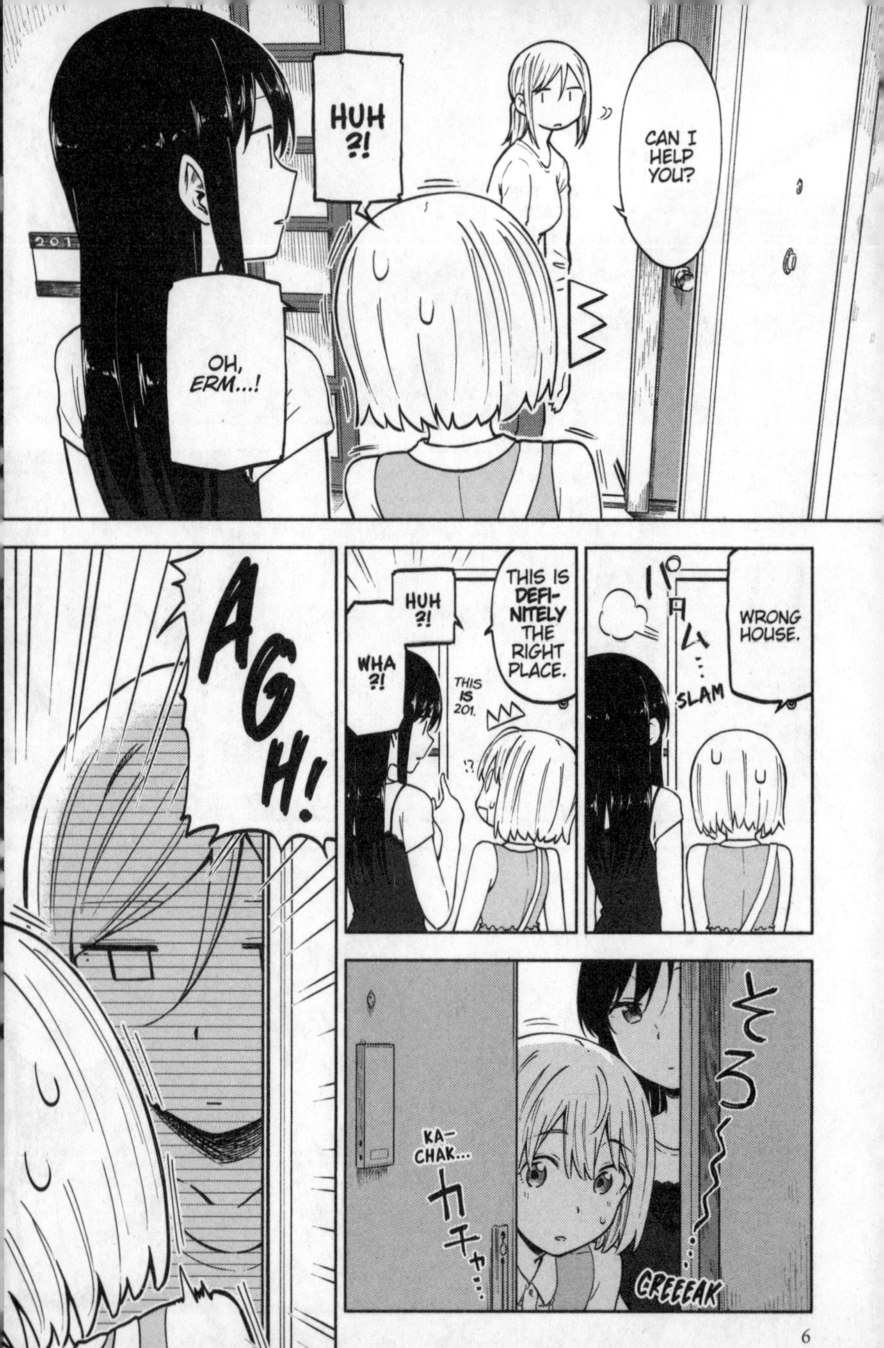
CAN I HELP YOU?
HUH ?!
201
OH, ERM...!
WRONG HOUSE.
SLAM
THIS IS DEFINITELY THE RIGHT PLACE.
HUH ?!
THIS IS 201.
WHA ?!
CREEEAK
KA-CHAK...
カチャ...
AGH!

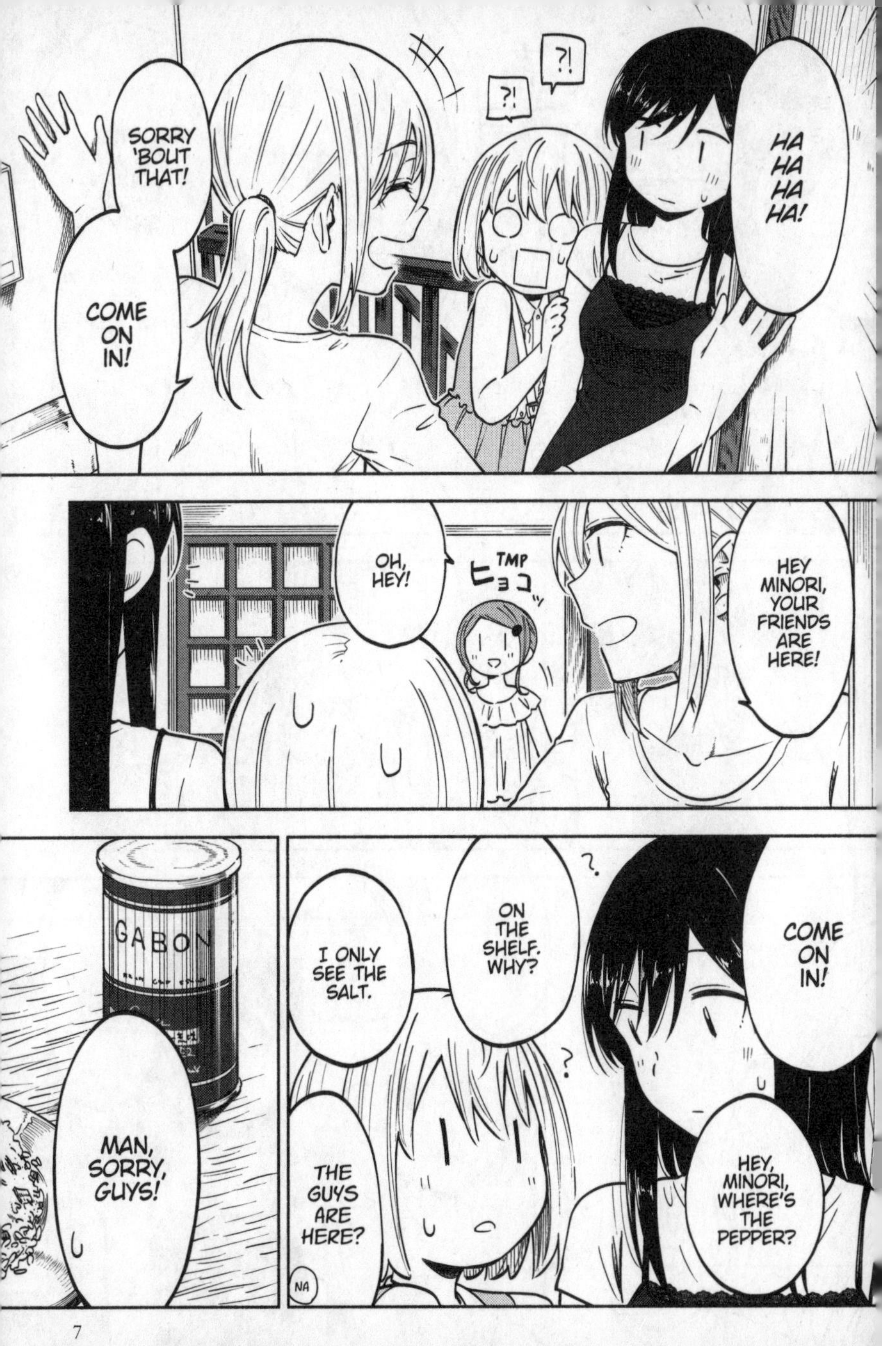
HA HA HA HA!
?!
?!
SORRY 'BOUT THAT!
COME ON IN!
HEY MINORI, YOUR FRIENDS ARE HERE!
TMP
ヒョコッ
OH, HEY!
COME ON IN!
HEY, MINORI, WHERE'S THE PEPPER?
?
ON THE SHELF. WHY?
?
I ONLY SEE THE SALT.
THE GUYS ARE HERE?
NA
GABON
MAN, SORRY, GUYS!

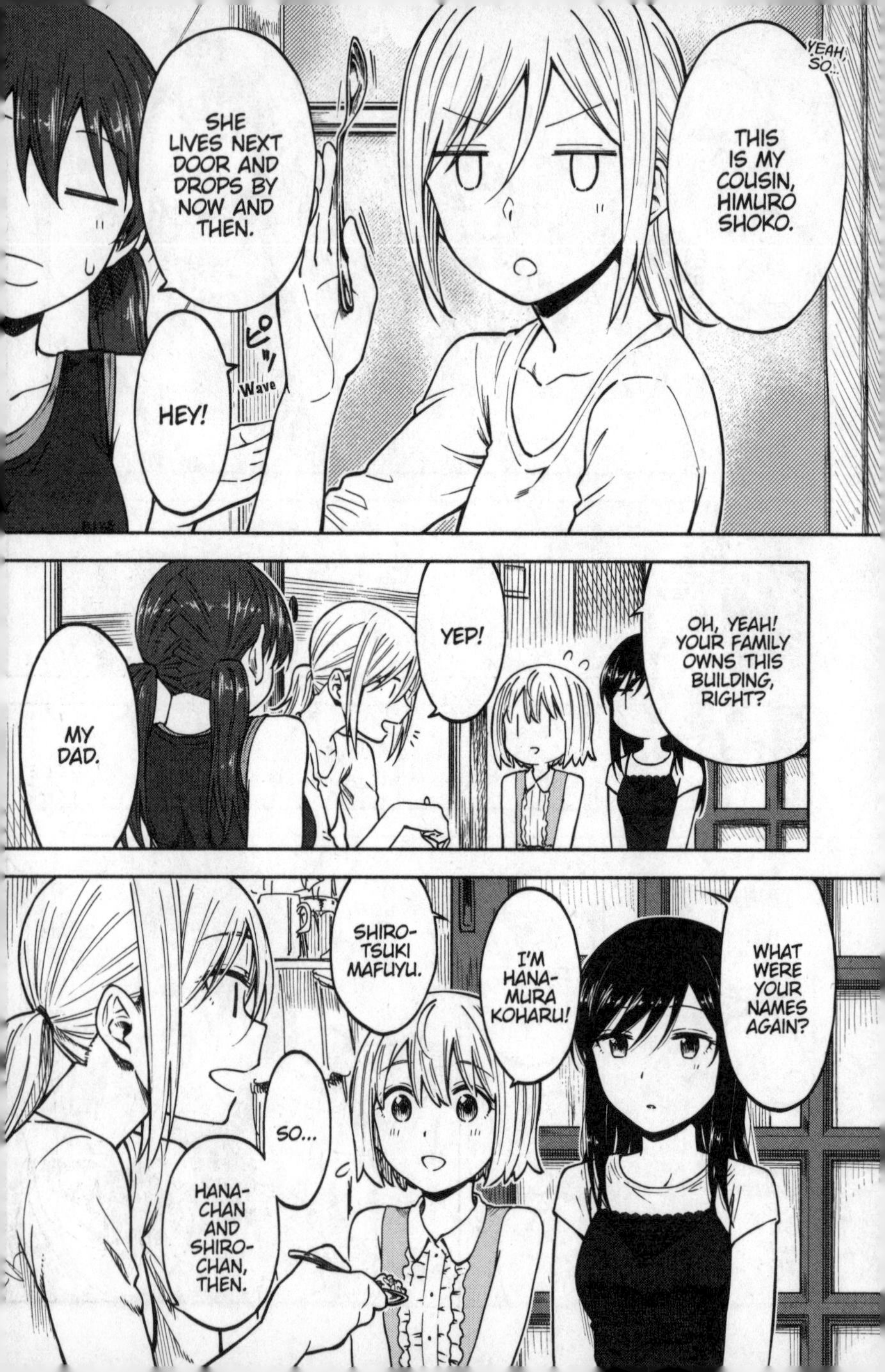
YEAH, SO...
THIS IS MY COUSIN, HIMURO SHOKO.
SHE LIVES NEXT DOOR AND DROPS BY NOW AND THEN.
ピッ
Wave
HEY!
OH, YEAH! YOUR FAMILY OWNS THIS BUILDING, RIGHT?
YEP!
MY DAD.
WHAT WERE YOUR NAMES AGAIN?
I'M HANAMURA KOHARU!
SHIROTSUKI MAFUYU.
SO...
HANA-CHAN AND SHIRO-CHAN, THEN.

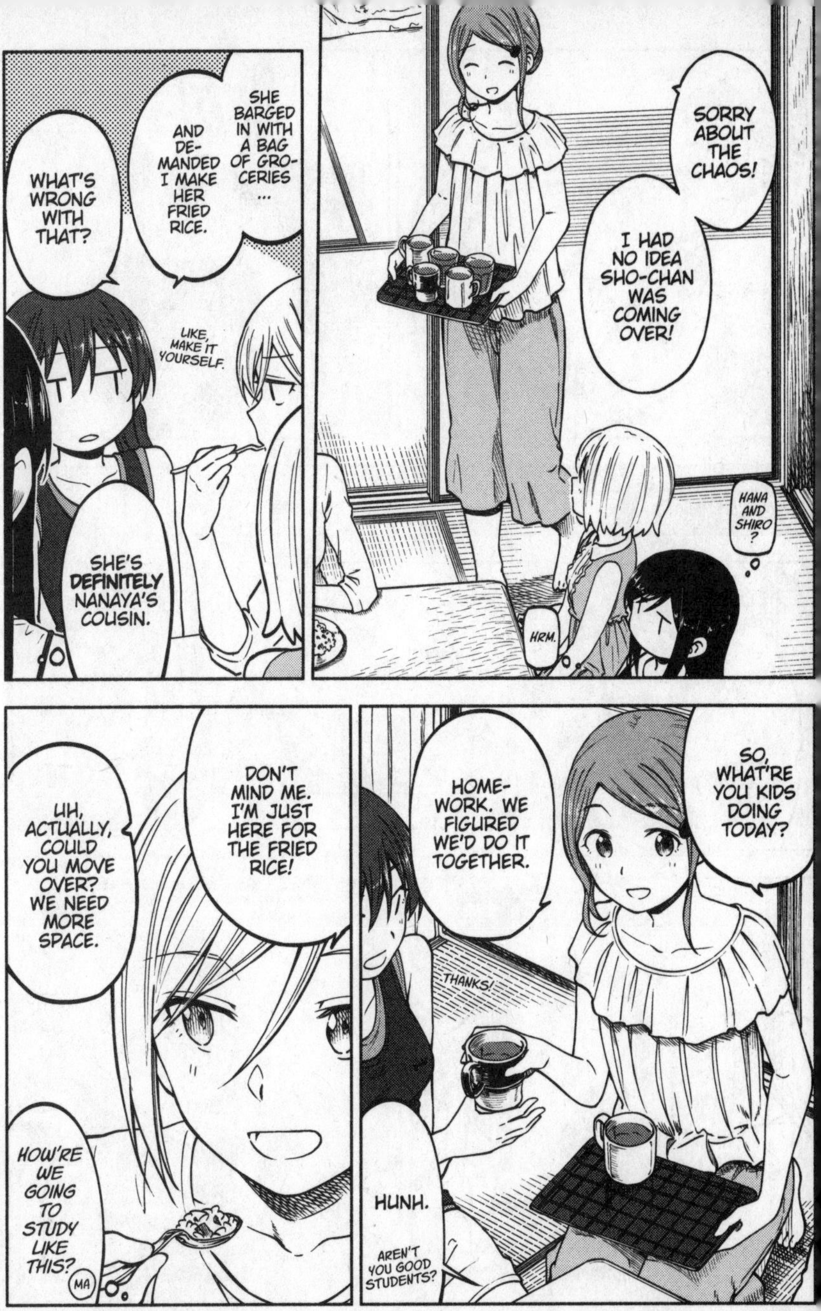
SORRY ABOUT THE CHAOS!
I HAD NO IDEA SHO-CHAN WAS COMING OVER!
HANA AND SHIRO?
HRM.
SHE BARGED IN WITH A BAG OF GROCERIES...
AND DEMANDED I MAKE HER FRIED RICE.
WHAT'S WRONG WITH THAT?
LIKE, MAKE IT YOURSELF.
SHE'S **DEFINITELY** NANAYA'S COUSIN.
SO, WHAT'RE YOU KIDS DOING TODAY?
HOMEWORK. WE FIGURED WE'D DO IT TOGETHER.
THANKS!
HUNH.
AREN'T YOU GOOD STUDENTS?
DON'T MIND ME. I'M JUST HERE FOR THE FRIED RICE!
UH, ACTUALLY, COULD YOU MOVE OVER? WE NEED MORE SPACE.
HOW'RE WE GOING TO STUDY LIKE THIS?
MA

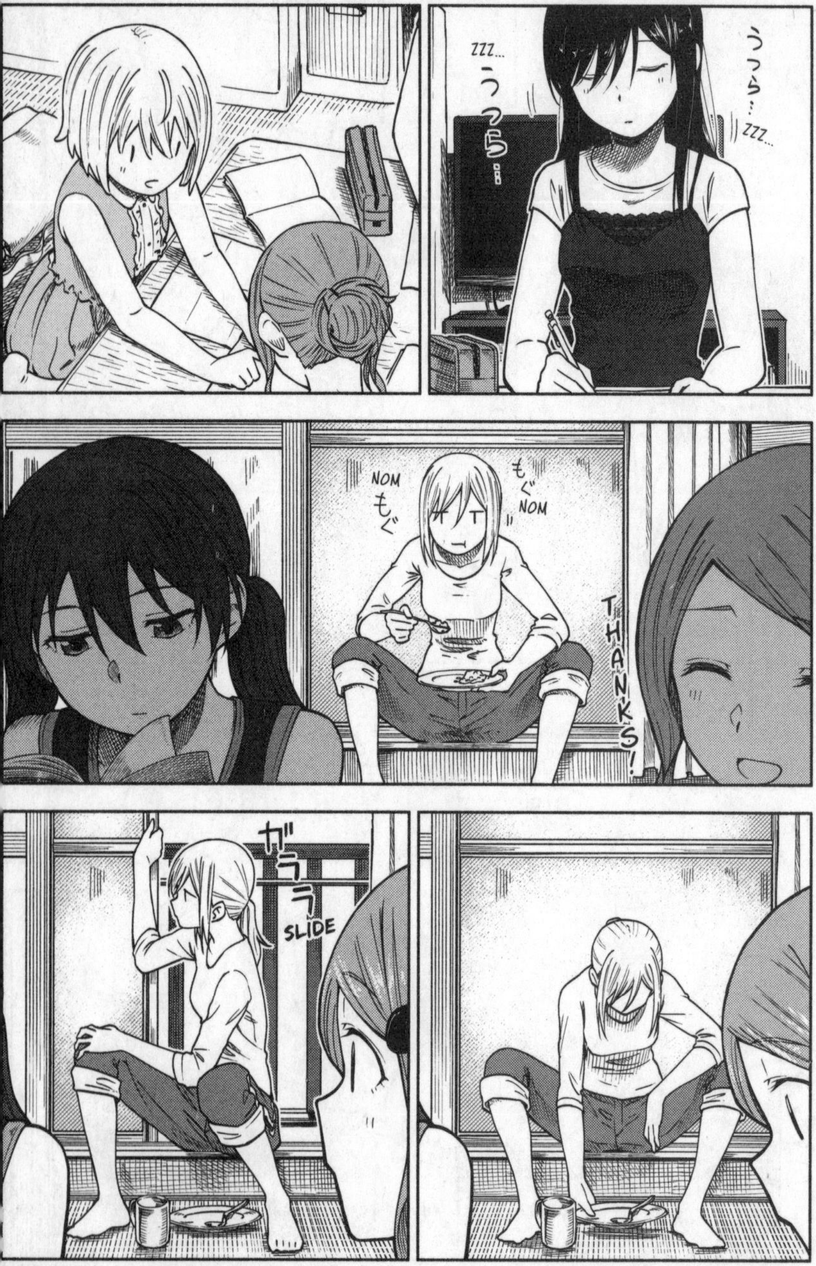
うつら… ZZZ…
ZZZ… うつら…
THANKS!
もぐ NOM
NOM もぐ
ガララ
SLIDE

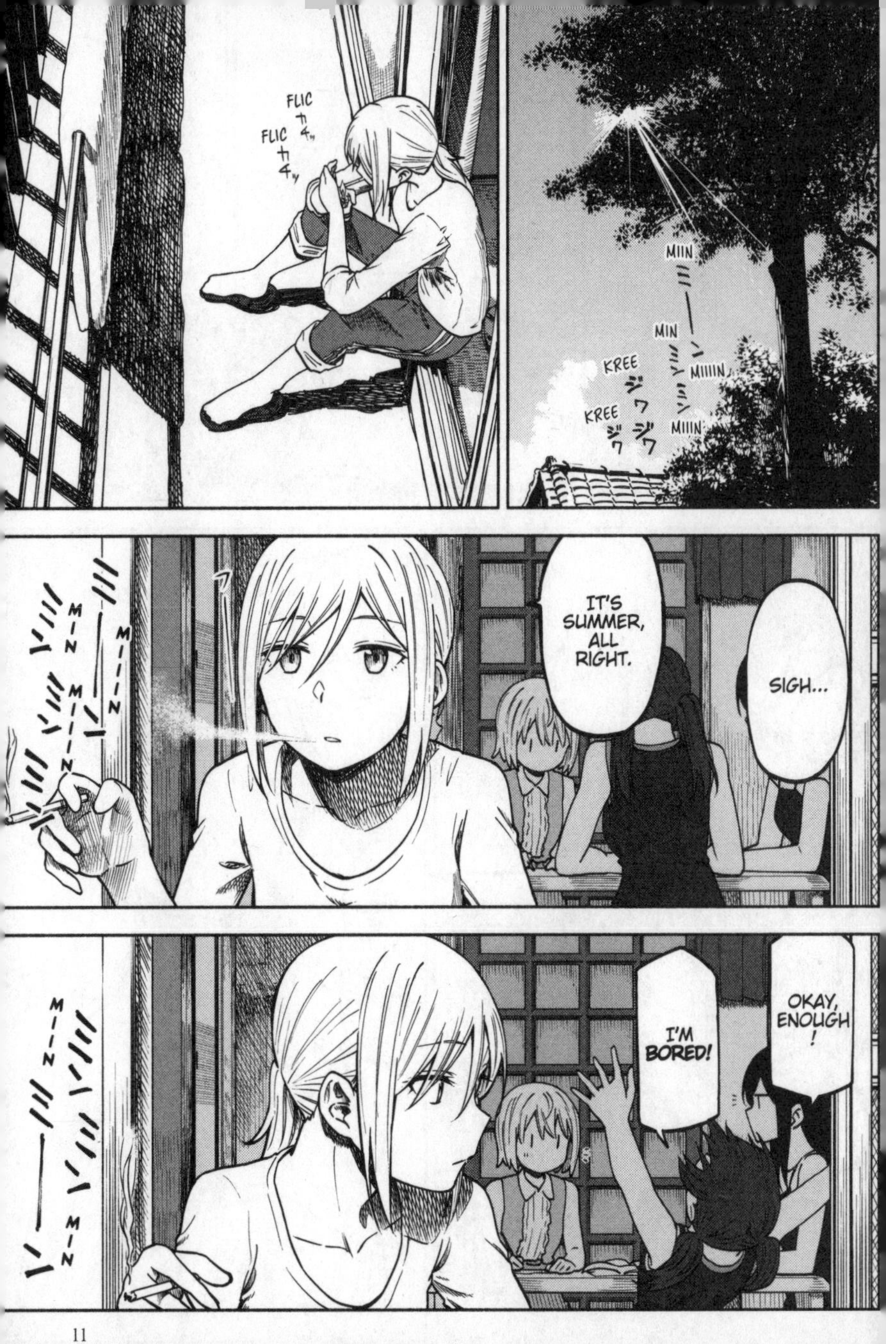
MIIN
MIN
MIIIN
MIIIN
KREE
KREE
FLIC
FLIC
SIGH...
IT'S SUMMER, ALL RIGHT.
M-I-N
M-I-I-N
M-I-I-N
OKAY, ENOUGH!
I'M BORED!
M-I-N
M-I-N

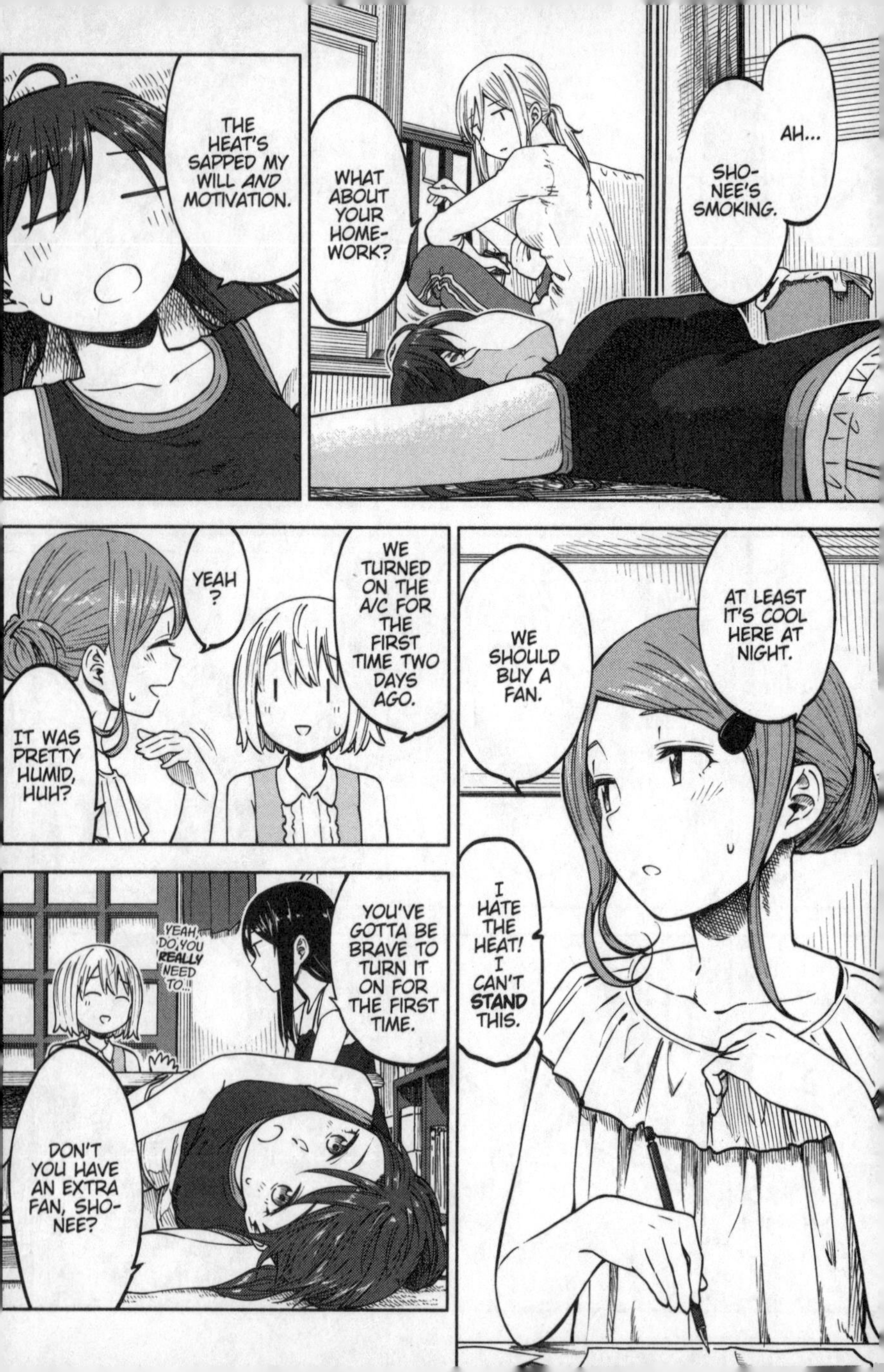
AH...
SHO-NEE'S SMOKING.
WHAT ABOUT YOUR HOMEWORK?
THE HEAT'S SAPPED MY WILL *AND* MOTIVATION.
AT LEAST IT'S COOL HERE AT NIGHT.
WE SHOULD BUY A FAN.
I HATE THE HEAT! I CAN'T **STAND** THIS.
WE TURNED ON THE A/C FOR THE FIRST TIME TWO DAYS AGO.
YEAH?
IT WAS PRETTY HUMID, HUH?
YOU'VE GOTTA BE BRAVE TO TURN IT ON FOR THE FIRST TIME.
YEAH, DO YOU **REALLY** NEED TO...!
DON'T YOU HAVE AN EXTRA FAN, SHO-NEE?

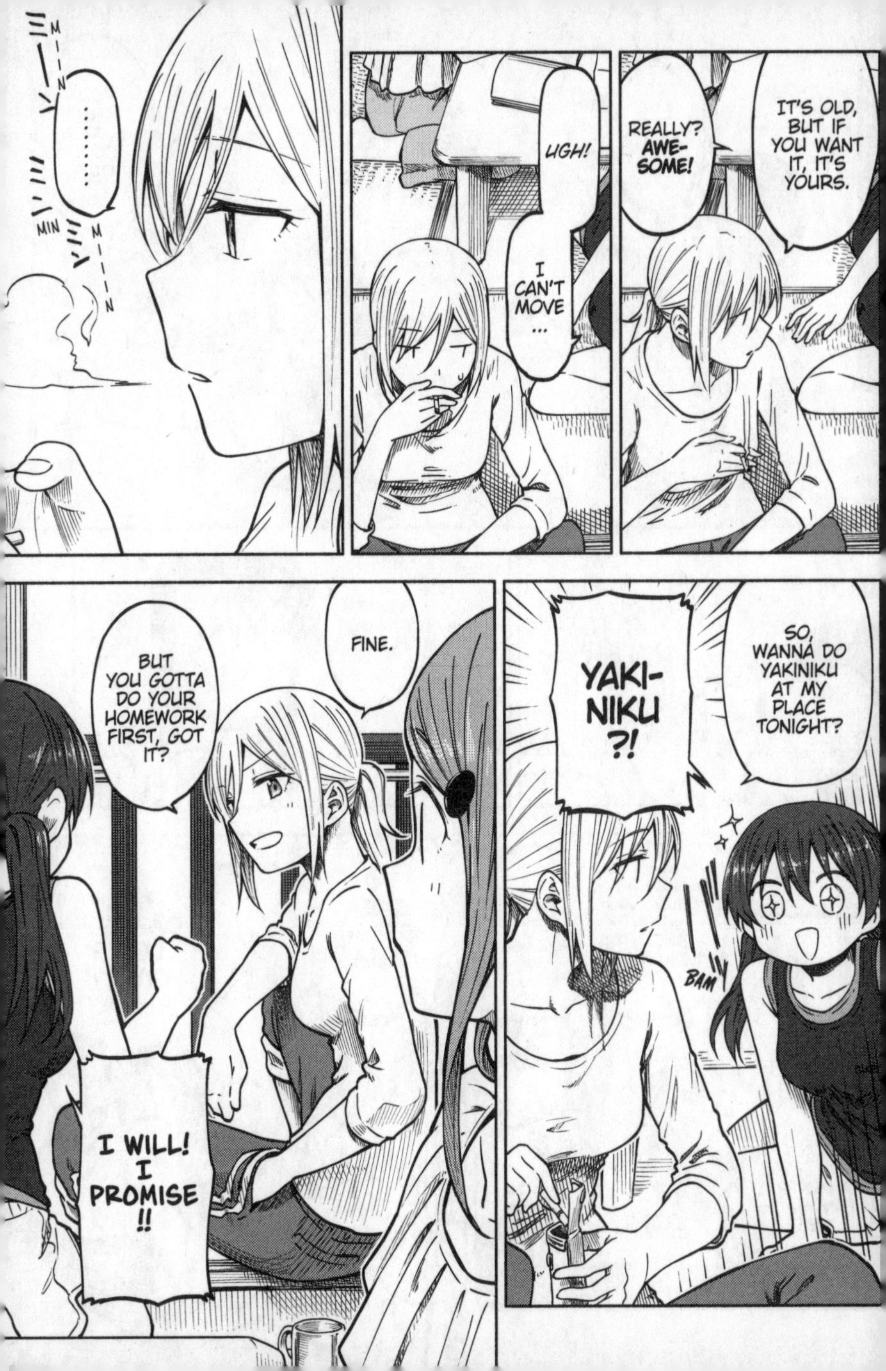
IT'S OLD, BUT IF YOU WANT IT, IT'S YOURS.
REALLY? AWE-SOME!
UGH!
I CAN'T MOVE ...
M-I-N
......
MIN
M-I-N
SO, WANNA DO YAKINIKU AT MY PLACE TONIGHT?
YAKI-NIKU?!
BAM
FINE.
BUT YOU GOTTA DO YOUR HOMEWORK FIRST, GOT IT?
I WILL! I PROMISE!!

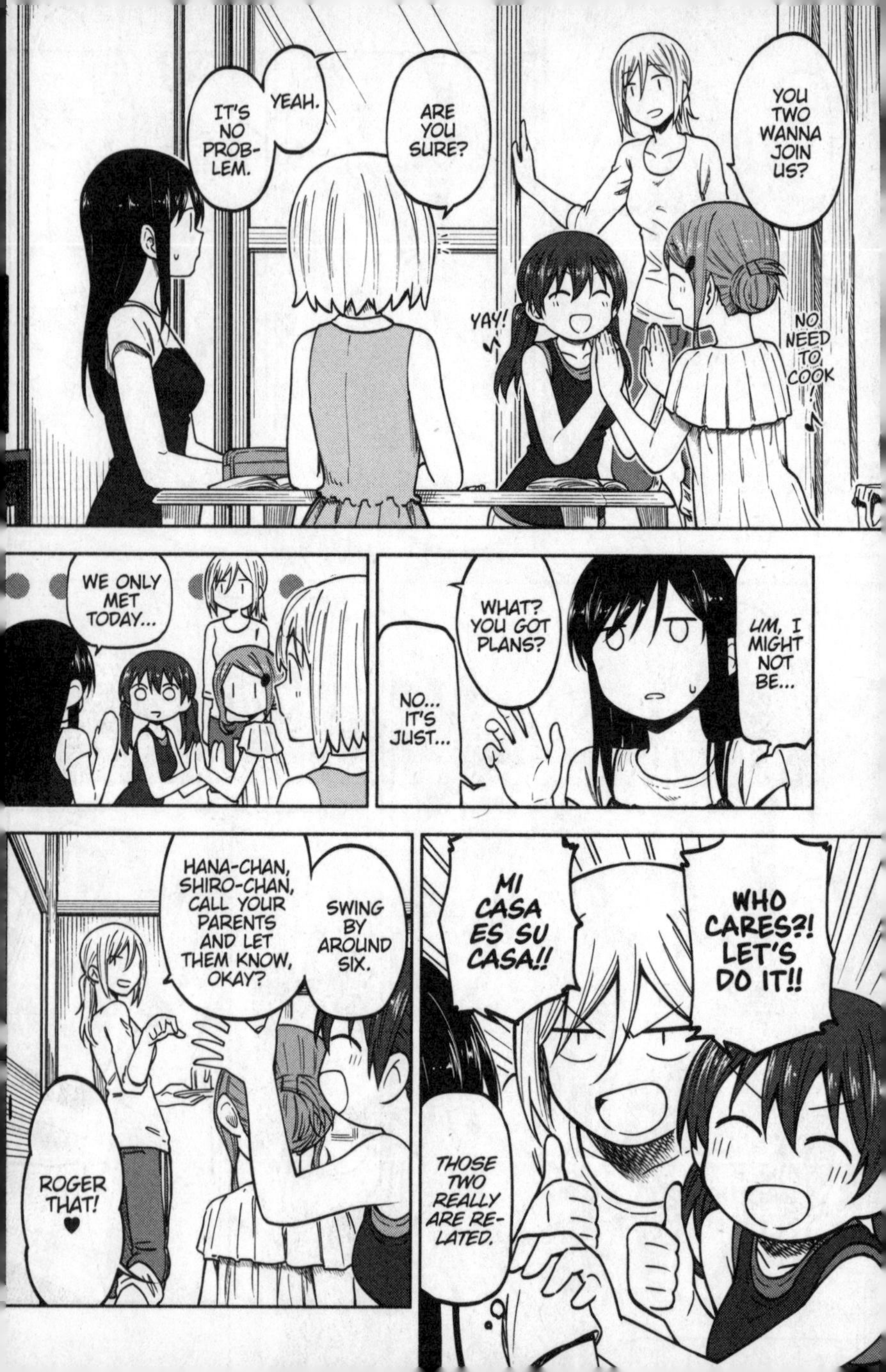
YOU TWO WANNA JOIN US?
NO NEED TO COOK!
YAY!
ARE YOU SURE?
YEAH.
IT'S NO PROB-LEM.
UM, I MIGHT NOT BE...
WHAT? YOU GOT PLANS?
NO... IT'S JUST...
WE ONLY MET TODAY...
WHO CARES?! LET'S DO IT!!
MI CASA ES SU CASA!!
THOSE TWO REALLY ARE RE-LATED.
SWING BY AROUND SIX.
HANA-CHAN, SHIRO-CHAN, CALL YOUR PARENTS AND LET THEM KNOW, OKAY?
ROGER THAT! ♥

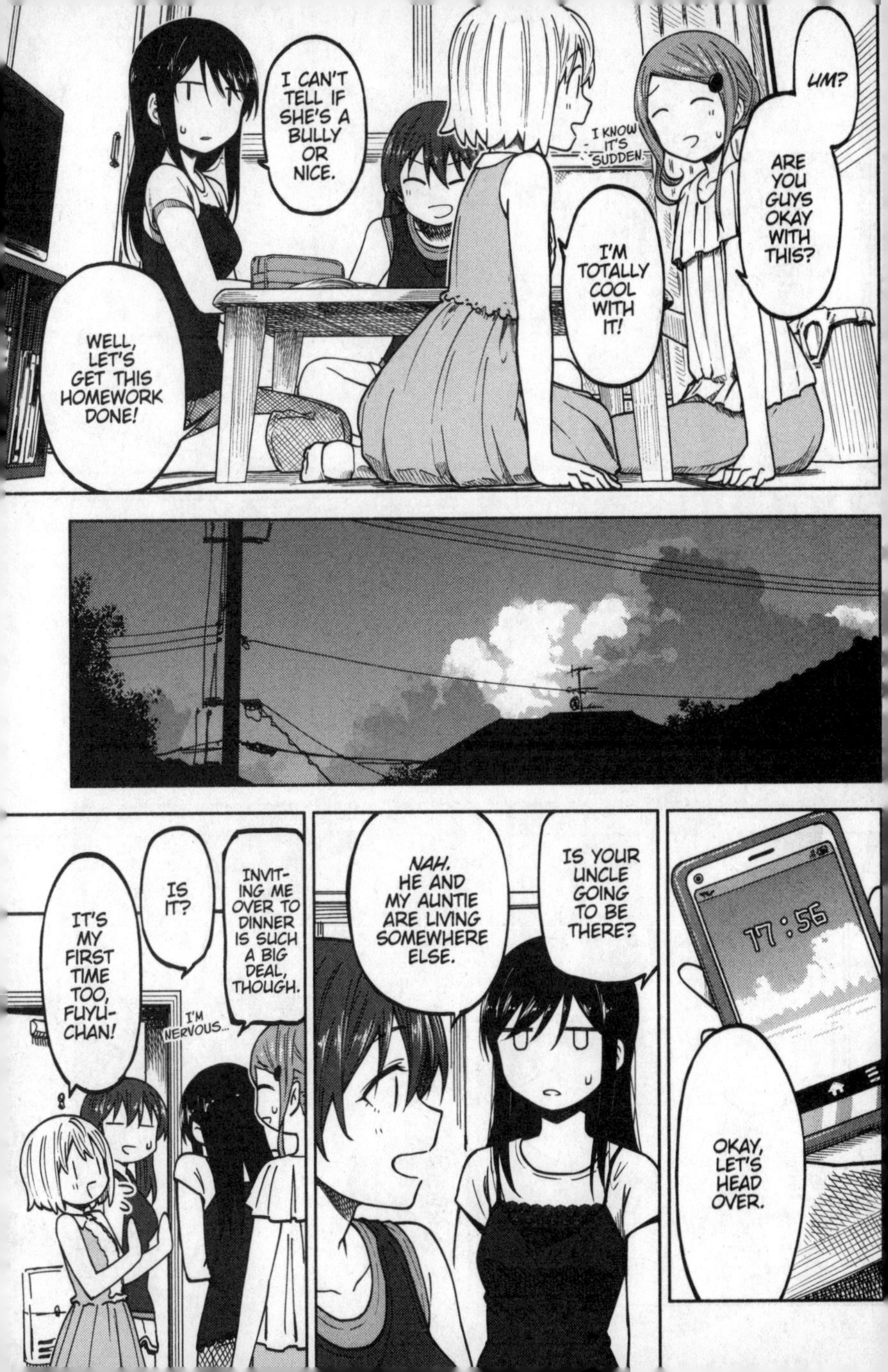
UM?
ARE YOU GUYS OKAY WITH THIS?
I KNOW IT'S SUDDEN.
I'M TOTALLY COOL WITH IT!
I CAN'T TELL IF SHE'S A BULLY OR NICE.
WELL, LET'S GET THIS HOMEWORK DONE!
17:56
OKAY, LET'S HEAD OVER.
IS YOUR UNCLE GOING TO BE THERE?
NAH. HE AND MY AUNTIE ARE LIVING SOMEWHERE ELSE.
INVITING ME OVER TO DINNER IS SUCH A BIG DEAL, THOUGH.
IS IT?
I'M NERVOUS...
IT'S MY FIRST TIME TOO, FUYU-CHAN!

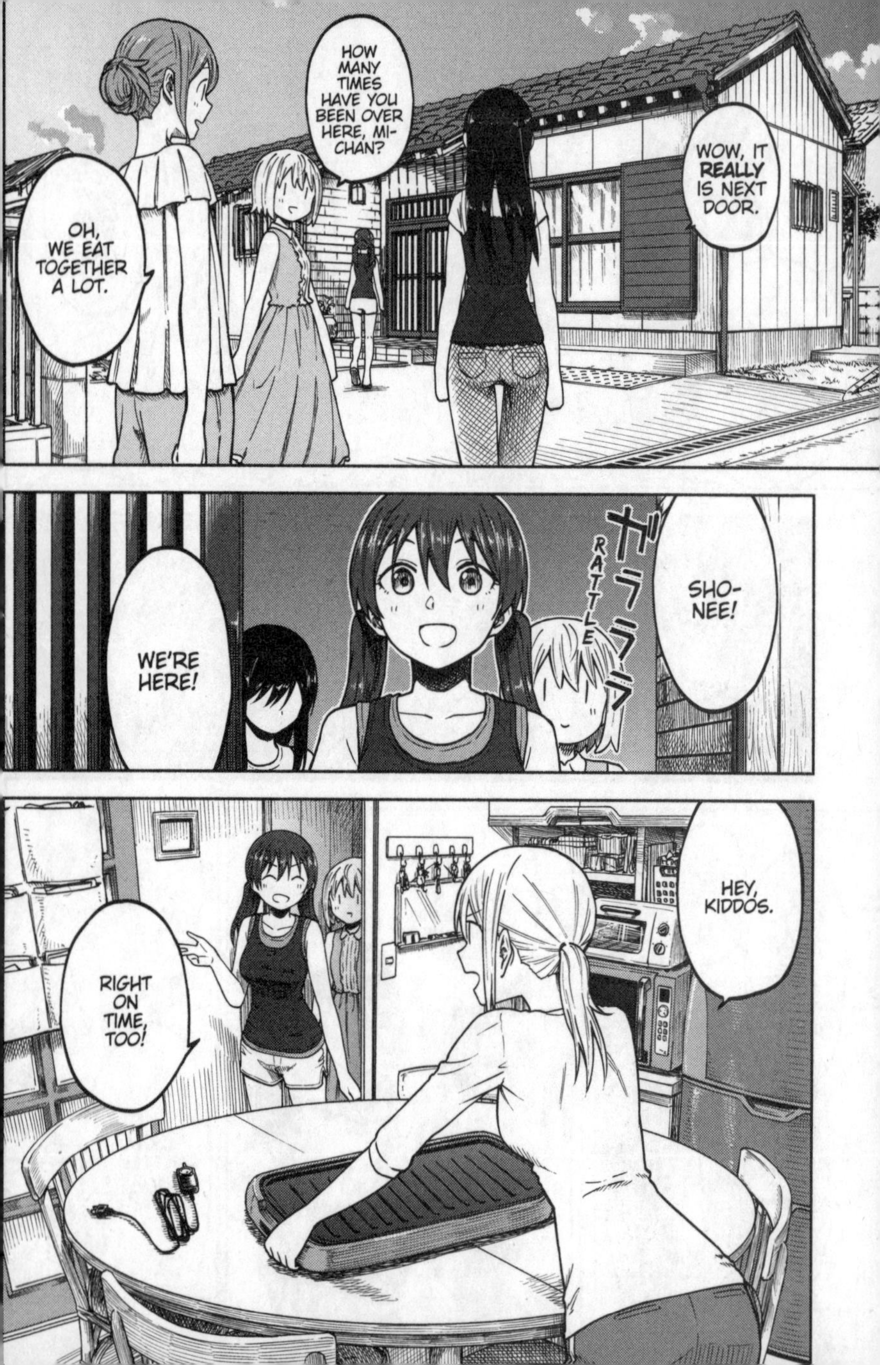
WOW, IT REALLY IS NEXT DOOR.
HOW MANY TIMES HAVE YOU BEEN OVER HERE, MI-CHAN?
OH, WE EAT TOGETHER A LOT.
SHO-NEE!
ガラララ
RATTLE
WE'RE HERE!
HEY, KIDDOS.
RIGHT ON TIME, TOO!

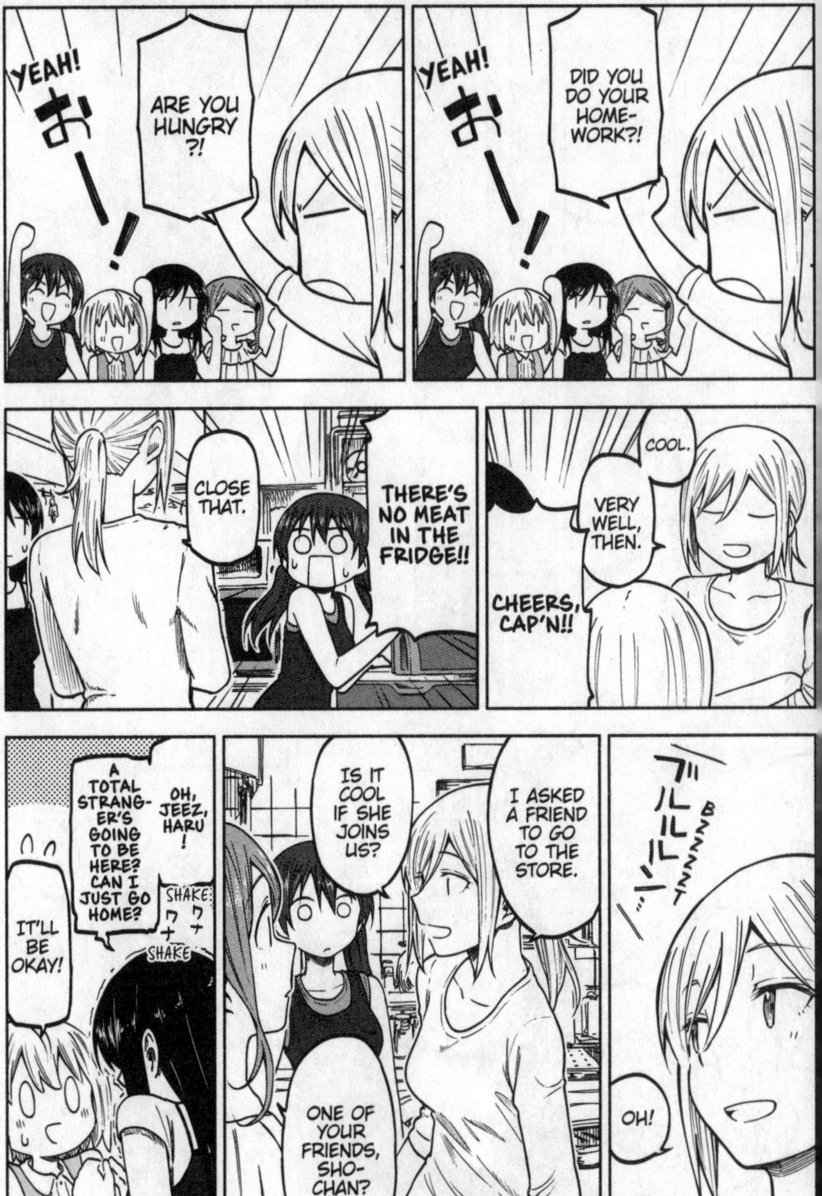

DID YOU DO YOUR HOMEWORK?!
YEAH! おー!
ARE YOU HUNGRY?!
YEAH! おー!
COOL.
VERY WELL, THEN.
CHEERS, CAP'N!!
THERE'S NO MEAT IN THE FRIDGE!!
CLOSE THAT.
ブルルル…
BZZZZZT
OH!
I ASKED A FRIEND TO GO TO THE STORE.
IS IT COOL IF SHE JOINS US?
ONE OF YOUR FRIENDS, SHO-CHAN?
OH, JEEZ, HARU!
A TOTAL STRANGER'S GOING TO BE HERE? CAN I JUST GO HOME?
SHAKE ワナ ワナ SHAKE
IT'LL BE OKAY!

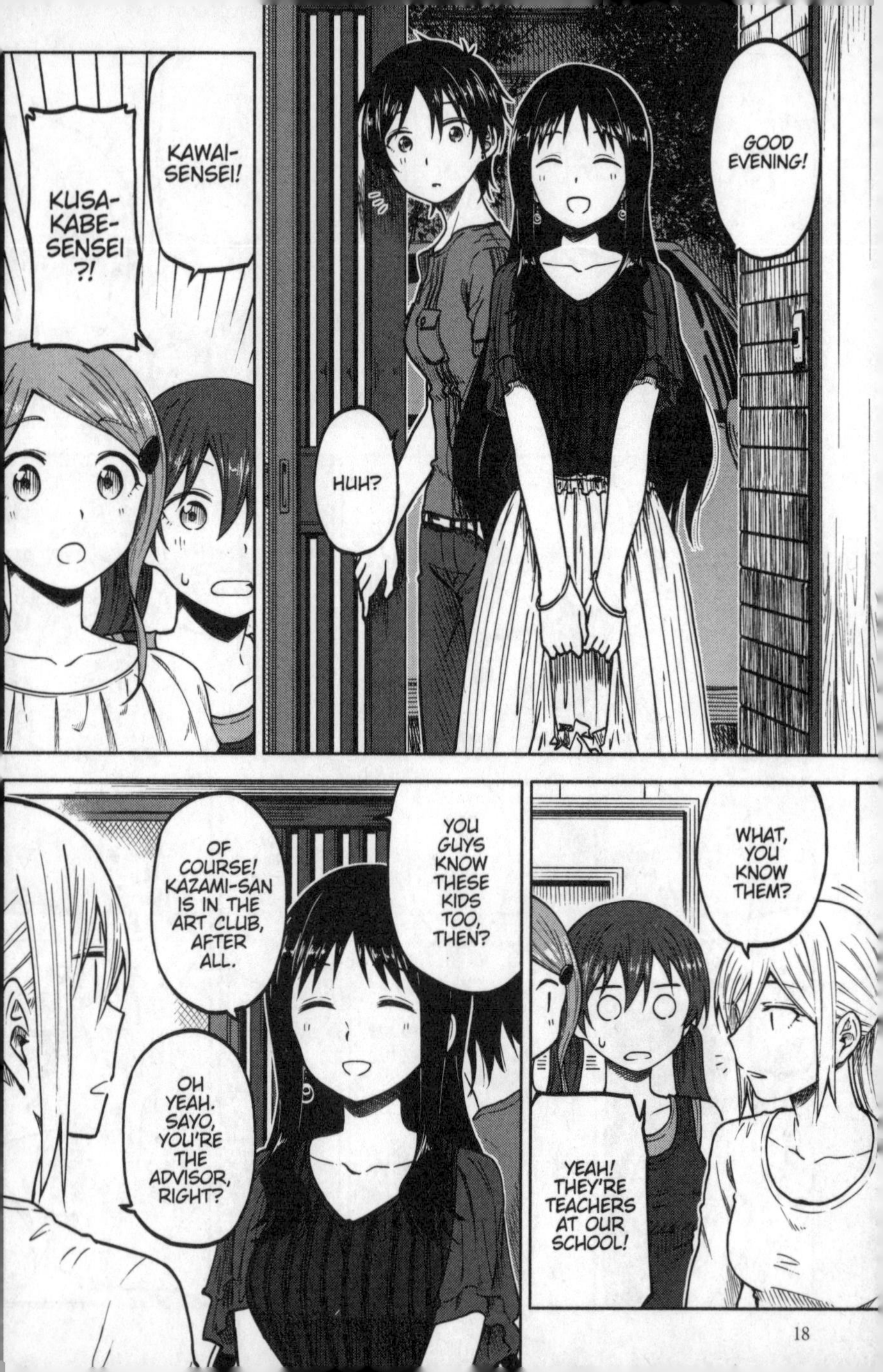
GOOD EVENING!
HUH?
KAWAI-SENSEI!
KUSA-KABE-SENSEI?!
WHAT, YOU KNOW THEM?
YEAH! THEY'RE TEACHERS AT OUR SCHOOL!
YOU GUYS KNOW THESE KIDS TOO, THEN?
OF COURSE! KAZAMI-SAN IS IN THE ART CLUB, AFTER ALL.
OH YEAH. SAYO, YOU'RE THE ADVISOR, RIGHT?

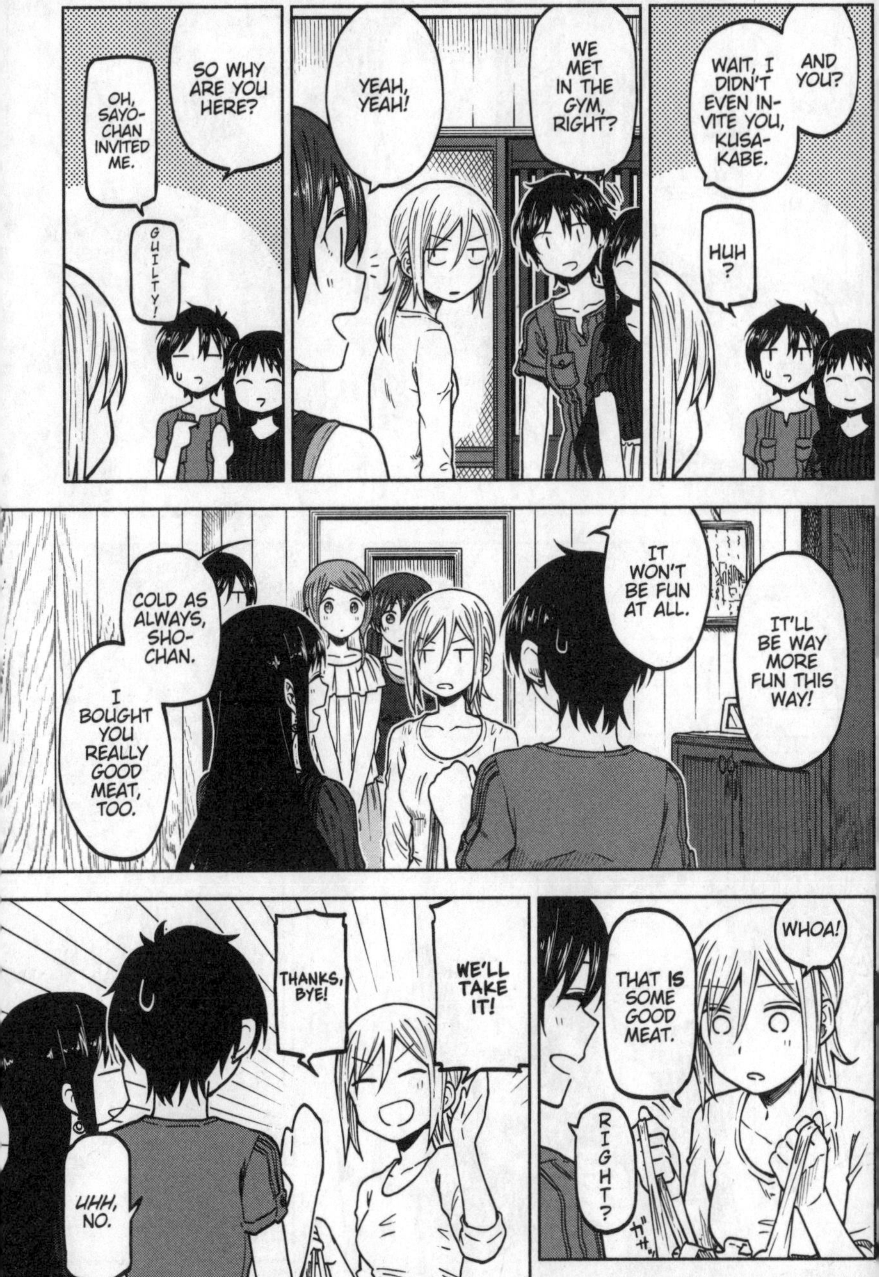
AND YOU?
WAIT, I DIDN'T EVEN INVITE YOU, KUSAKABE.
HUH?
WE MET IN THE GYM, RIGHT?
YEAH, YEAH!
SO WHY ARE YOU HERE?
OH, SAYO-CHAN INVITED ME.
GUILTY!
IT'LL BE WAY MORE FUN THIS WAY!
IT WON'T BE FUN AT ALL.
COLD AS ALWAYS, SHO-CHAN.
I BOUGHT YOU REALLY GOOD MEAT, TOO.
WHOA!
THAT IS SOME GOOD MEAT.
RIGHT?
WE'LL TAKE IT!
THANKS, BYE!
UHH, NO.

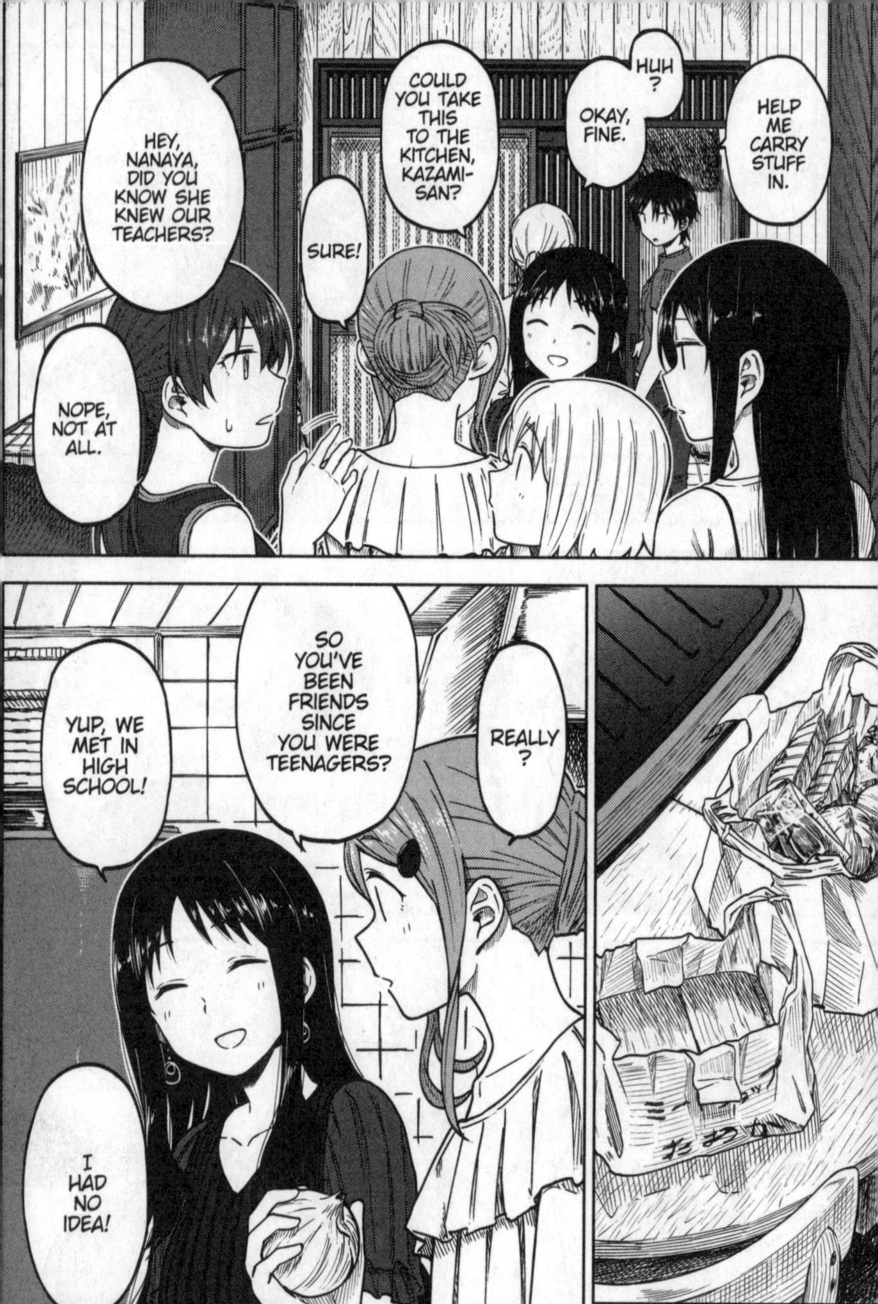
HELP ME CARRY STUFF IN.
HUH?
OKAY, FINE.
COULD YOU TAKE THIS TO THE KITCHEN, KAZAMI-SAN?
SURE!
HEY, NANAYA, DID YOU KNOW SHE KNEW OUR TEACHERS?
NOPE, NOT AT ALL.
REALLY?
SO YOU'VE BEEN FRIENDS SINCE YOU WERE TEENAGERS?
YUP, WE MET IN HIGH SCHOOL!
I HAD NO IDEA!

Bag: Taoka's Meat Shop

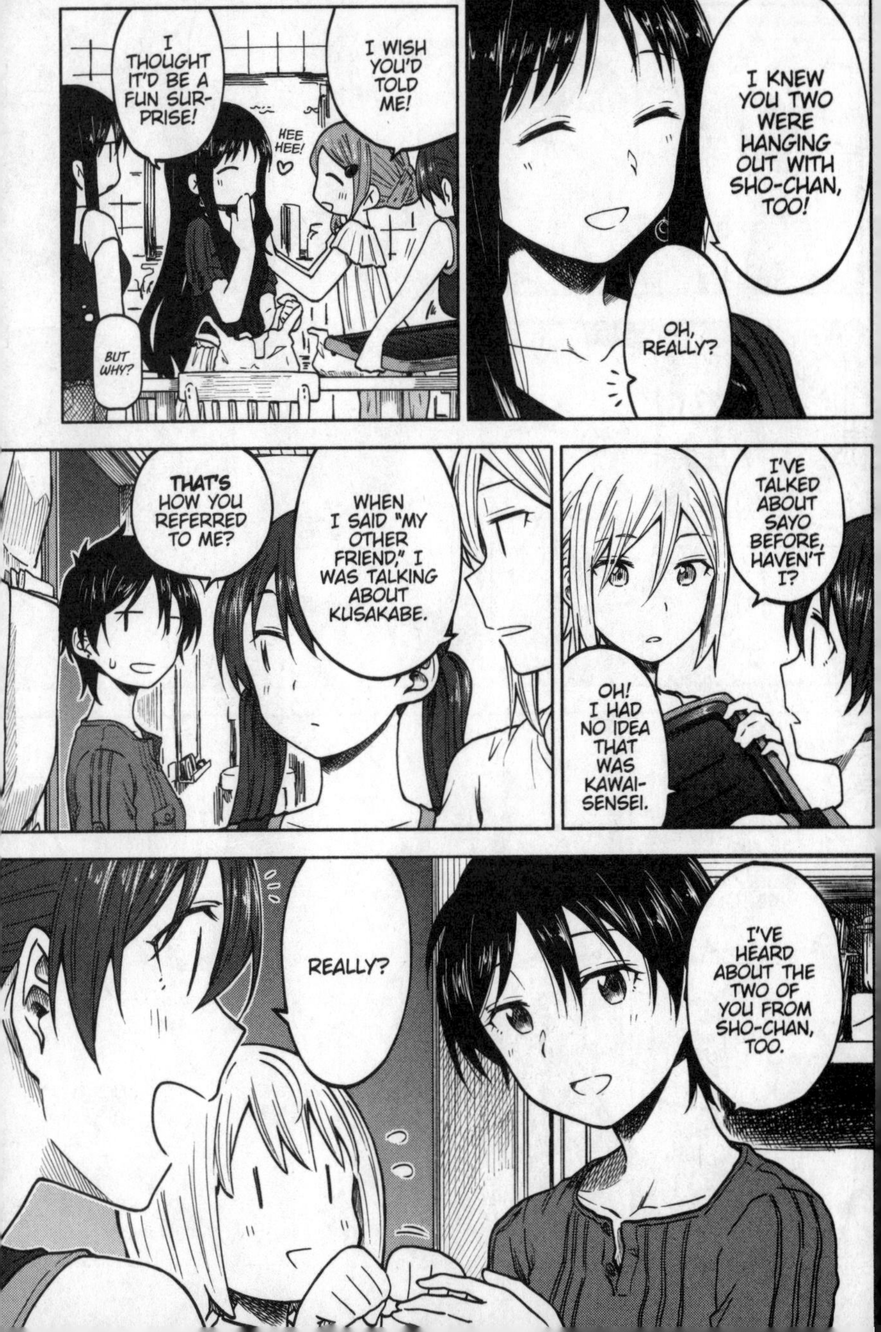
I KNEW YOU TWO WERE HANGING OUT WITH SHO-CHAN, TOO!
OH, REALLY?
I WISH YOU'D TOLD ME!
I THOUGHT IT'D BE A FUN SUR-PRISE!
HEE HEE!
BUT WHY?
I'VE TALKED ABOUT SAYO BEFORE, HAVEN'T I?
OH! I HAD NO IDEA THAT WAS KAWAI-SENSEI.
WHEN I SAID "MY OTHER FRIEND," I WAS TALKING ABOUT KUSAKABE.
THAT'S HOW YOU REFERRED TO ME?
I'VE HEARD ABOUT THE TWO OF YOU FROM SHO-CHAN, TOO.
REALLY?

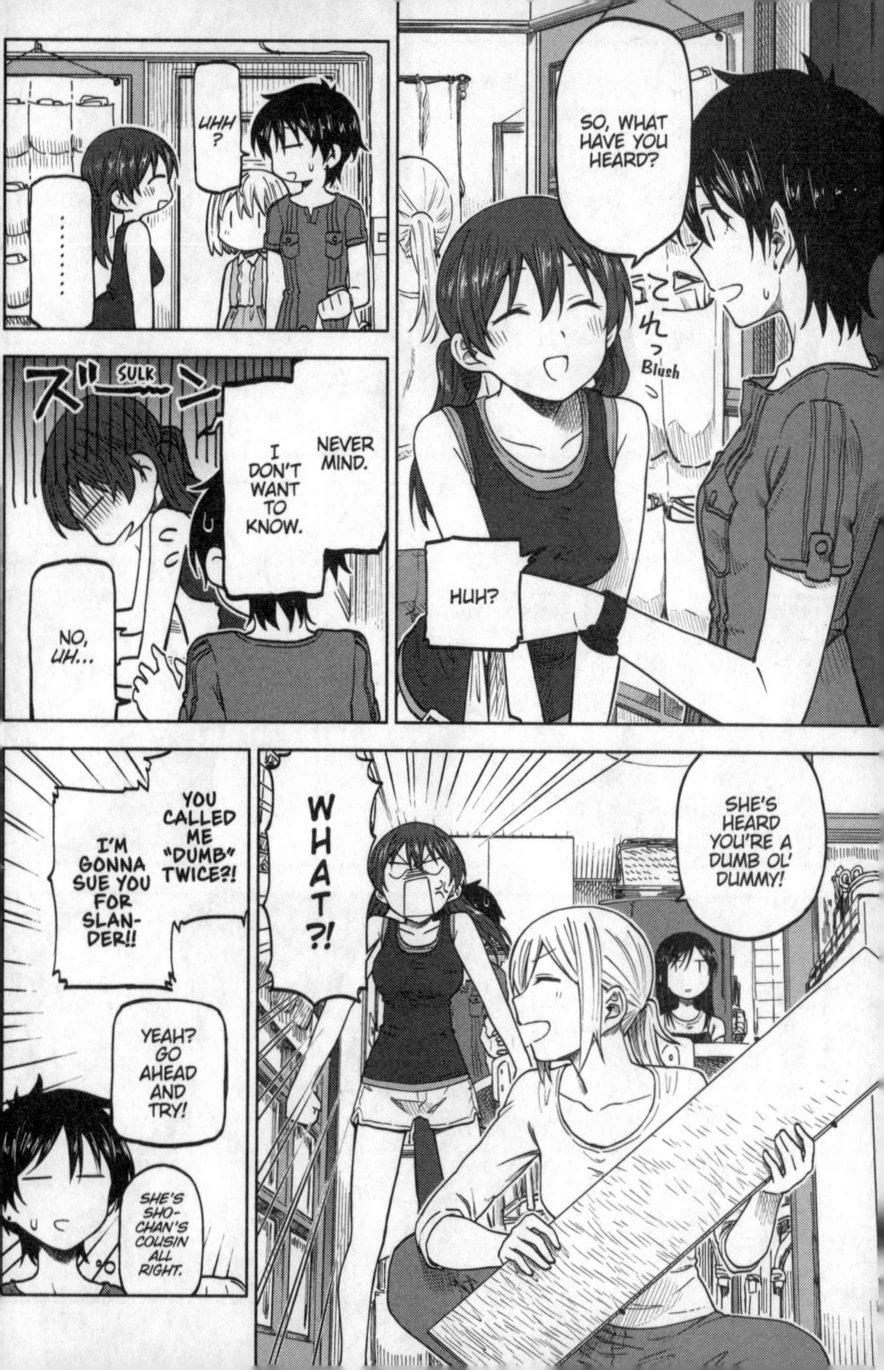
SO, WHAT HAVE YOU HEARD?
てれっ
Blush
HUH?
UHH?
......
ズーン
SULK
NEVER MIND. I DON'T WANT TO KNOW.
NO, UH...
SHE'S HEARD YOU'RE A DUMB OL' DUMMY!
WHAT?!
YOU CALLED ME "DUMB" TWICE?!
I'M GONNA SUE YOU FOR SLANDER!!
YEAH? GO AHEAD AND TRY!
SHE'S SHO-CHAN'S COUSIN ALL RIGHT.

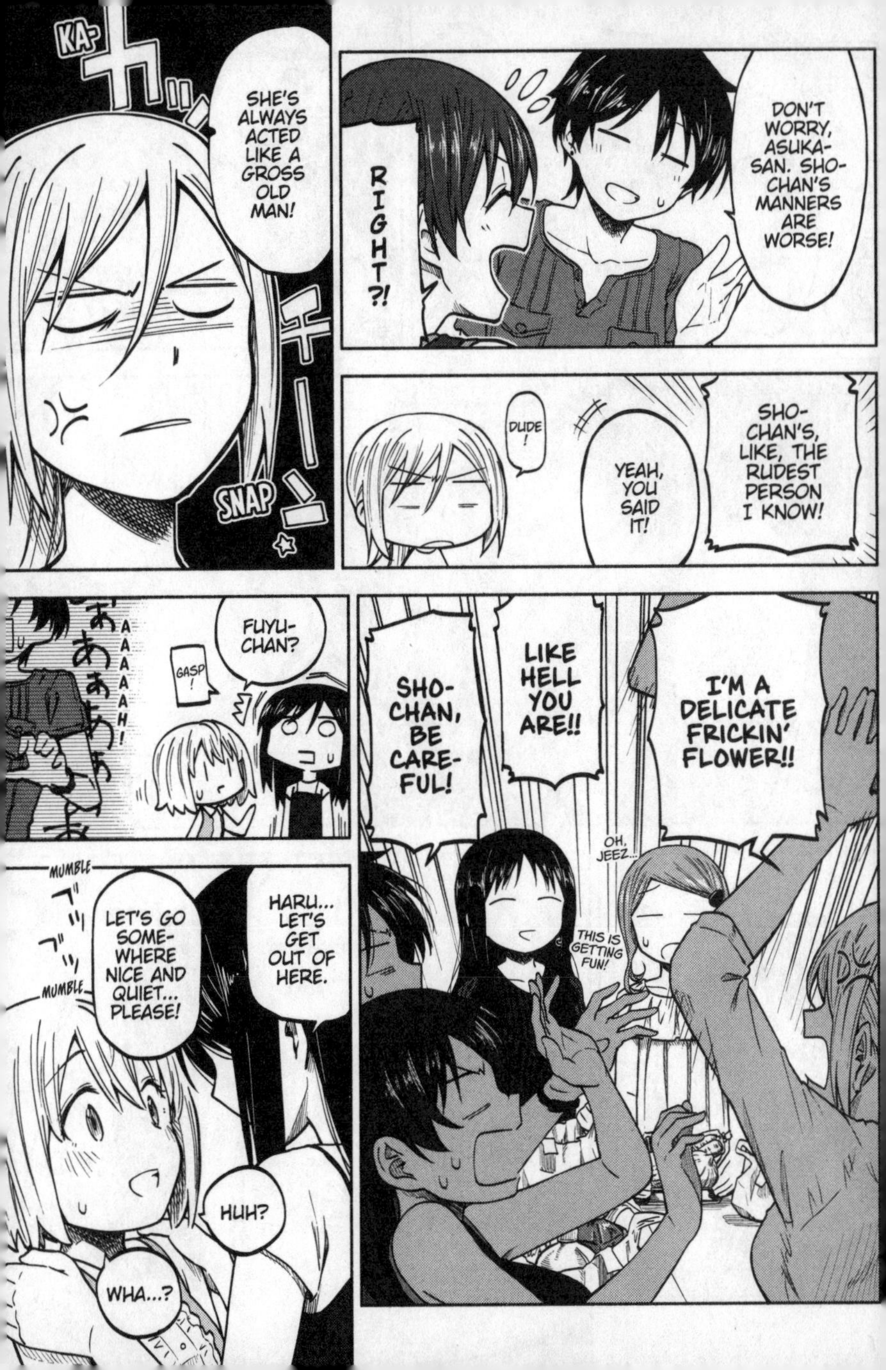
DON'T WORRY, ASUKA-SAN. SHO-CHAN'S MANNERS ARE WORSE!
RIGHT?!
SHO-CHAN'S, LIKE, THE RUDEST PERSON I KNOW!
YEAH, YOU SAID IT!
DUDE!
KA-
SHE'S ALWAYS ACTED LIKE A GROSS OLD MAN!
SNAP
I'M A DELICATE FRICKIN' FLOWER!!
LIKE HELL YOU ARE!!
SHO-CHAN, BE CARE-FUL!
OH, JEEZ...
THIS IS GETTING FUN!
FUYU-CHAN?
GASP!
AAAAAAH!
HARU... LET'S GET OUT OF HERE.
MUMBLE
LET'S GO SOME-WHERE NICE AND QUIET... PLEASE!
MUMBLE
HUH?
WHA...?

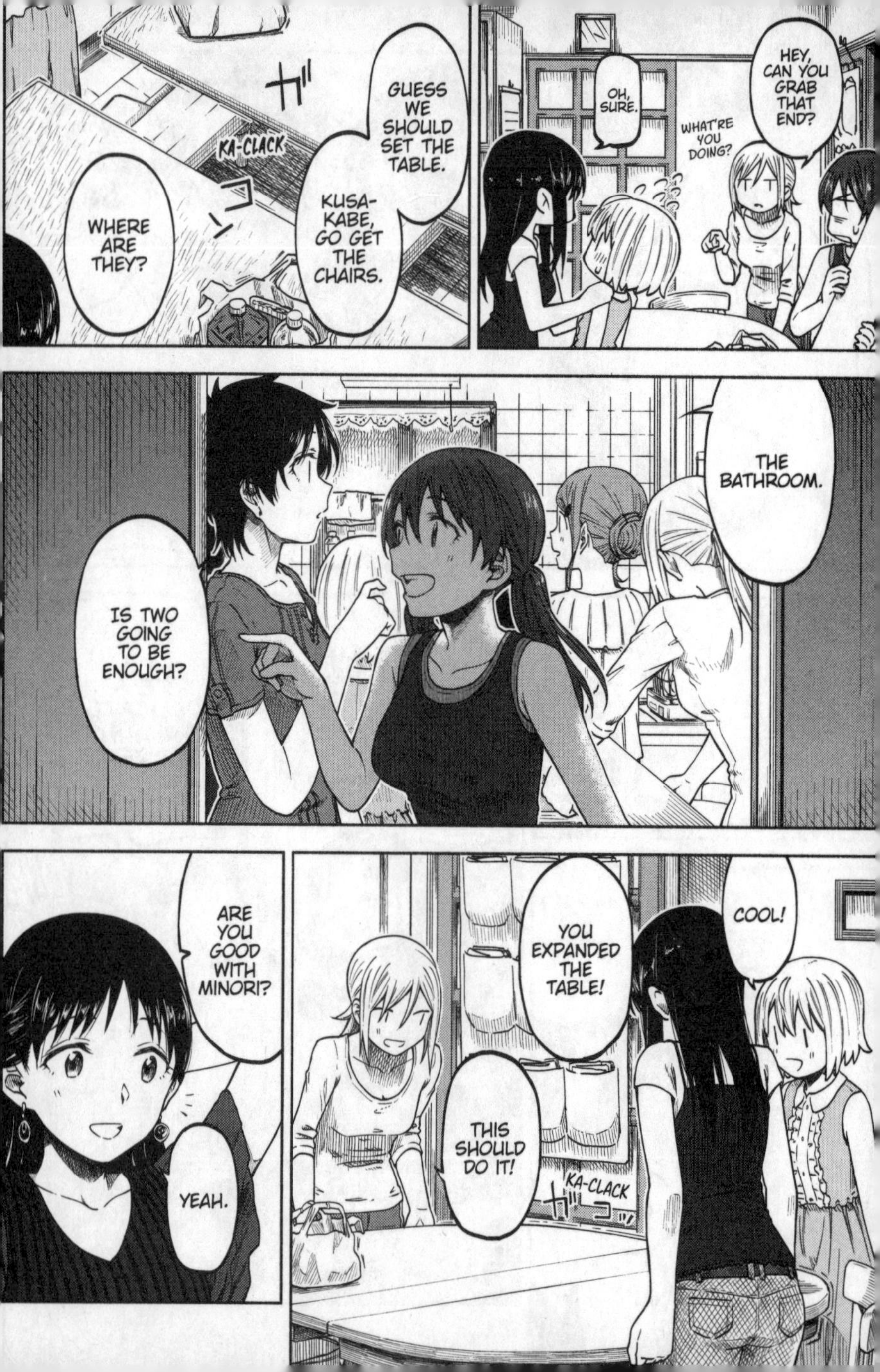
HEY, CAN YOU GRAB THAT END?
WHAT'RE YOU DOING?
OH, SURE.
GUESS WE SHOULD SET THE TABLE.
KA-CLACK
KUSA-KABE, GO GET THE CHAIRS.
WHERE ARE THEY?
THE BATHROOM.
IS TWO GOING TO BE ENOUGH?
COOL!
YOU EXPANDED THE TABLE!
THIS SHOULD DO IT!
KA-CLACK
ARE YOU GOOD WITH MINORI?
YEAH.

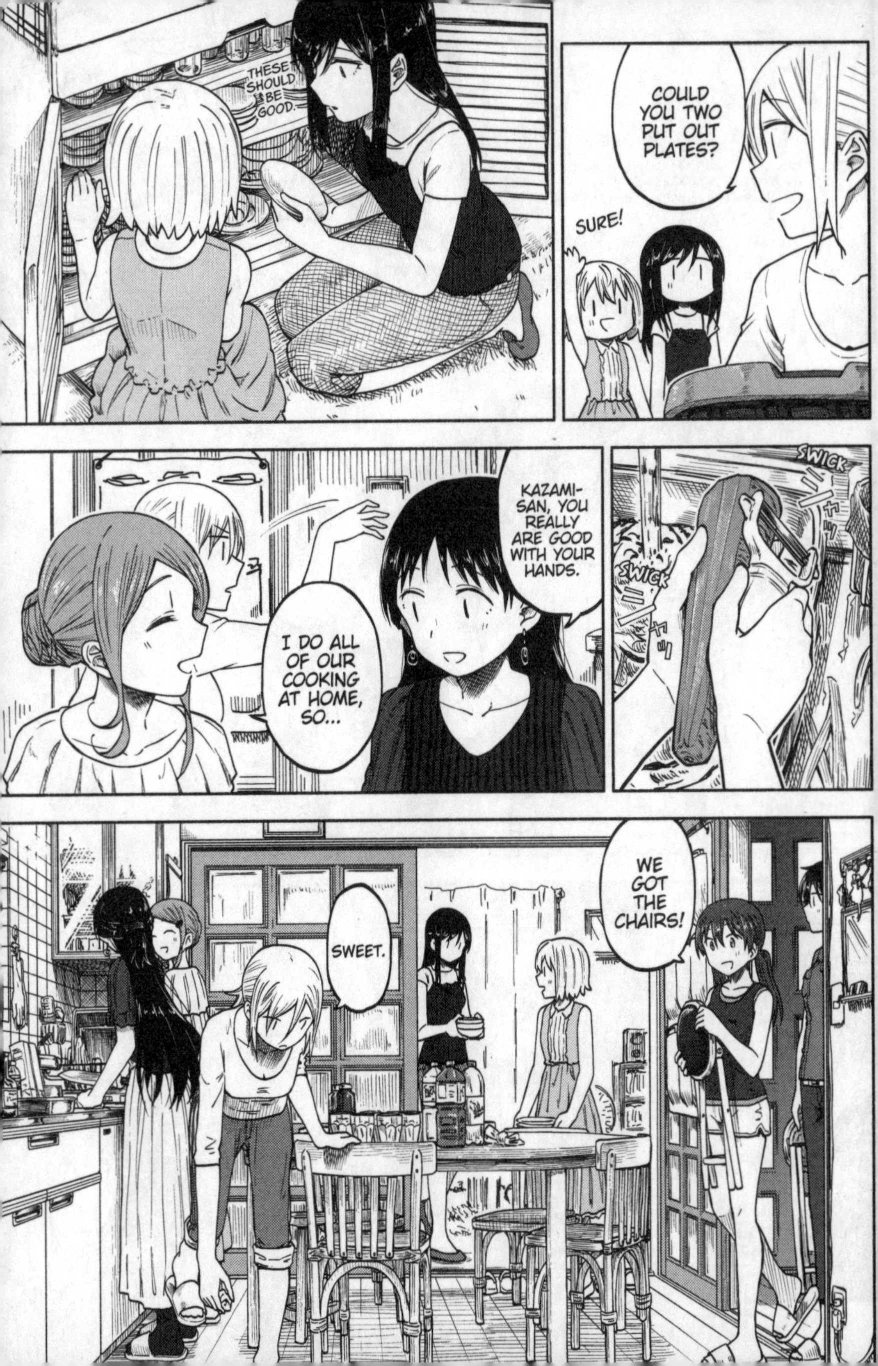
COULD YOU TWO PUT OUT PLATES?
SURE!
THESE SHOULD BE GOOD.
SWICK
SWICK
KAZAMI-SAN, YOU REALLY ARE GOOD WITH YOUR HANDS.
I DO ALL OF OUR COOKING AT HOME, SO...
WE GOT THE CHAIRS!
SWEET.

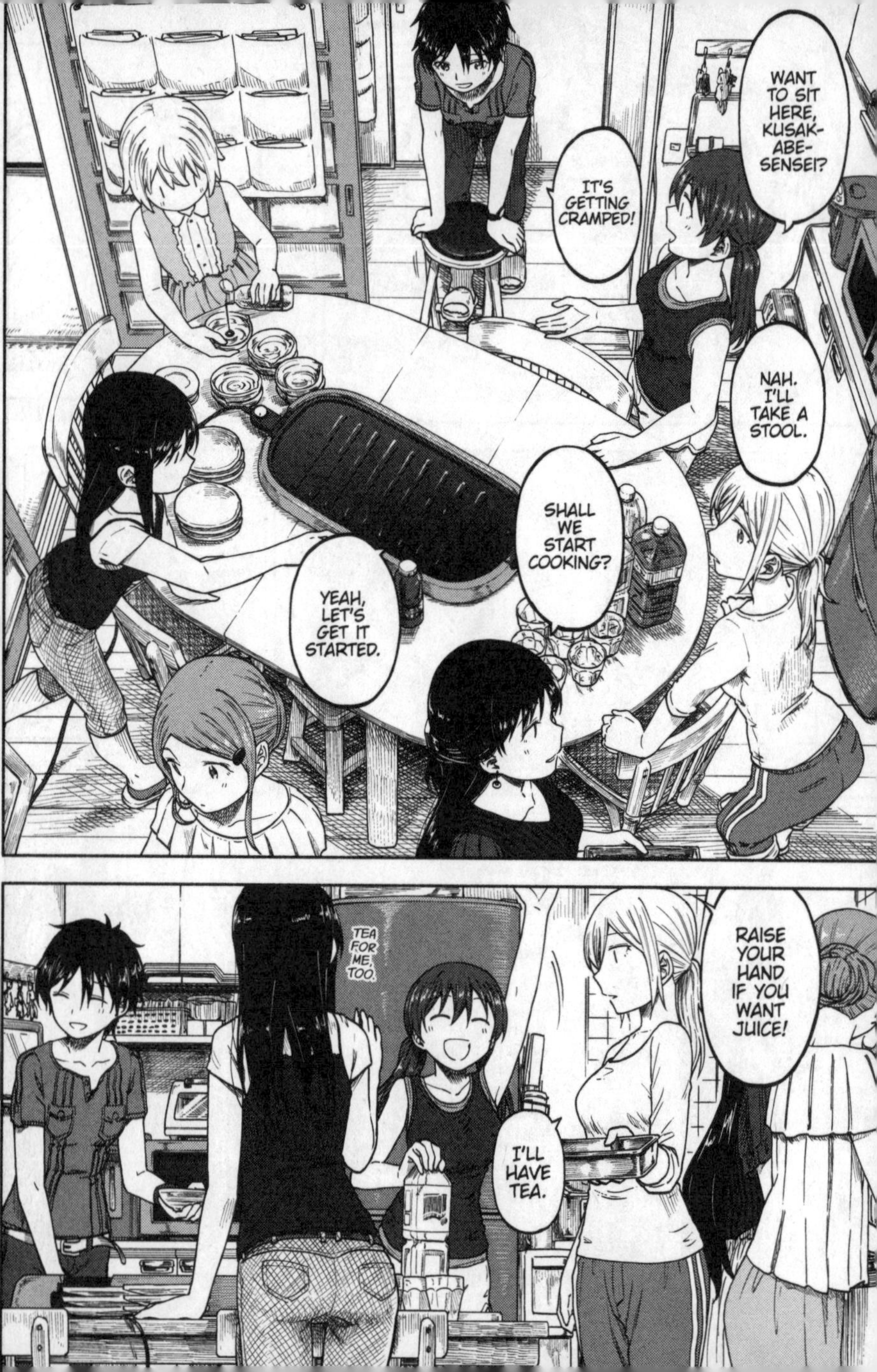
WANT TO SIT HERE, KUSAKABE-SENSEI?
IT'S GETTING CRAMPED!
NAH. I'LL TAKE A STOOL.
SHALL WE START COOKING?
YEAH, LET'S GET IT STARTED.
RAISE YOUR HAND IF YOU WANT JUICE!
I'LL HAVE TEA.
TEA FOR ME, TOO.

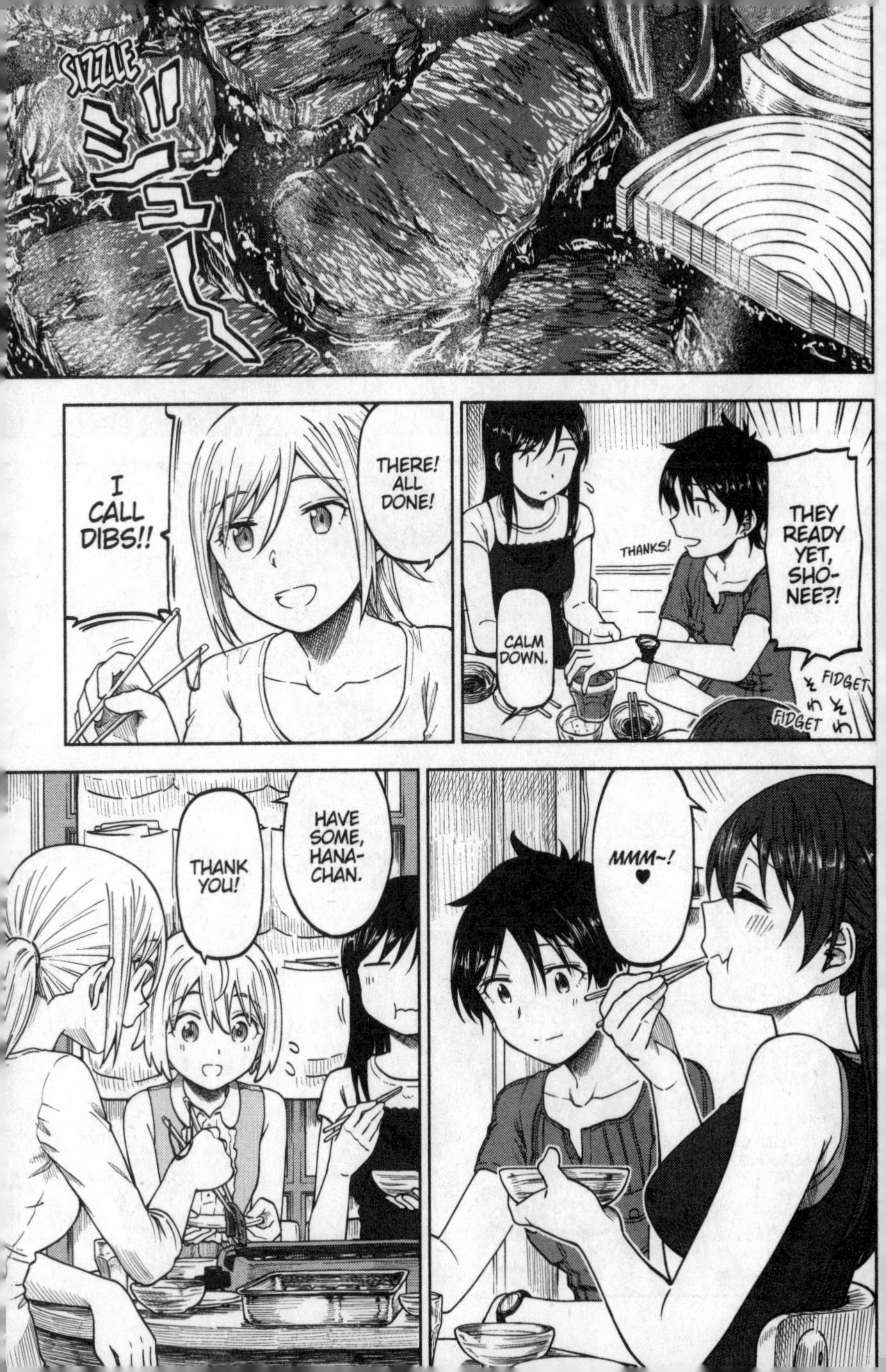
SIZZLE
THEY READY YET, SHO-NEE?!
THANKS!
CALM DOWN.
FIDGET
FIDGET
THERE! ALL DONE!
I CALL DIBS!!
MMM~! ♥
HAVE SOME, HANA-CHAN.
THANK YOU!

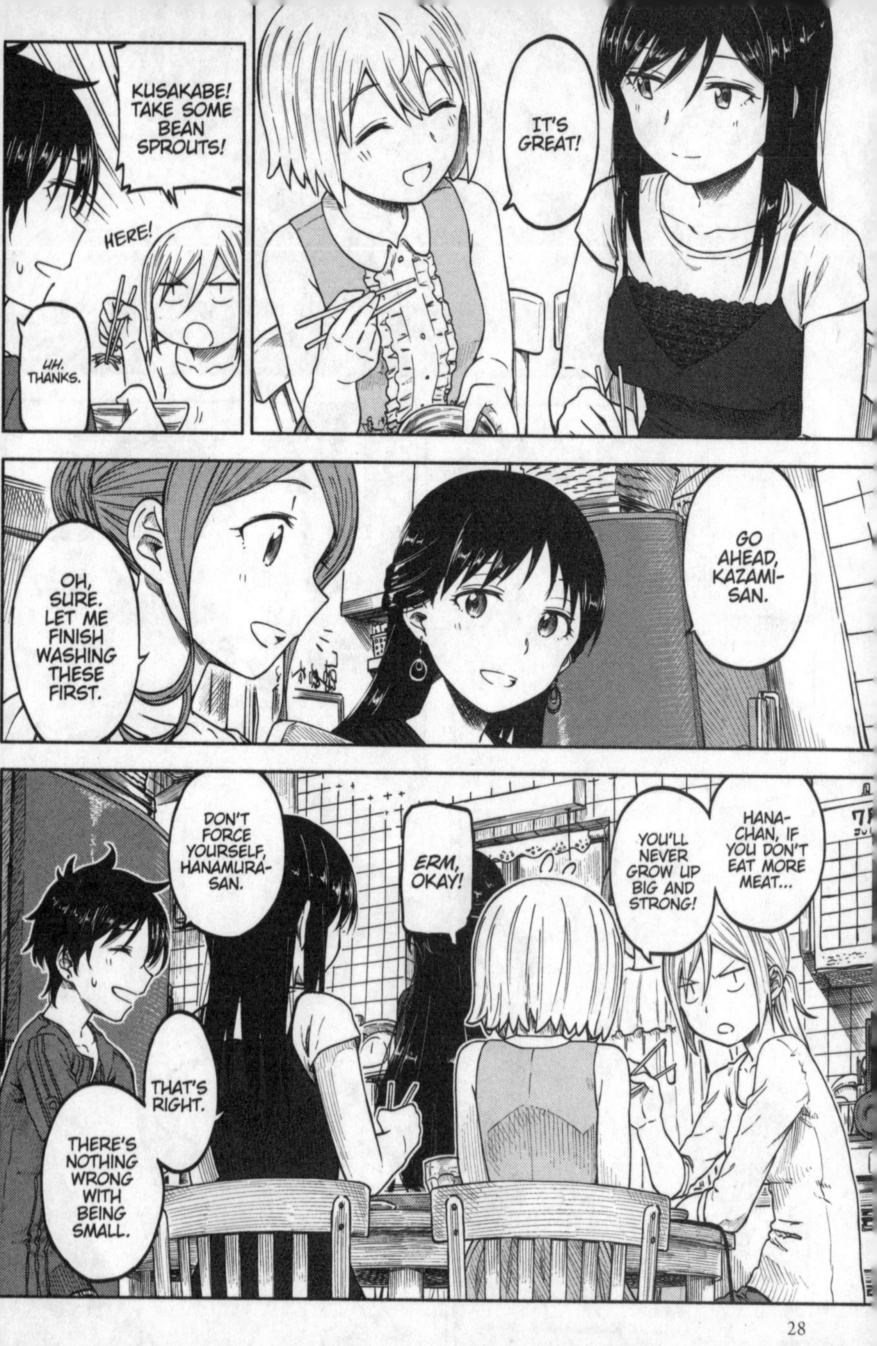
IT'S GREAT!
KUSAKABE! TAKE SOME BEAN SPROUTS!
HERE!
UH. THANKS.
GO AHEAD, KAZAMI-SAN.
OH, SURE. LET ME FINISH WASHING THESE FIRST.
HANA-CHAN, IF YOU DON'T EAT MORE MEAT...
YOU'LL NEVER GROW UP BIG AND STRONG!
ERM, OKAY!
DON'T FORCE YOURSELF, HANAMURA-SAN.
THAT'S RIGHT.
THERE'S NOTHING WRONG WITH BEING SMALL.

Our Wonderful Days

story & art by Kei Hamuro

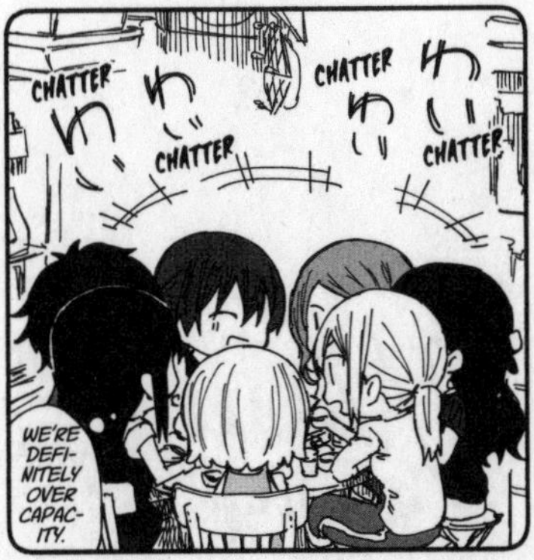
CHATTER
CHATTER
CHATTER
CHATTER
WE'RE DEFINITELY OVER CAPACITY.

Our Wonderful Days

Tsurezure Biyori

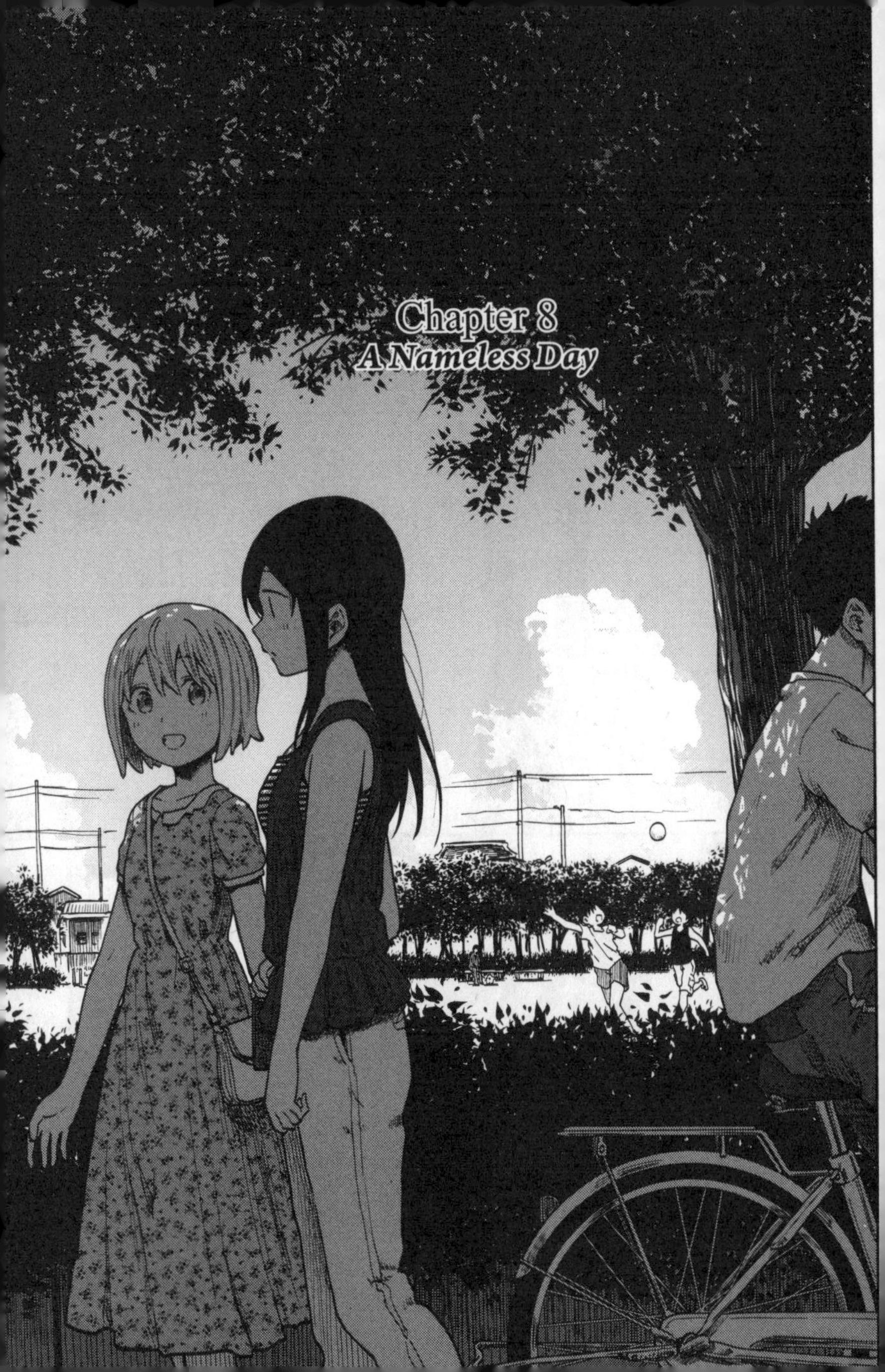
Chapter 8
A Nameless Day

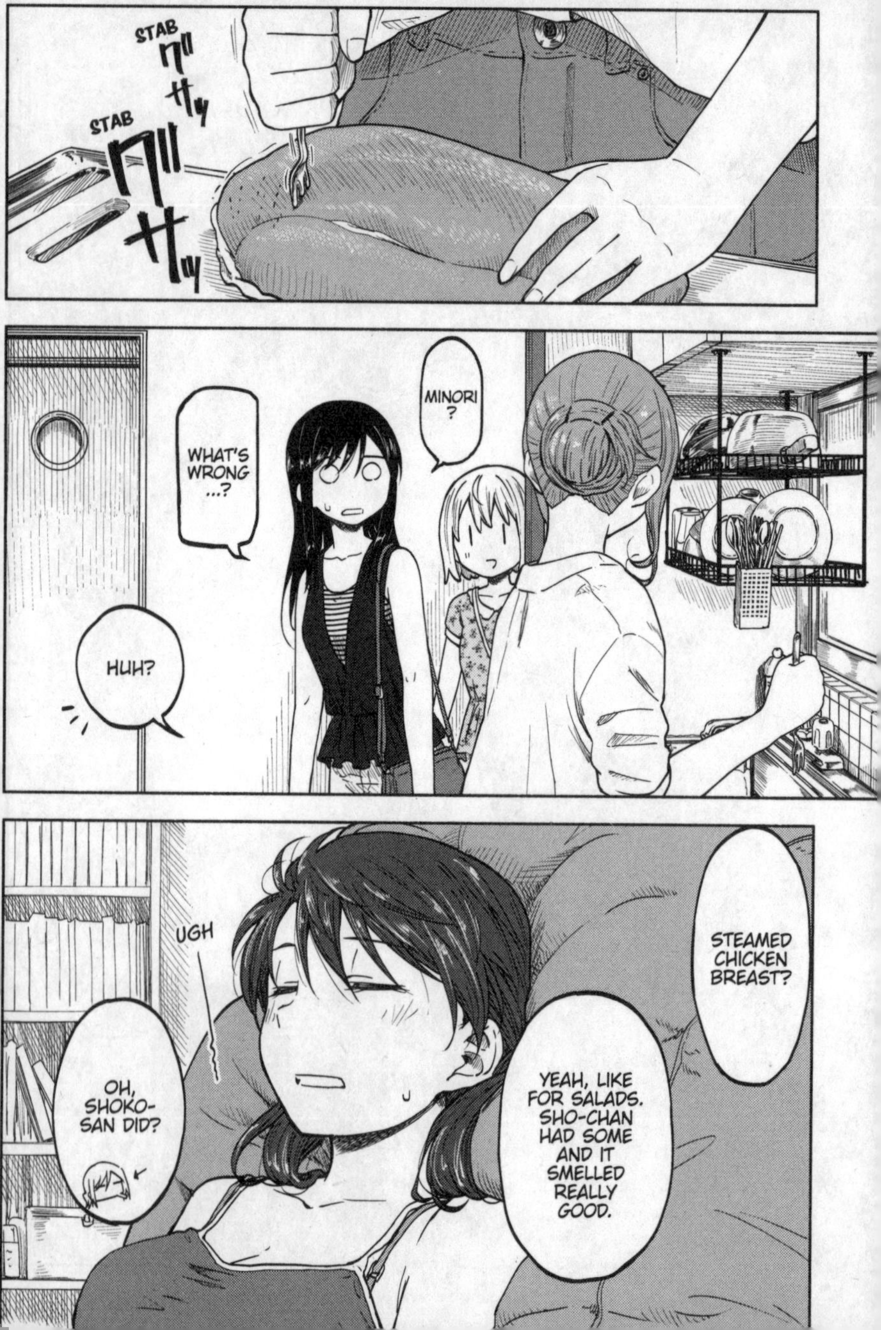
STAB ガッ
STAB ガッ
MINORI?
WHAT'S WRONG...?
HUH?
STEAMED CHICKEN BREAST?
YEAH, LIKE FOR SALADS. SHO-CHAN HAD SOME AND IT SMELLED REALLY GOOD.
UGH
OH, SHOKO-SAN DID?

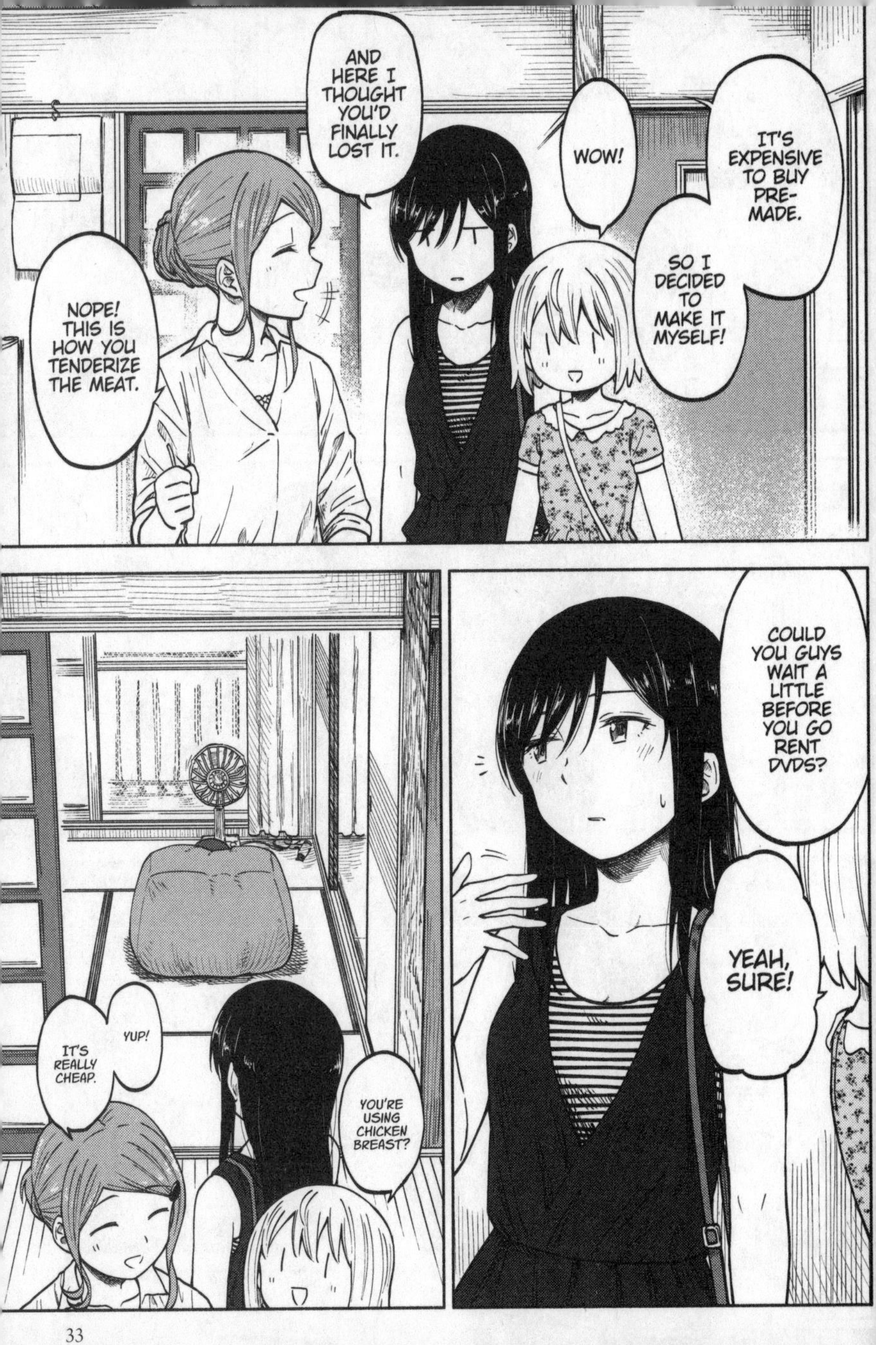
IT'S EXPENSIVE TO BUY PRE-MADE.
SO I DECIDED TO MAKE IT MYSELF!
WOW!
AND HERE I THOUGHT YOU'D FINALLY LOST IT.
NOPE! THIS IS HOW YOU TENDERIZE THE MEAT.
COULD YOU GUYS WAIT A LITTLE BEFORE YOU GO RENT DVDS?
YEAH, SURE!
YOU'RE USING CHICKEN BREAST?
YUP!
IT'S REALLY CHEAP.

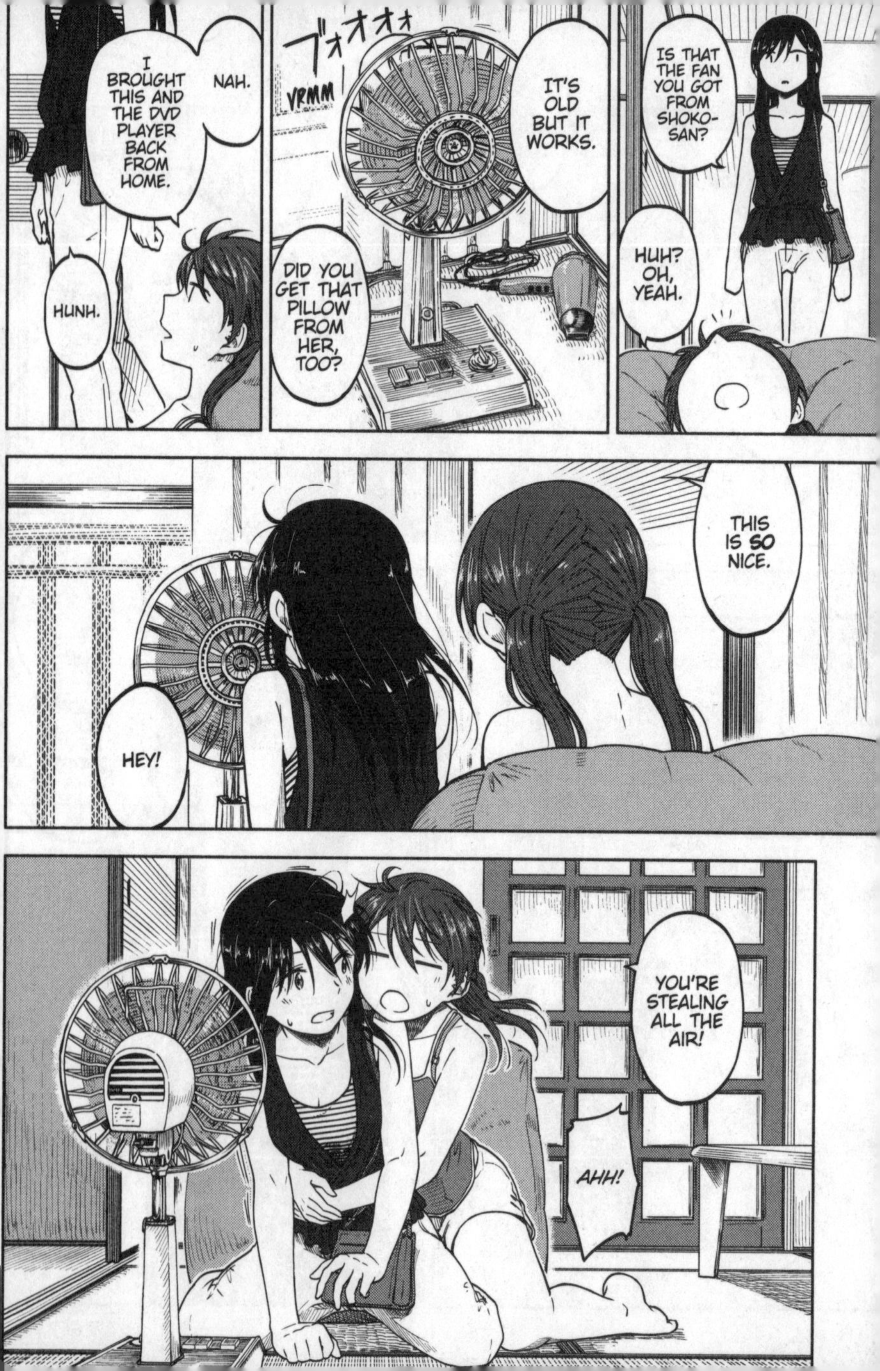
IS THAT THE FAN YOU GOT FROM SHOKO-SAN?
HUH? OH, YEAH.
ブォオオォ
VRMM
IT'S OLD BUT IT WORKS.
DID YOU GET THAT PILLOW FROM HER, TOO?
NAH.
I BROUGHT THIS AND THE DVD PLAYER BACK FROM HOME.
HUNH.
THIS IS SO NICE.
HEY!
YOU'RE STEALING ALL THE AIR!
AHH!

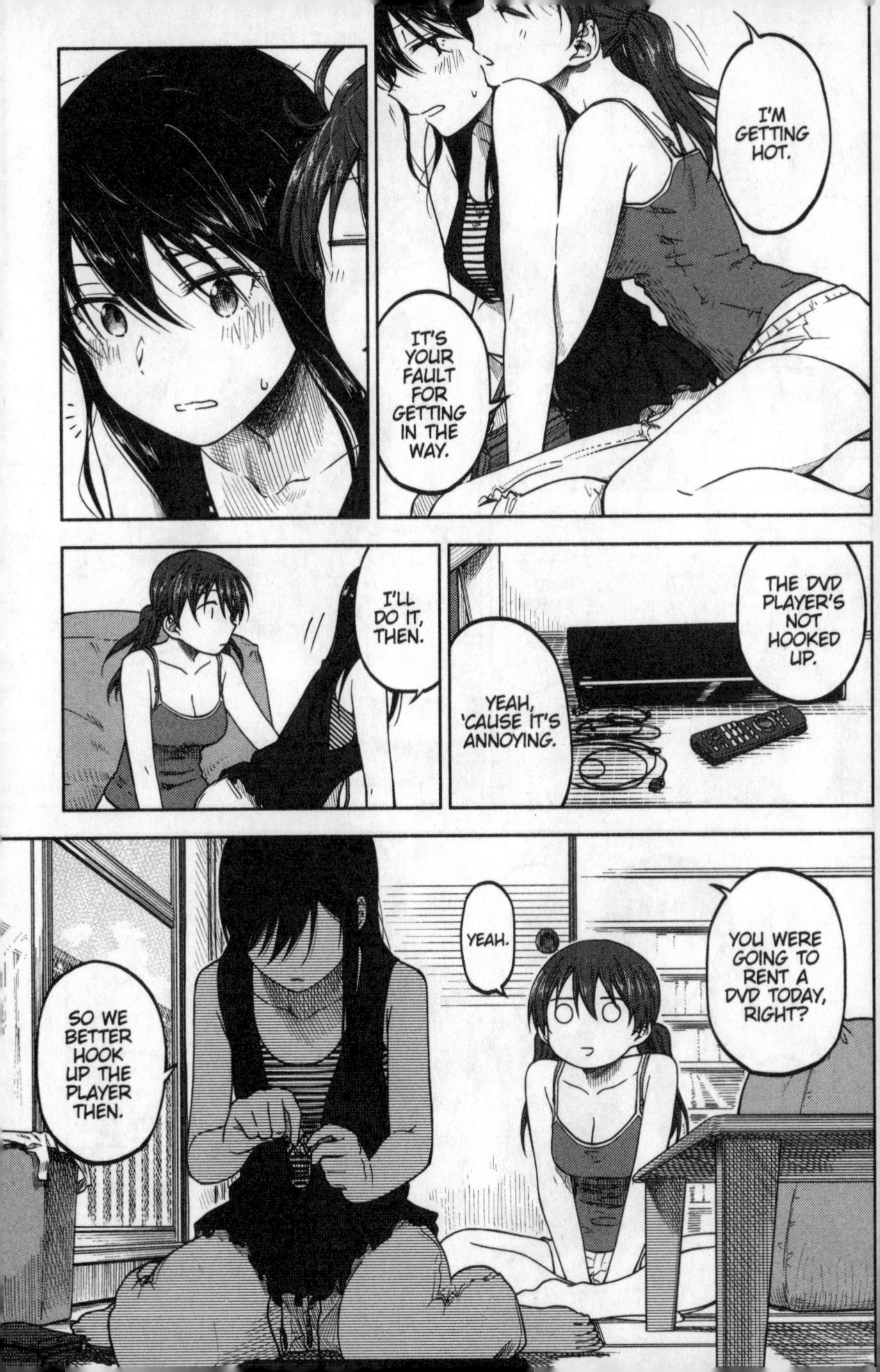
I'M GETTING HOT.
IT'S YOUR FAULT FOR GETTING IN THE WAY.
THE DVD PLAYER'S NOT HOOKED UP.
YEAH, 'CAUSE IT'S ANNOYING.
I'LL DO IT, THEN.
YOU WERE GOING TO RENT A DVD TODAY, RIGHT?
YEAH.
SO WE BETTER HOOK UP THE PLAYER THEN.

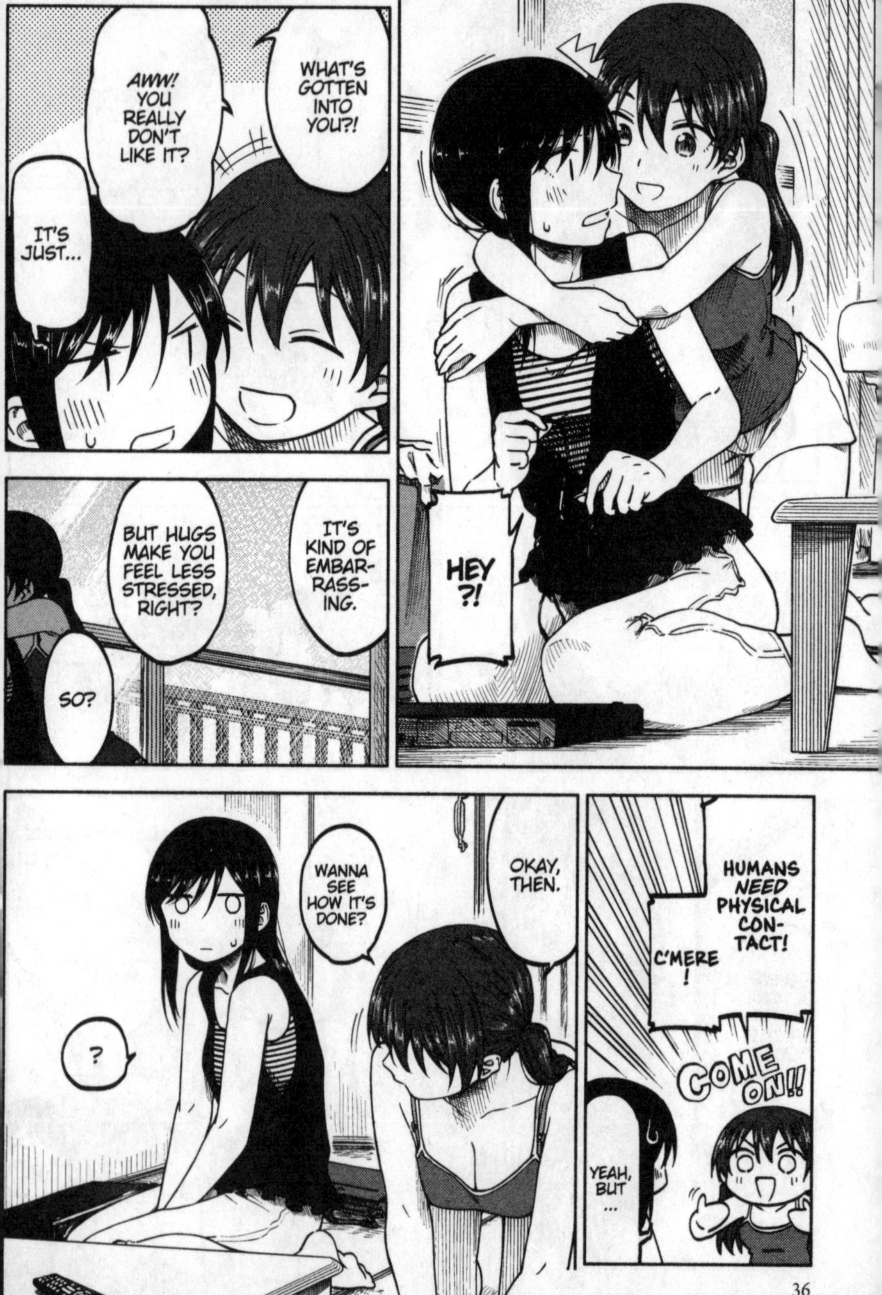
HEY ?!
WHAT'S GOTTEN INTO YOU?!
AWW! YOU REALLY DON'T LIKE IT?
IT'S JUST...
IT'S KIND OF EMBARRASSING.
BUT HUGS MAKE YOU FEEL LESS STRESSED, RIGHT?
SO?
HUMANS NEED PHYSICAL CONTACT!
C'MERE!
COME ON!!
YEAH, BUT ...
OKAY, THEN.
WANNA SEE HOW IT'S DONE?
?

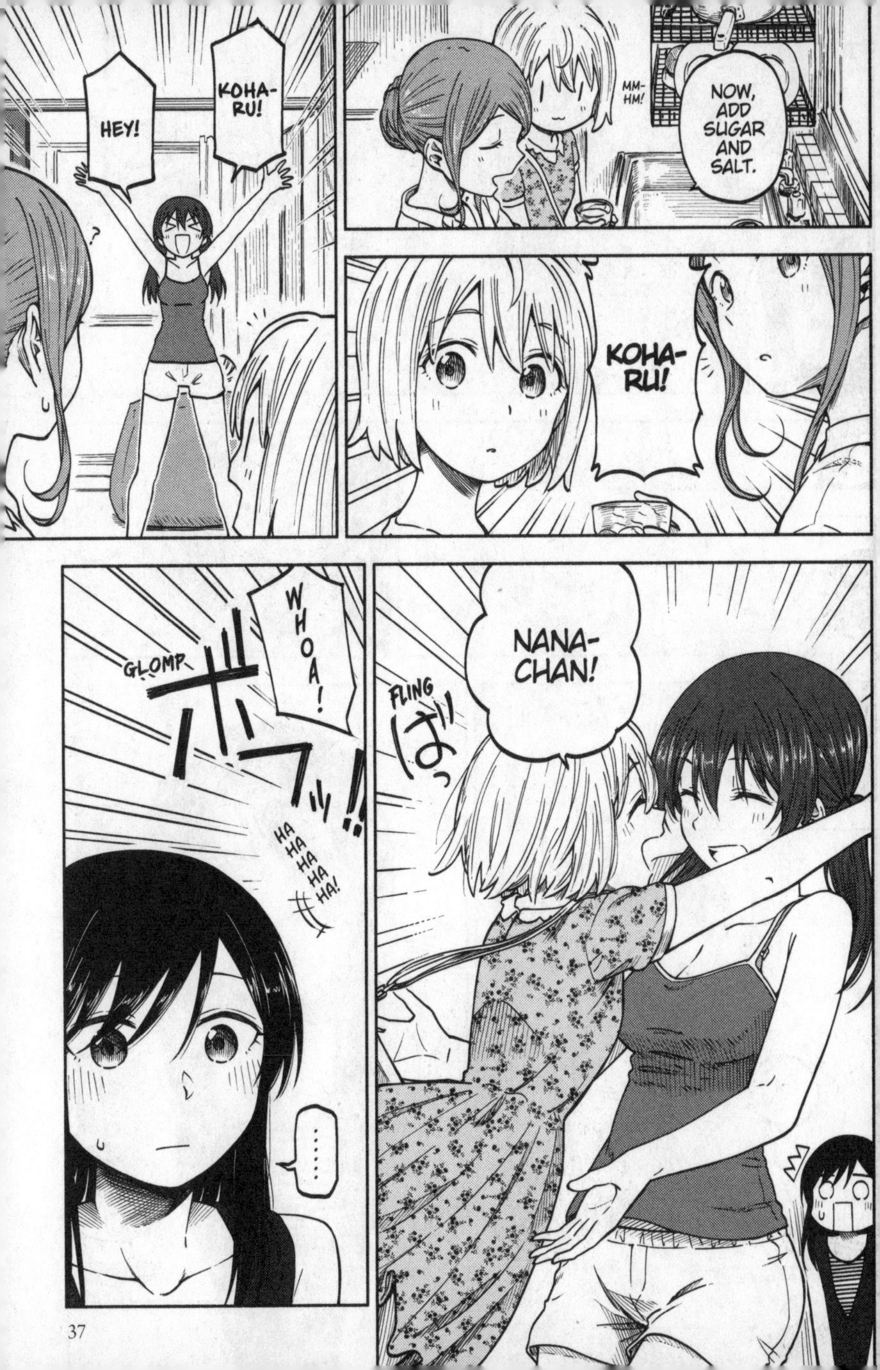
NOW, ADD SUGAR AND SALT.
MM-HM!
KOHA-RU!
KOHA-RU!
HEY!
?
NANA-CHAN!
FLING
WHOA!
GLOMP
HA HA HA HA HA!
......

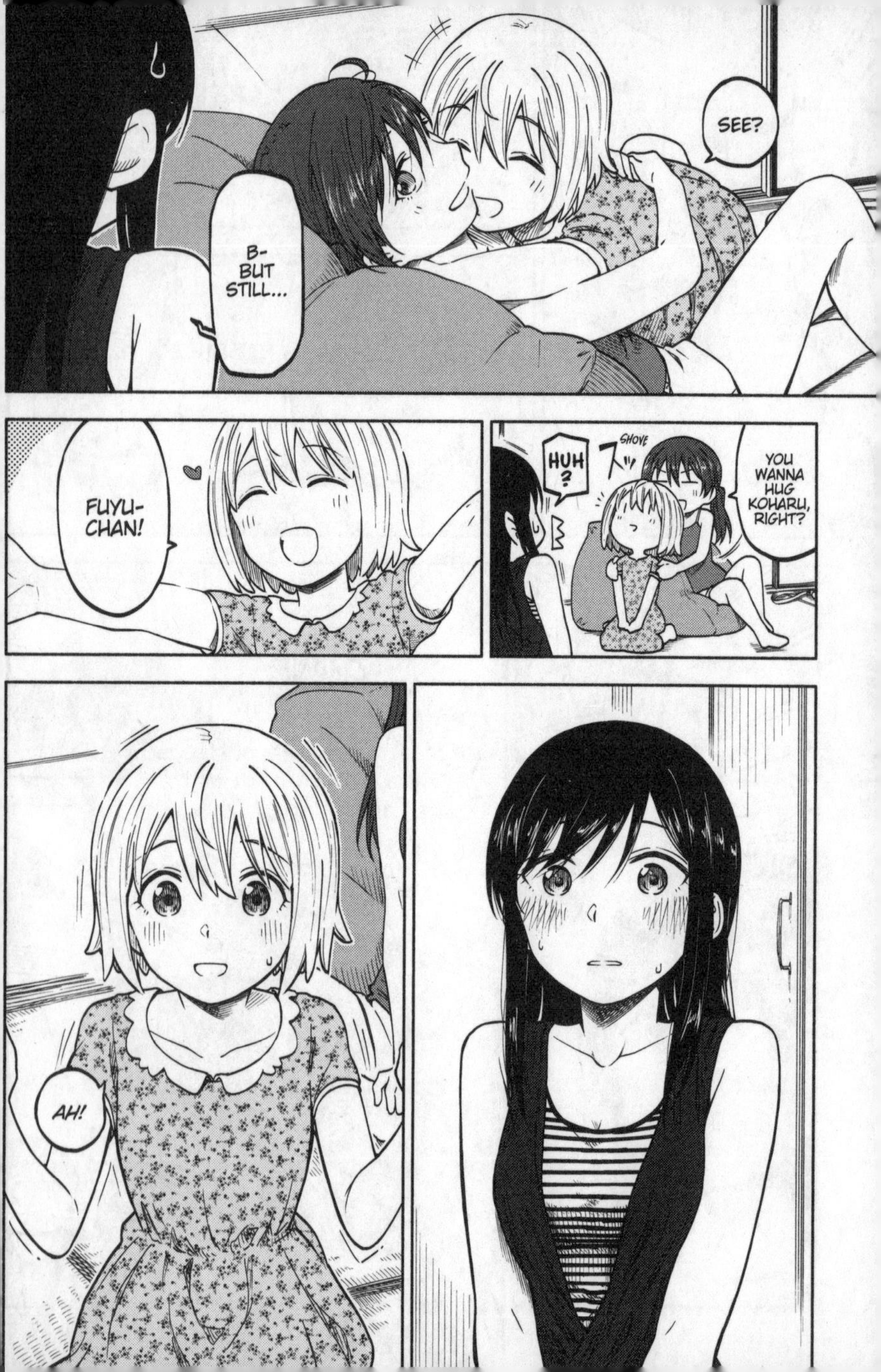
SEE?
B-BUT STILL...
YOU WANNA HUG KOHARU, RIGHT?
SHOVE
スッ
HUH?
FUYU-CHAN!
AH!

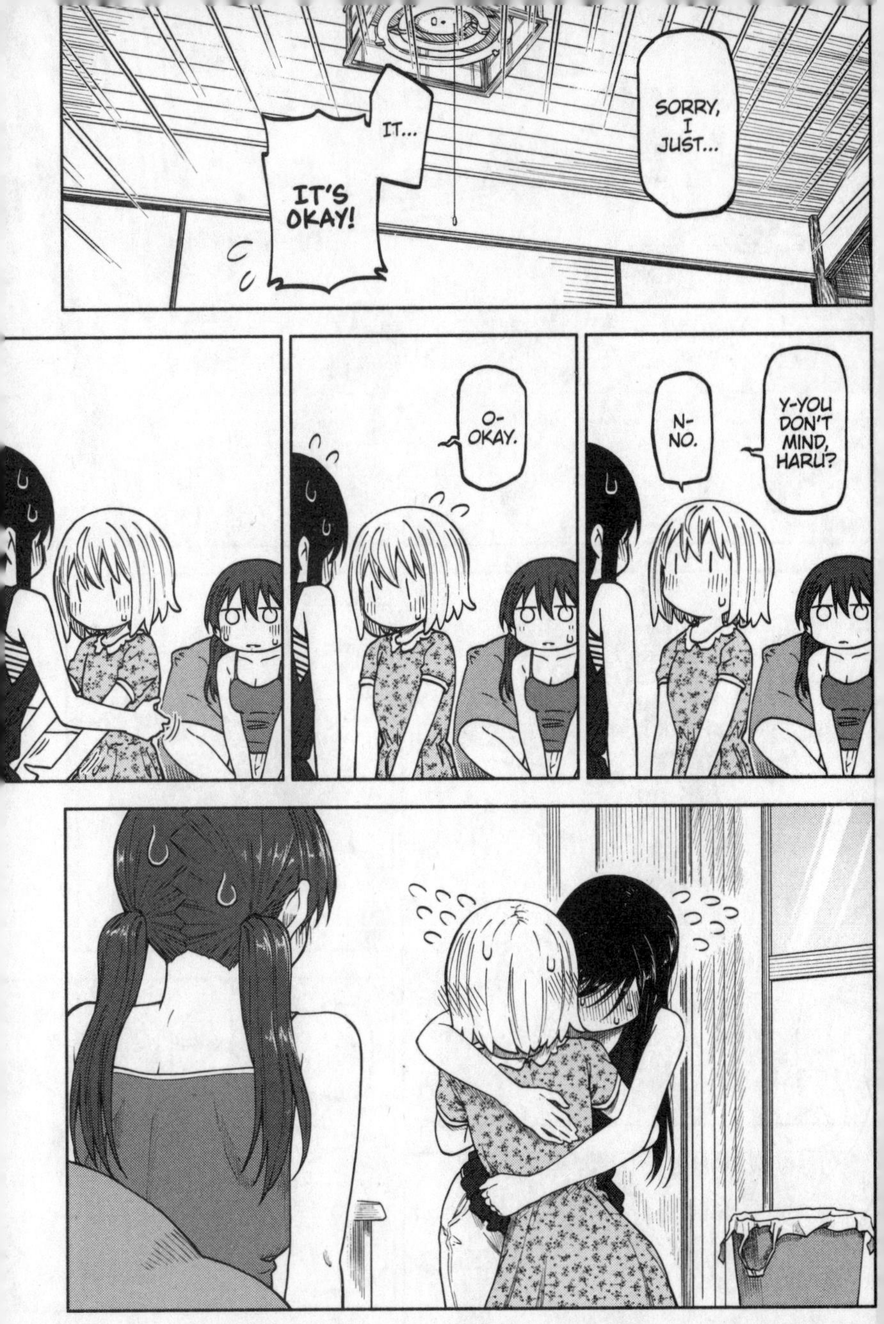
SORRY, I JUST...
IT...
IT'S OKAY!
Y-YOU DON'T MIND, HARU?
N-NO.
O-OKAY.

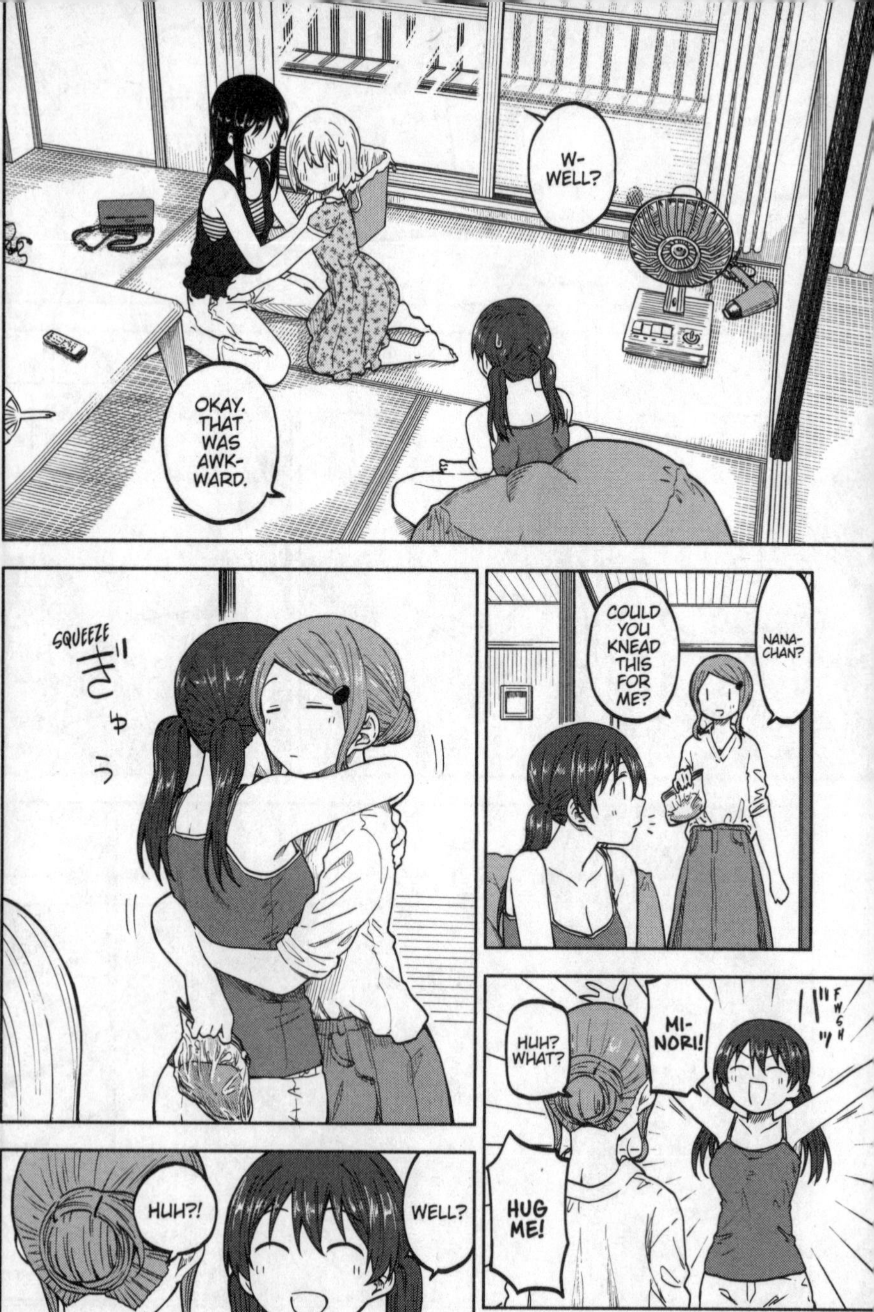
W-
WELL?
OKAY. THAT WAS AWK-WARD.
NANA-CHAN?
COULD YOU KNEAD THIS FOR ME?
FWSH
MI-NORI!
HUH? WHAT?
HUG ME!
SQUEEZE
ぎゅう
WELL?
HUH?!

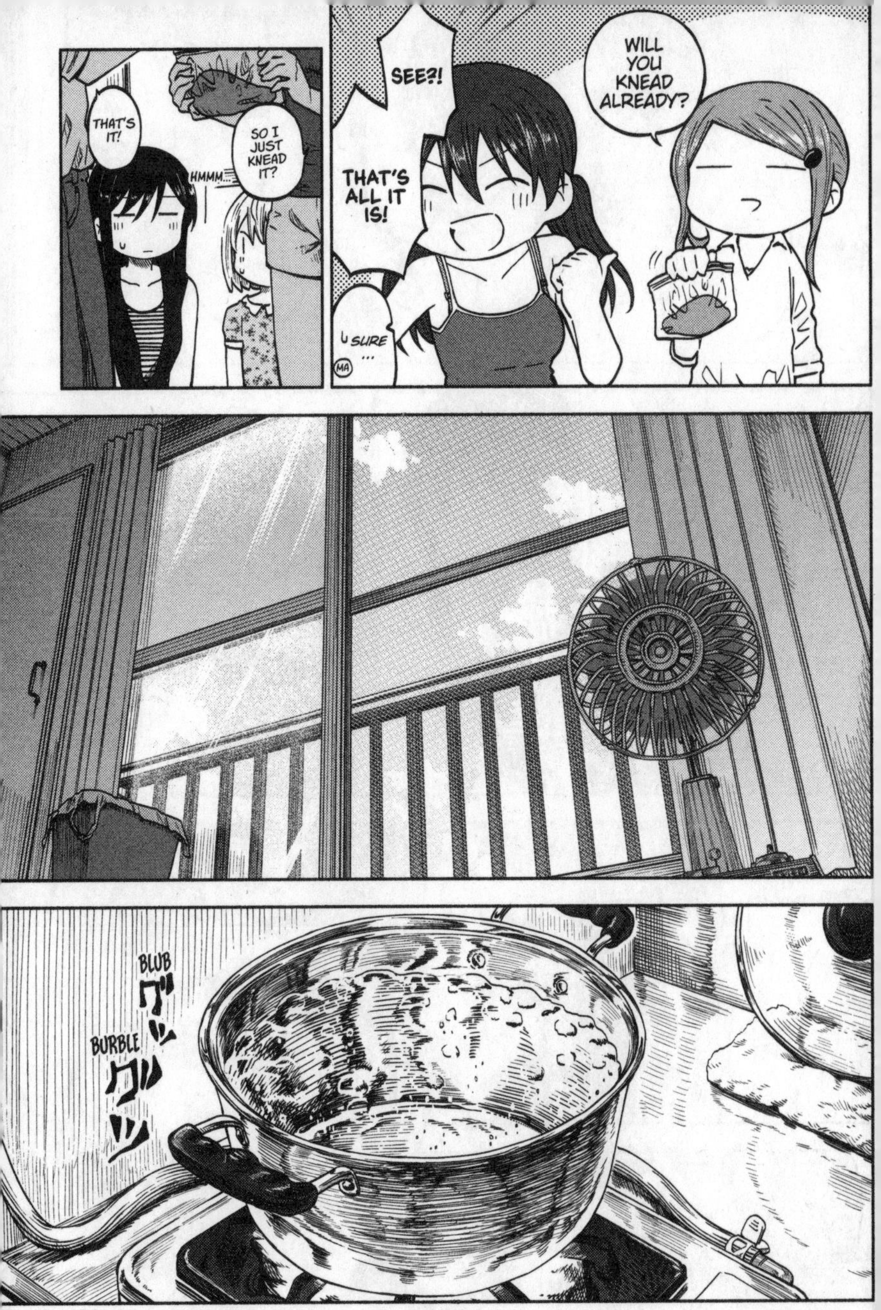
WILL YOU KNEAD ALREADY?
SEE?!
THAT'S ALL IT IS!
SURE...
MA
SO I JUST KNEAD IT?
THAT'S IT!
HMMM...
BLUB
BURBLE

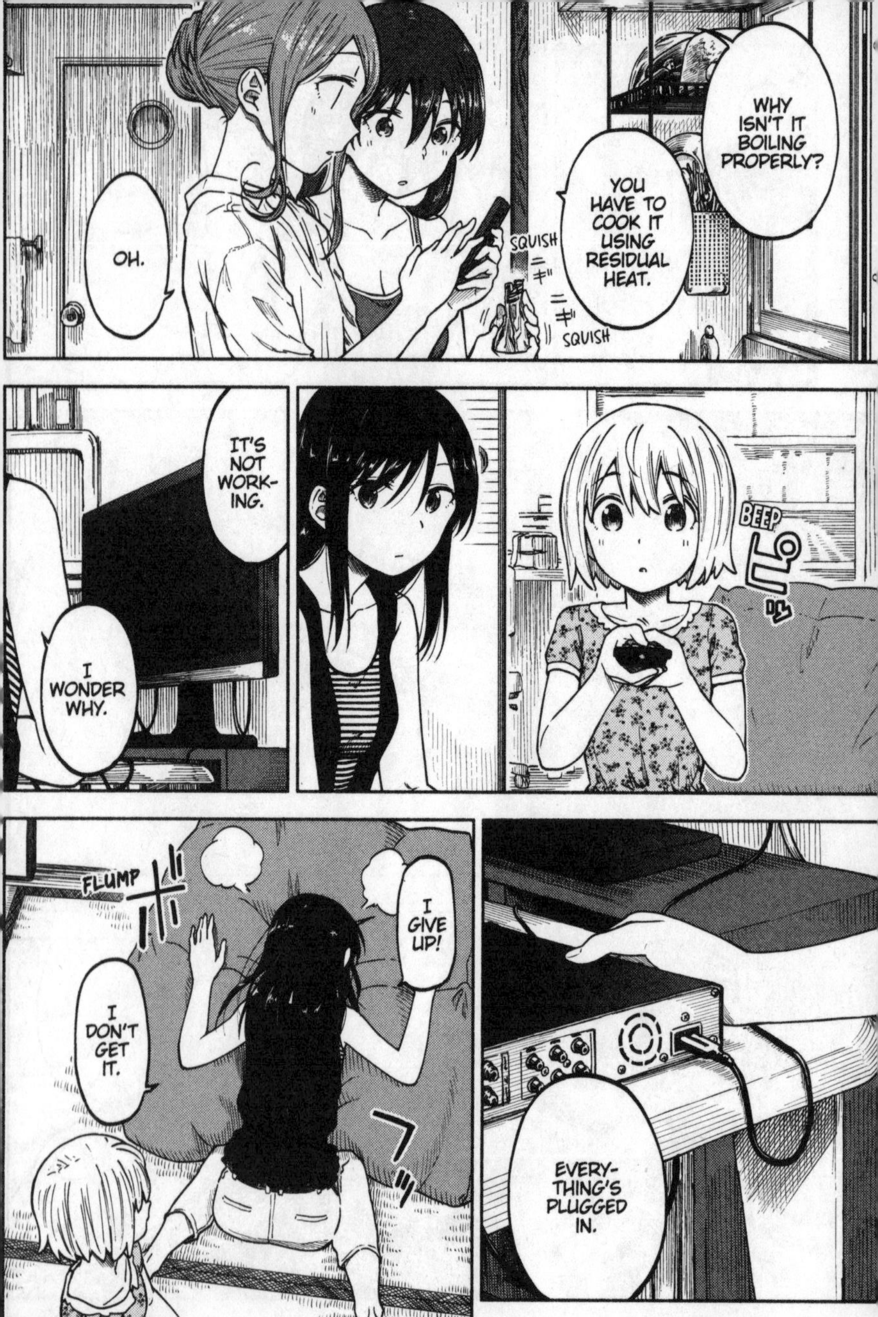
WHY ISN'T IT BOILING PROPERLY?
YOU HAVE TO COOK IT USING RESIDUAL HEAT.
SQUISH
SQUISH
OH.
BEEP
IT'S NOT WORK-ING.
I WONDER WHY.
EVERY-THING'S PLUGGED IN.
I GIVE UP!
FLUMP
I DON'T GET IT.

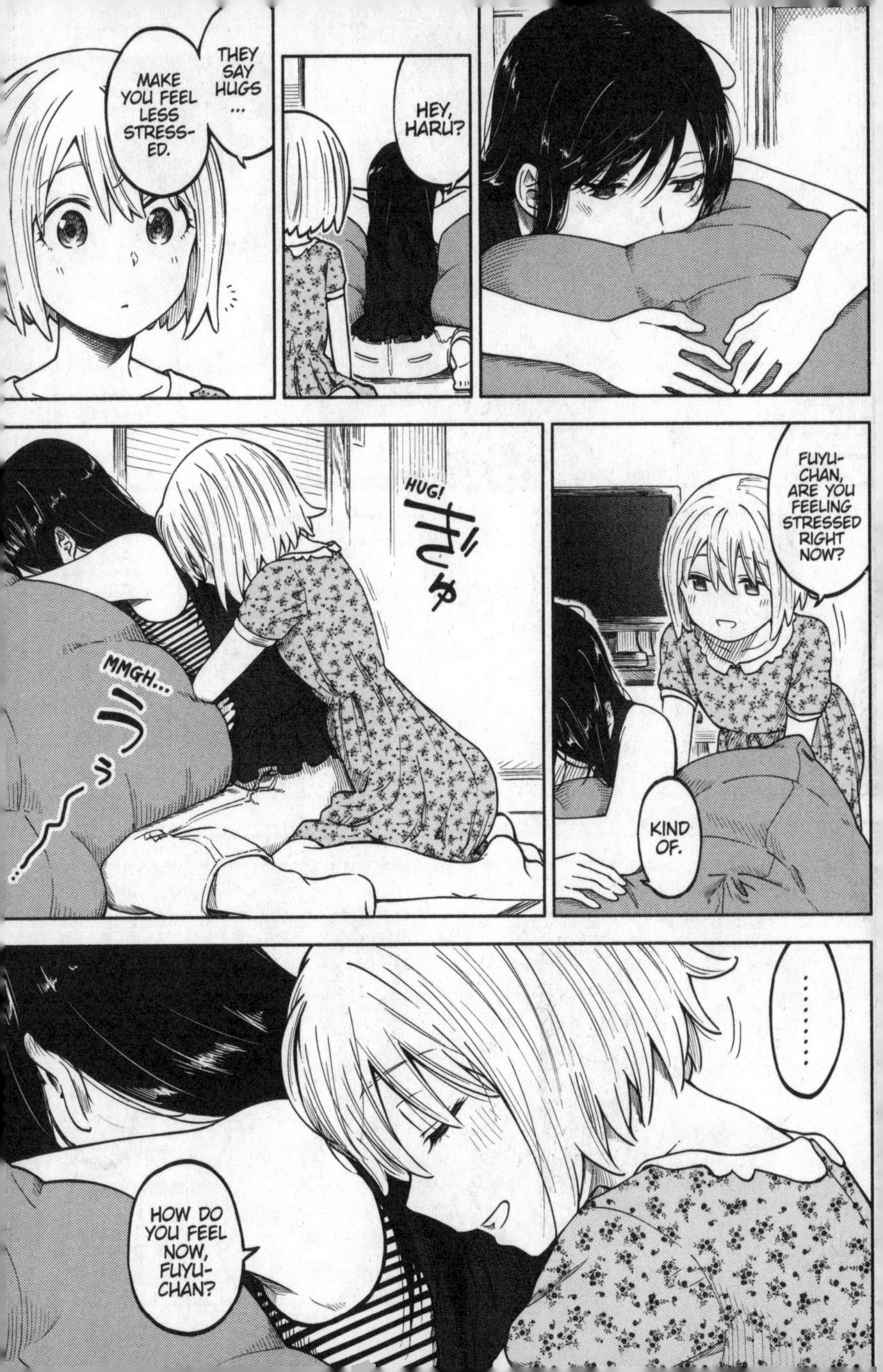
HEY, HARU?
THEY SAY HUGS ...
MAKE YOU FEEL LESS STRESS-ED.
FUYU-CHAN, ARE YOU FEELING STRESSED RIGHT NOW?
KIND OF.
HUG!
ぎゅ
MMGH...
......
HOW DO YOU FEEL NOW, FUYU-CHAN?

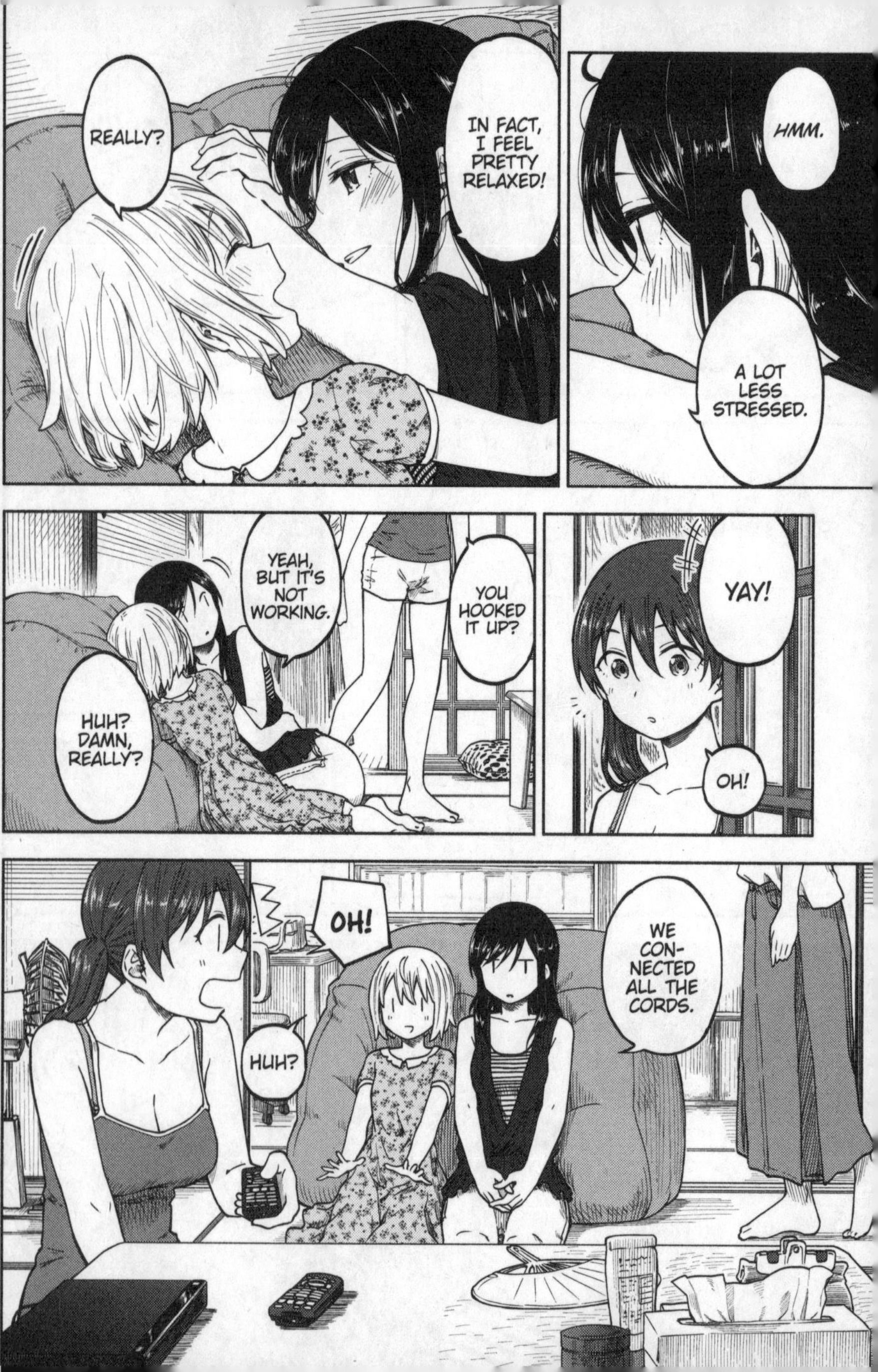
HMM.
A LOT LESS STRESSED.
IN FACT, I FEEL PRETTY RELAXED!
REALLY?
YAY!
OH!
YOU HOOKED IT UP?
YEAH, BUT IT'S NOT WORKING.
HUH? DAMN, REALLY?
WE CON-NECTED ALL THE CORDS.
OH!
HUH?

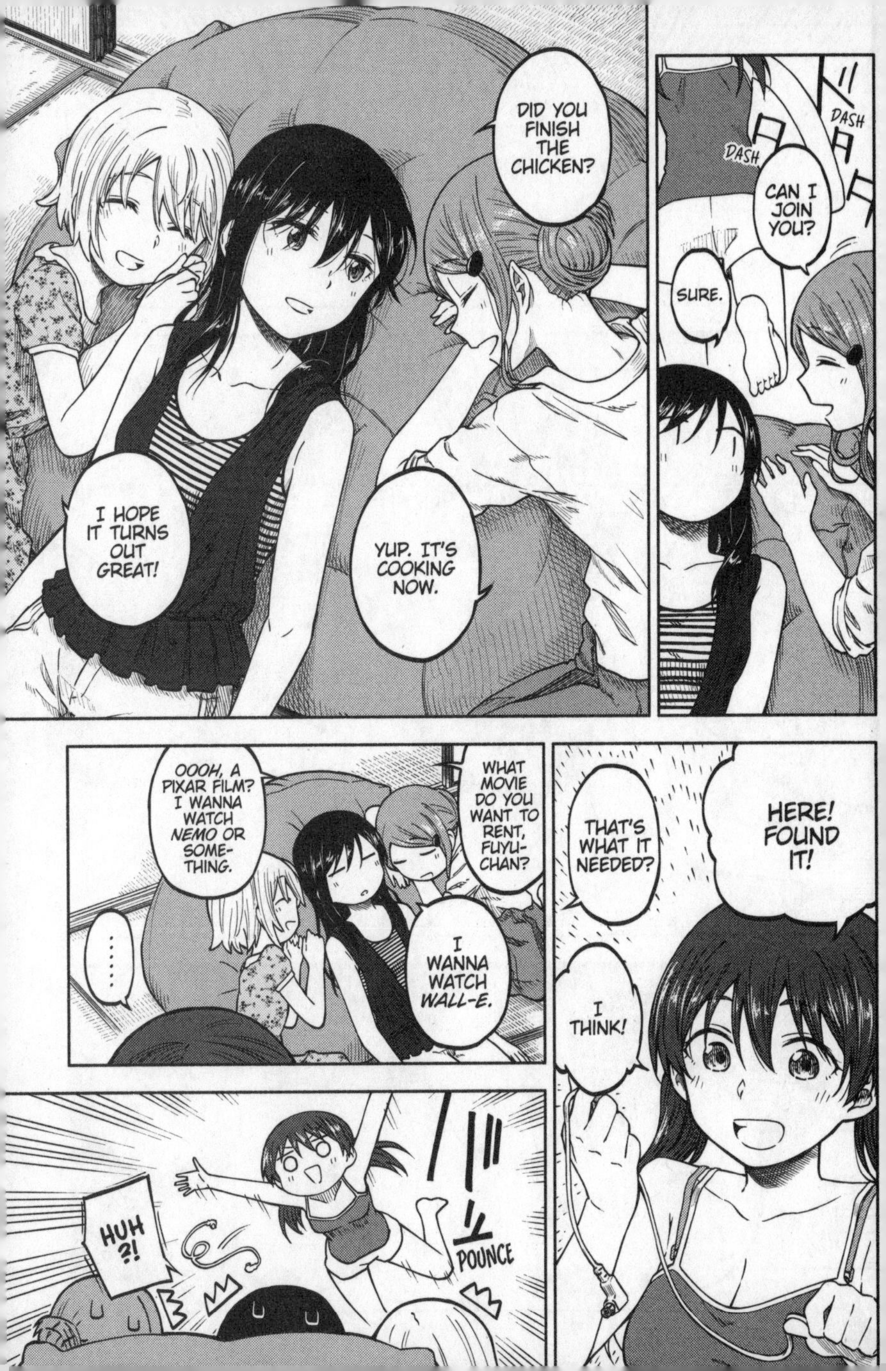
DASH
DASH
CAN I JOIN YOU?
SURE.
DID YOU FINISH THE CHICKEN?
YUP. IT'S COOKING NOW.
I HOPE IT TURNS OUT GREAT!
HERE! FOUND IT!
THAT'S WHAT IT NEEDED?
I THINK!
WHAT MOVIE DO YOU WANT TO RENT, FUYU-CHAN?
I WANNA WATCH *WALL-E*.
OOOH, A PIXAR FILM? I WANNA WATCH *NEMO* OR SOME-THING.
......
POUNCE
HUH?!

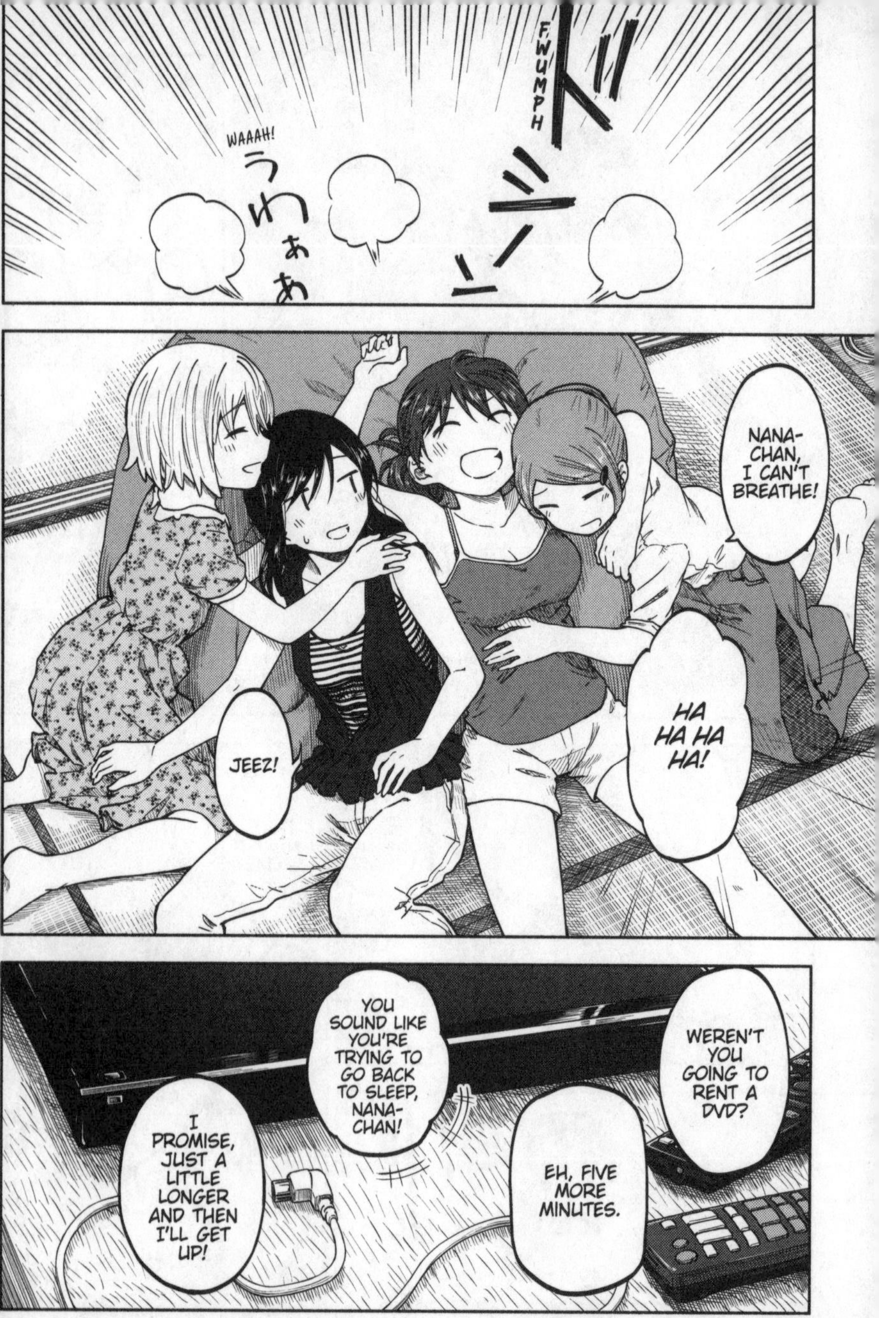
FWUMPH
WAAAH!
NANA-CHAN, I CAN'T BREATHE!
HA HA HA HA!
JEEZ!
WEREN'T YOU GOING TO RENT A DVD?
EH, FIVE MORE MINUTES.
YOU SOUND LIKE YOU'RE TRYING TO GO BACK TO SLEEP, NANA-CHAN!
I PROMISE, JUST A LITTLE LONGER AND THEN I'LL GET UP!

Our Wonderful Days

story & art by Kei Hamuro

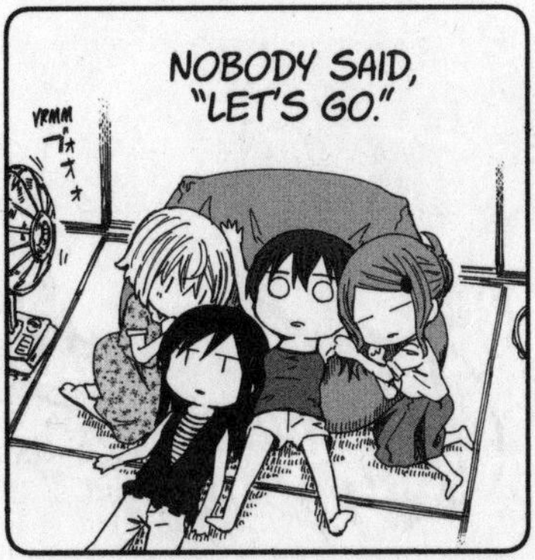
NOBODY SAID, "LET'S GO."
VRMM
ブオオォ

Our Wonderful Days
Tsurezure Biyori

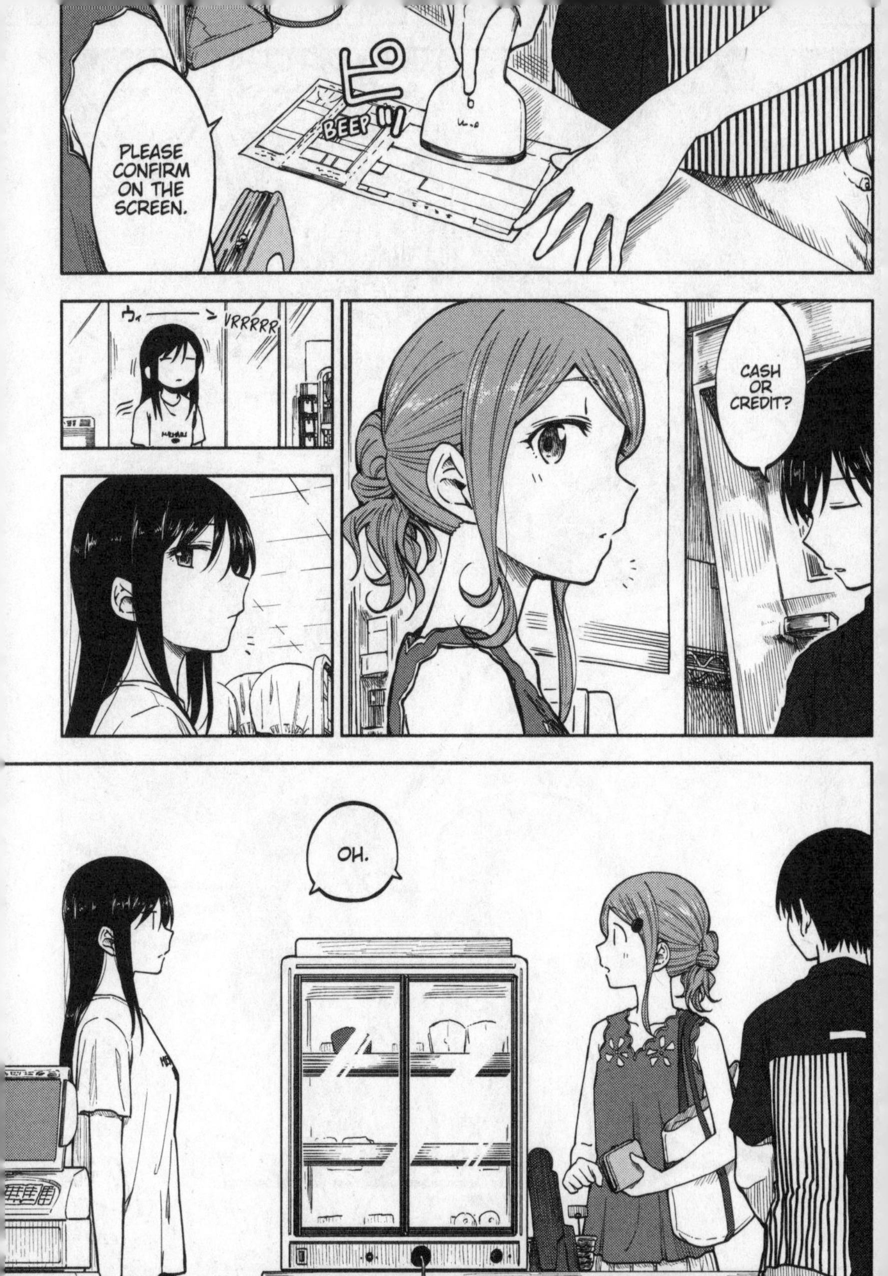
ピ
BEEP
PLEASE CONFIRM ON THE SCREEN.
CASH OR CREDIT?
ウィーー
VRRRRR
OH.

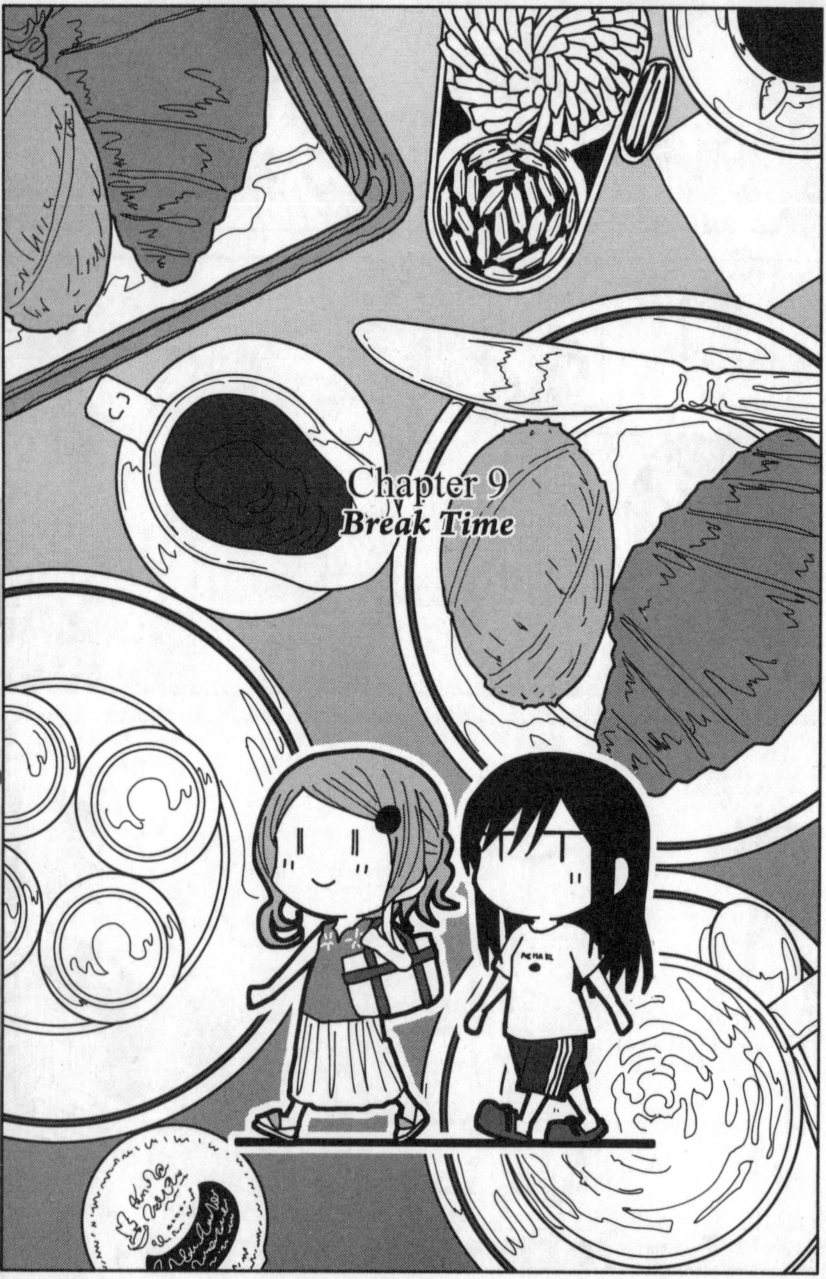
Chapter 9
Break Time

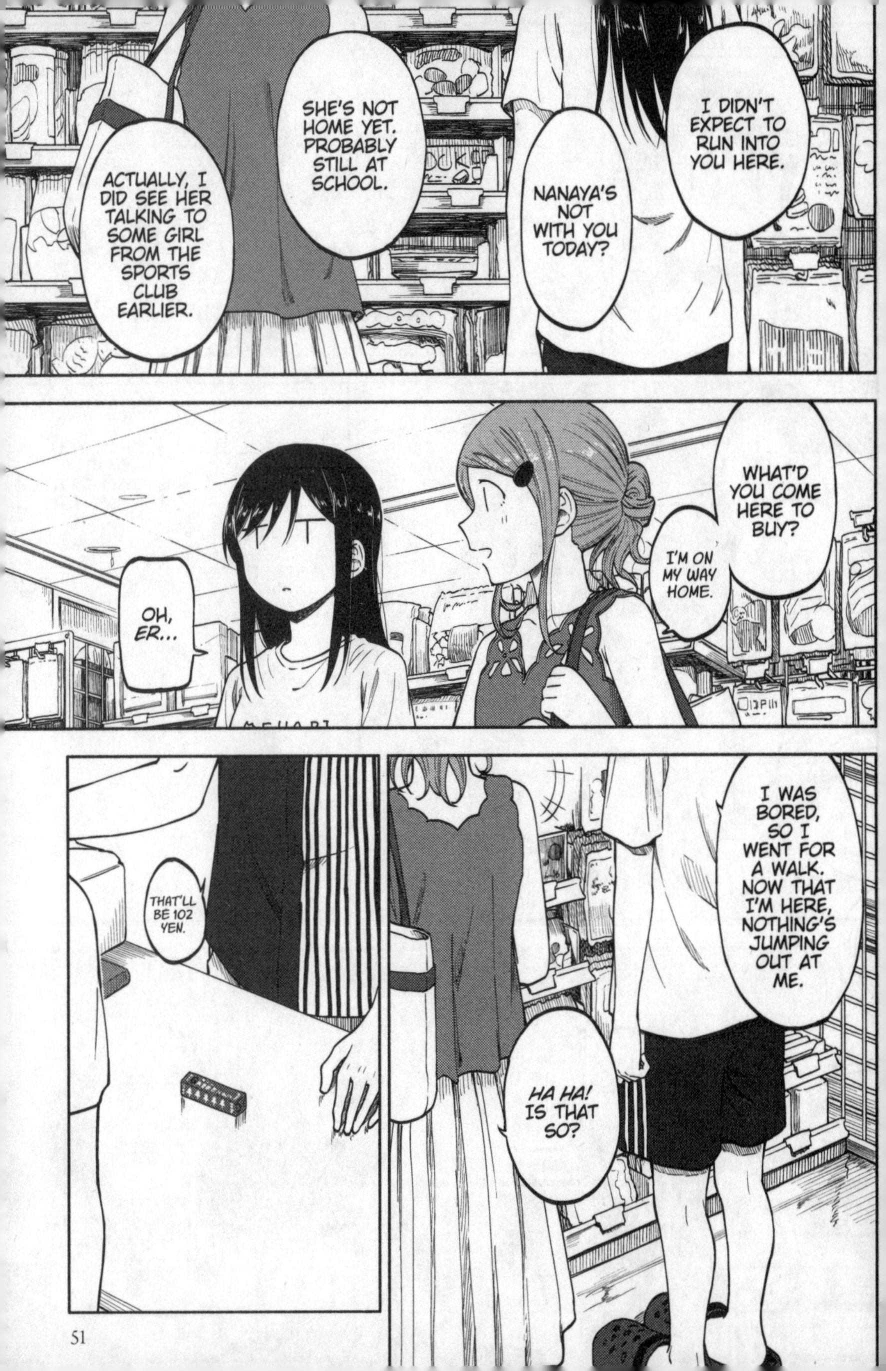
I DIDN'T EXPECT TO RUN INTO YOU HERE.
NANAYA'S NOT WITH YOU TODAY?
SHE'S NOT HOME YET. PROBABLY STILL AT SCHOOL.
ACTUALLY, I DID SEE HER TALKING TO SOME GIRL FROM THE SPORTS CLUB EARLIER.
WHAT'D YOU COME HERE TO BUY?
I'M ON MY WAY HOME.
OH, ER...
I WAS BORED, SO I WENT FOR A WALK. NOW THAT I'M HERE, NOTHING'S JUMPING OUT AT ME.
HA HA! IS THAT SO?
THAT'LL BE 102 YEN.

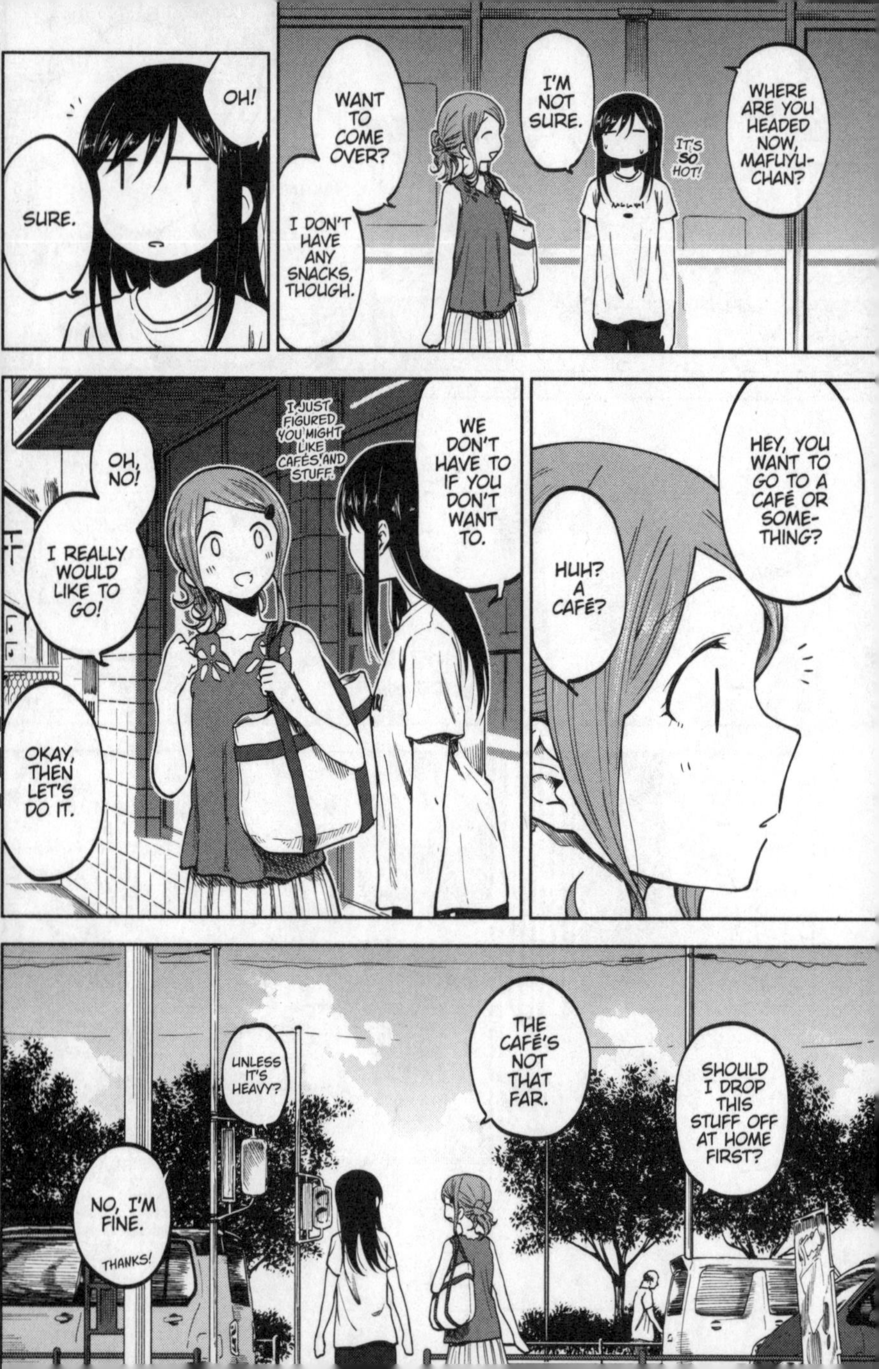
WHERE ARE YOU HEADED NOW, MAFUYU-CHAN?
IT'S SO HOT!
I'M NOT SURE.
WANT TO COME OVER?
I DON'T HAVE ANY SNACKS, THOUGH.
OH!
SURE.
HEY, YOU WANT TO GO TO A CAFÉ OR SOME-THING?
HUH? A CAFÉ?
WE DON'T HAVE TO IF YOU DON'T WANT TO.
I JUST FIGURED YOU MIGHT LIKE CAFÉS AND STUFF.
OH, NO!
I REALLY WOULD LIKE TO GO!
OKAY, THEN LET'S DO IT.
SHOULD I DROP THIS STUFF OFF AT HOME FIRST?
THE CAFÉ'S NOT THAT FAR.
UNLESS IT'S HEAVY?
NO, I'M FINE.
THANKS!

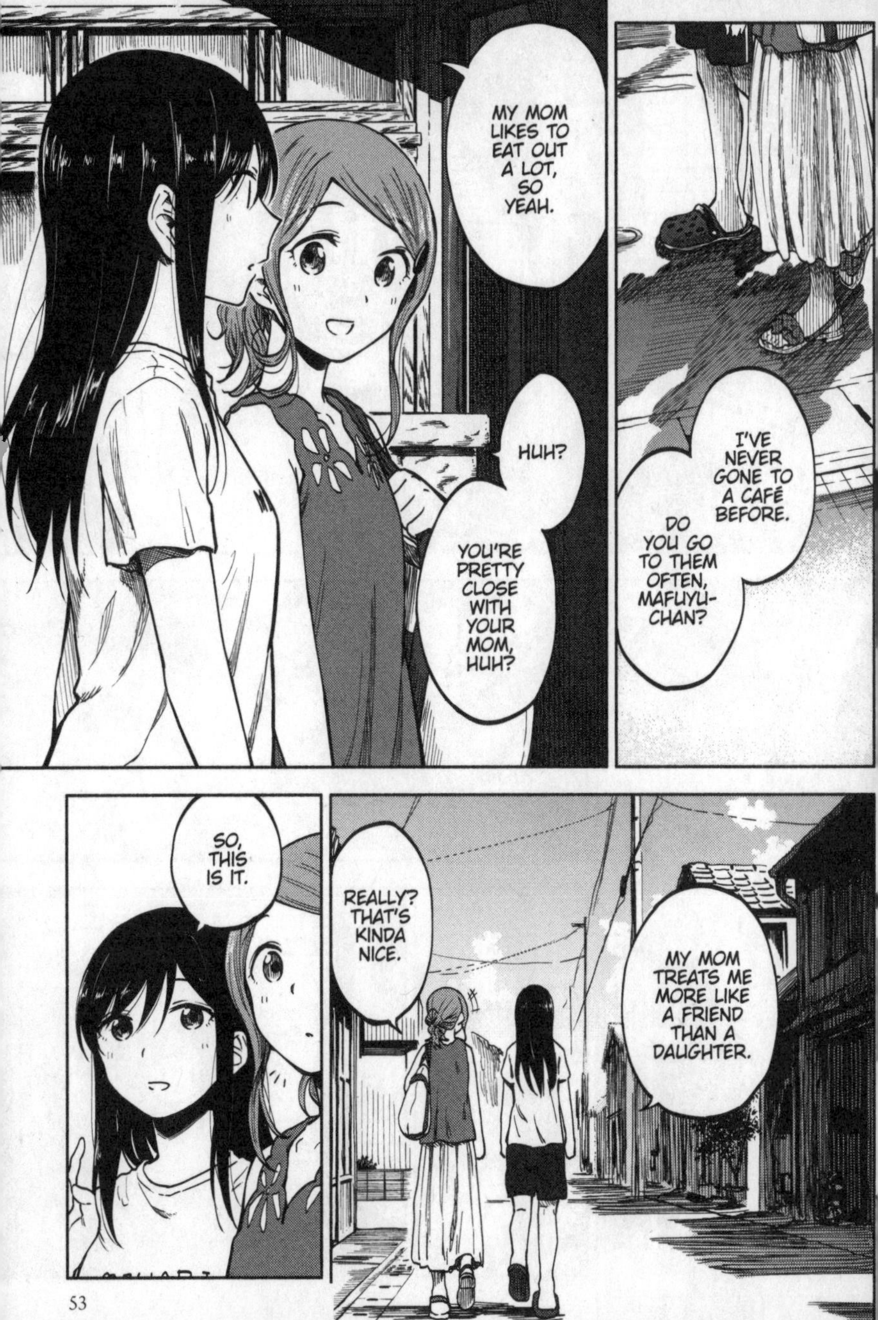
I'VE NEVER GONE TO A CAFÉ BEFORE.
DO YOU GO TO THEM OFTEN, MAFUYU-CHAN?
MY MOM LIKES TO EAT OUT A LOT, SO YEAH.
HUH?
YOU'RE PRETTY CLOSE WITH YOUR MOM, HUH?
MY MOM TREATS ME MORE LIKE A FRIEND THAN A DAUGHTER.
REALLY? THAT'S KINDA NICE.
SO, THIS IS IT.

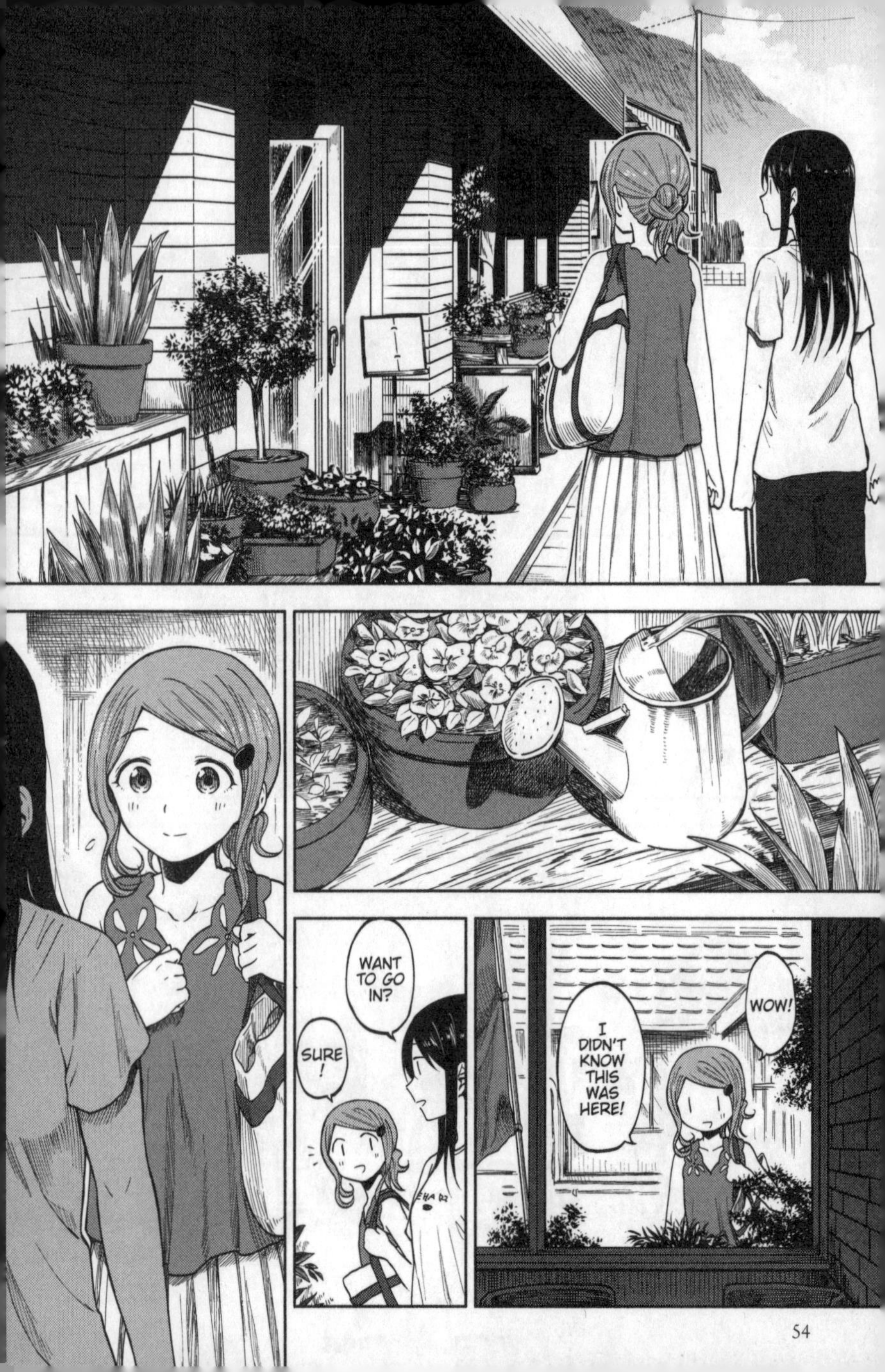
WOW!
I DIDN'T KNOW THIS WAS HERE!
WANT TO GO IN?
SURE!

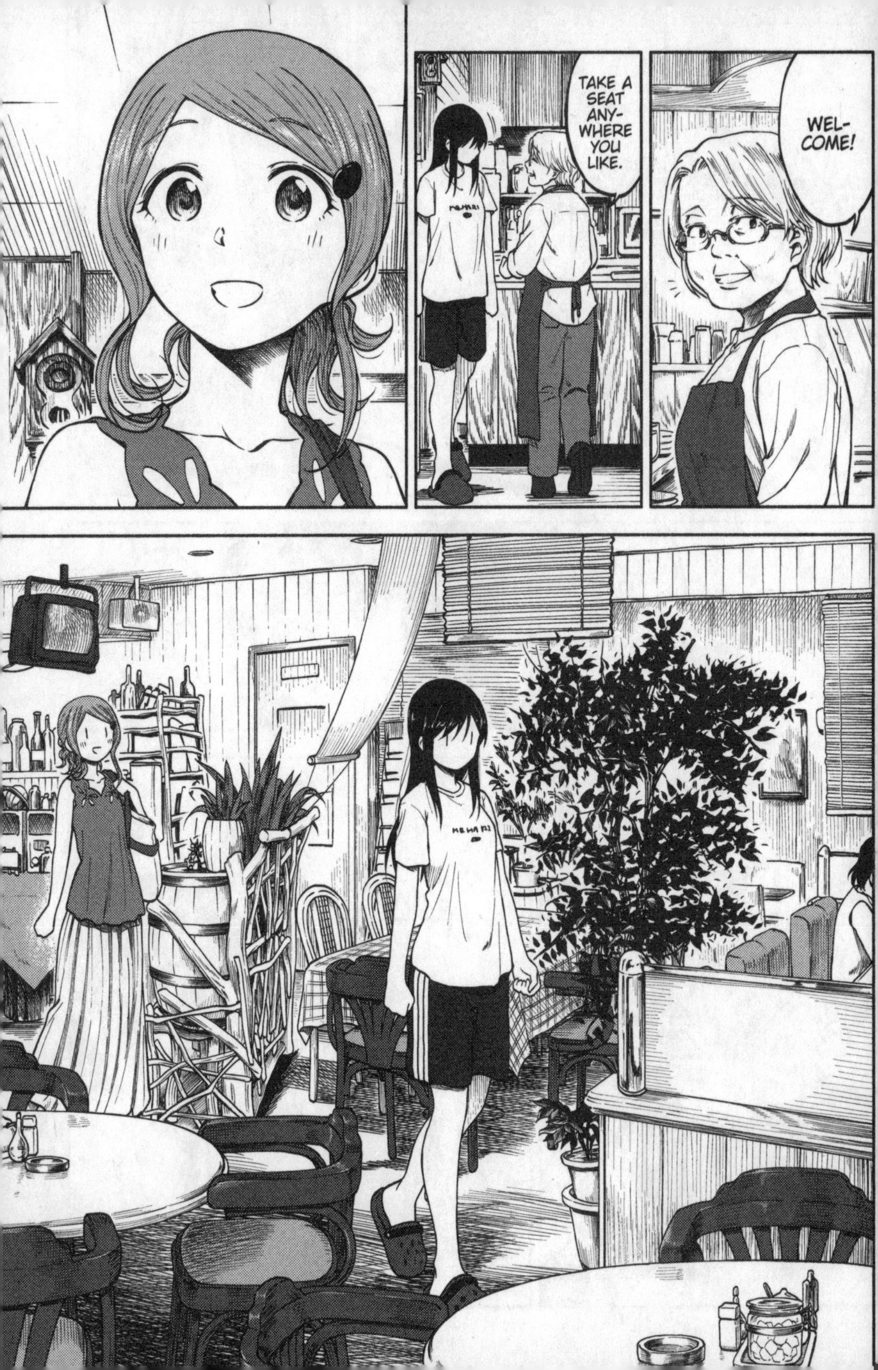
WEL-COME!
TAKE A SEAT ANY-WHERE YOU LIKE.

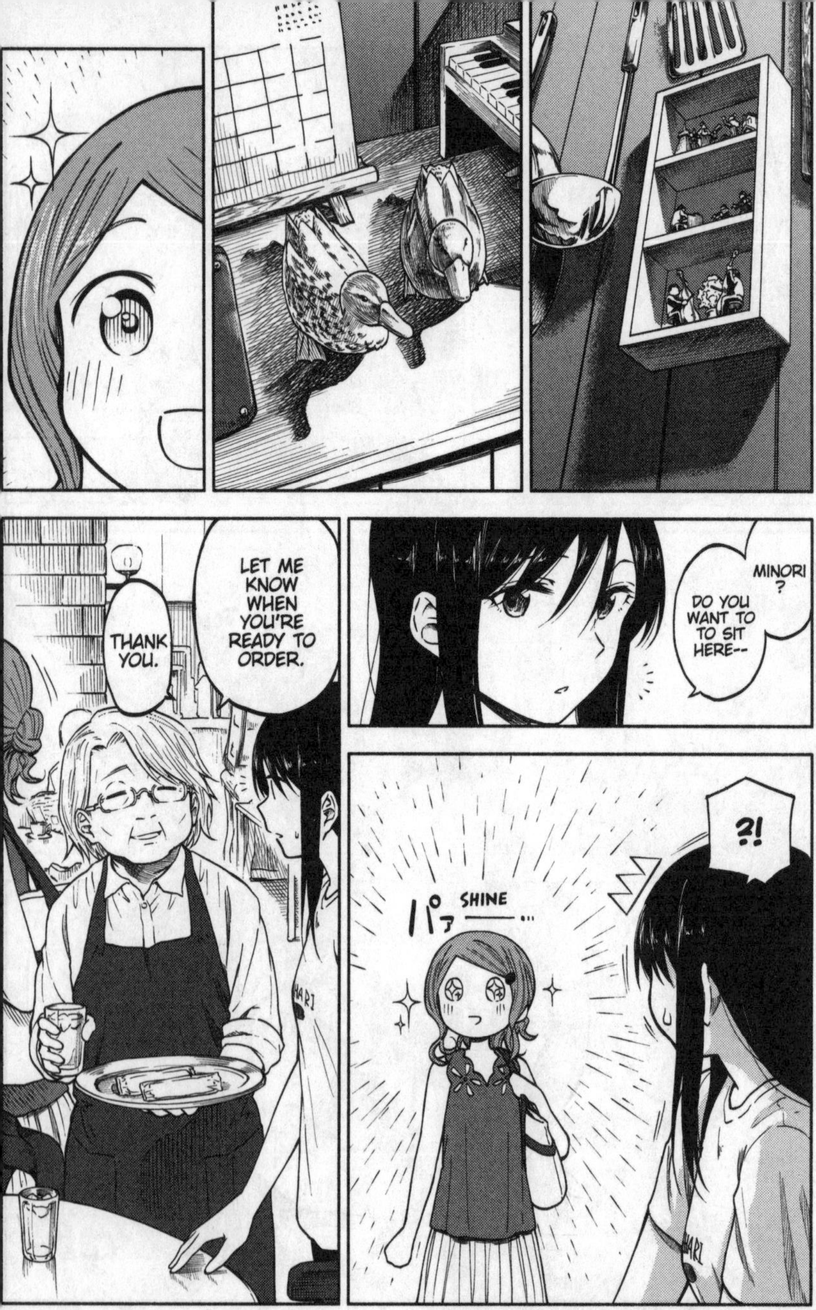
MINORI?
DO YOU WANT TO TO SIT HERE--
?!
パァ SHINE —...
LET ME KNOW WHEN YOU'RE READY TO ORDER.
THANK YOU.

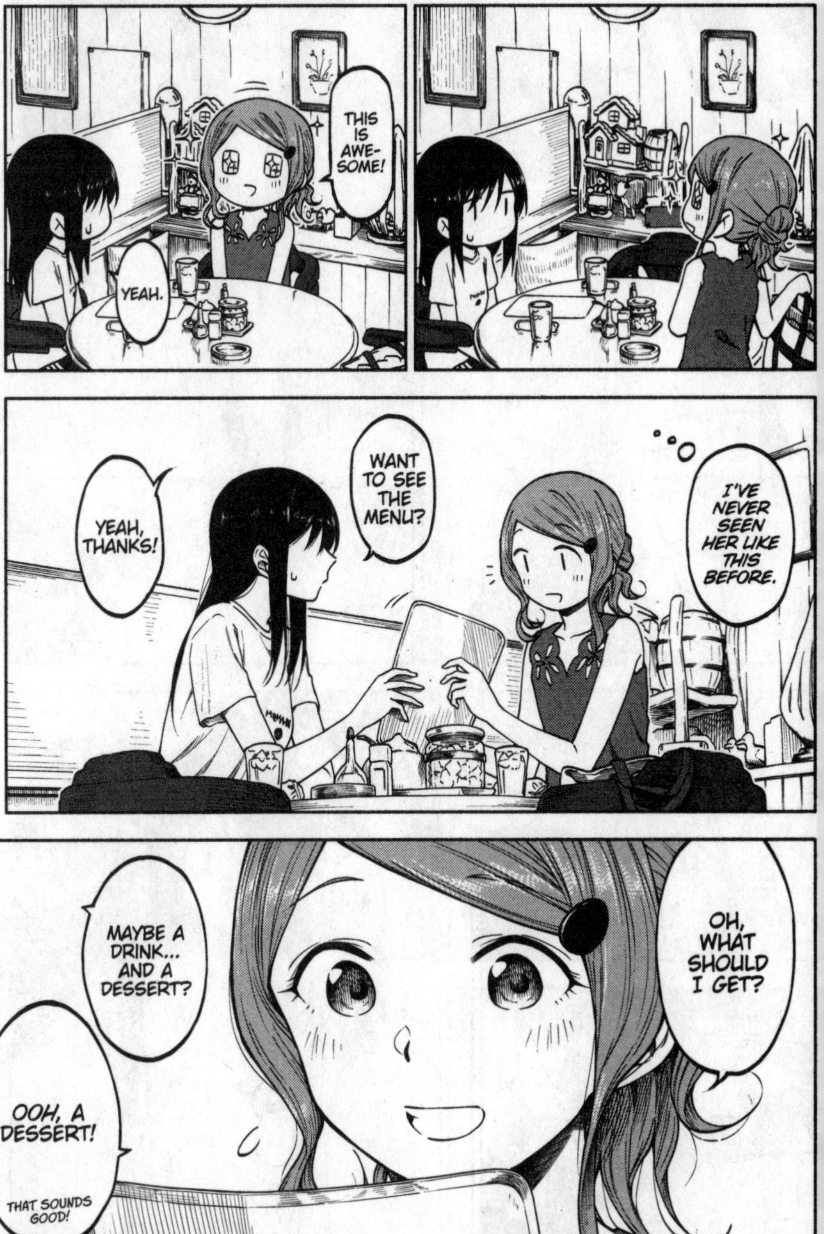
THIS IS AWE-SOME!
YEAH.
I'VE NEVER SEEN HER LIKE THIS BEFORE.
WANT TO SEE THE MENU?
YEAH, THANKS!
OH, WHAT SHOULD I GET?
MAYBE A DRINK... AND A DESSERT?
OOH, A DESSERT!
THAT SOUNDS GOOD!

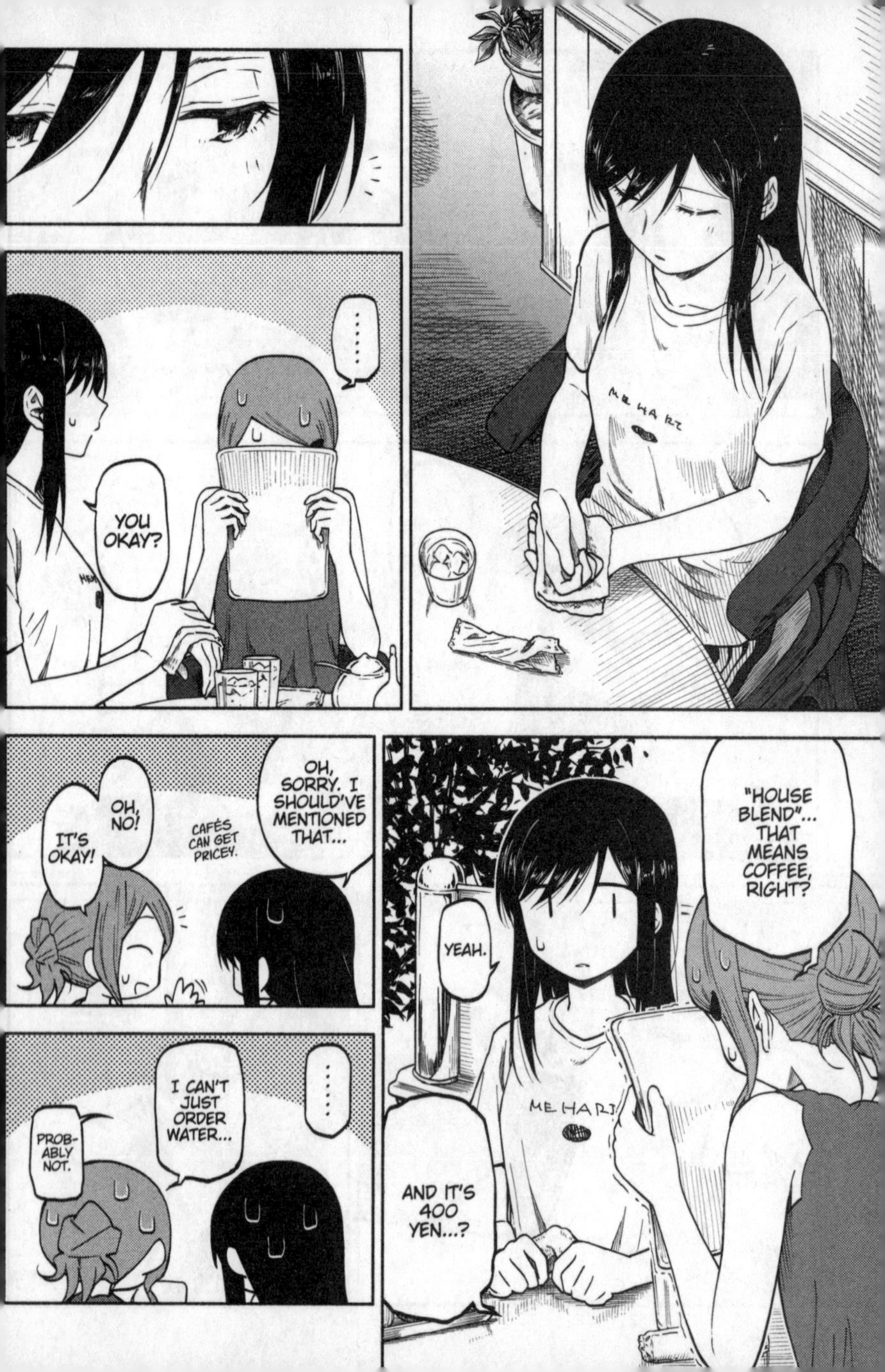
......
YOU OKAY?
"HOUSE BLEND"... THAT MEANS COFFEE, RIGHT?
YEAH.
ME HARI
AND IT'S 400 YEN...?
OH, SORRY. I SHOULD'VE MENTIONED THAT...
CAFÉS CAN GET PRICEY.
OH, NO!
IT'S OKAY!
......
I CAN'T JUST ORDER WATER...
PROB-ABLY NOT.

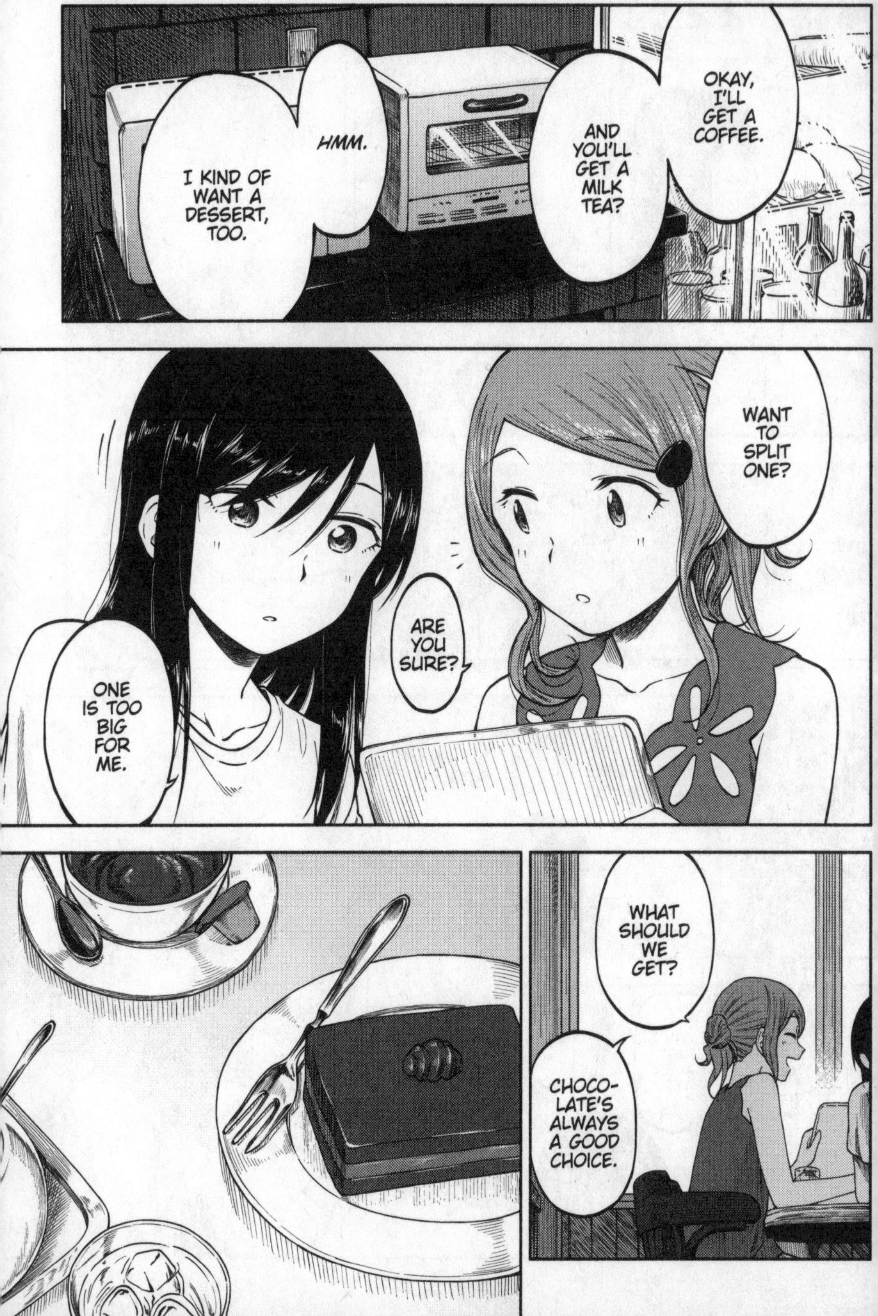
OKAY, I'LL GET A COFFEE.
AND YOU'LL GET A MILK TEA?
HMM.
I KIND OF WANT A DESSERT, TOO.
WANT TO SPLIT ONE?
ARE YOU SURE?
ONE IS TOO BIG FOR ME.
WHAT SHOULD WE GET?
CHOCO-LATE'S ALWAYS A GOOD CHOICE.

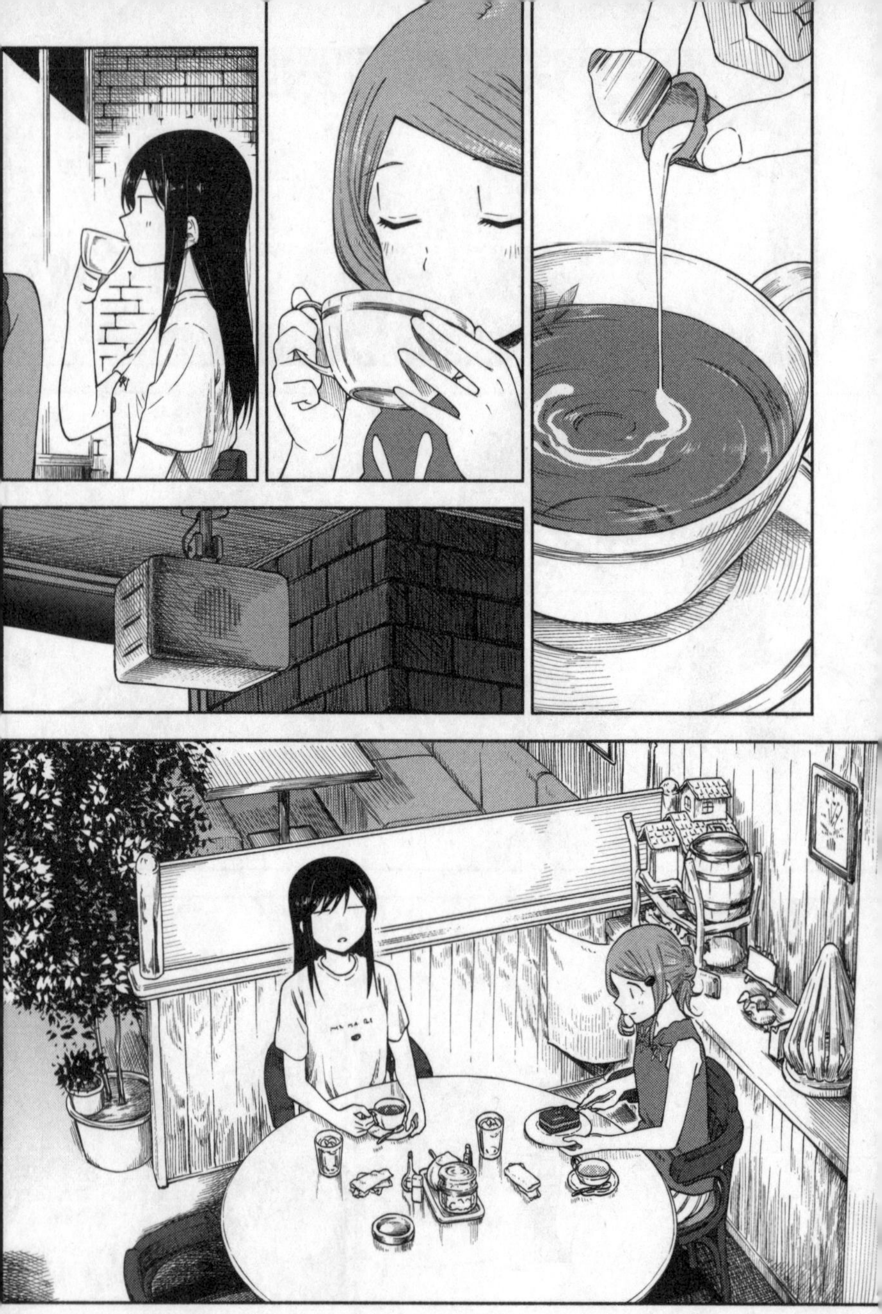

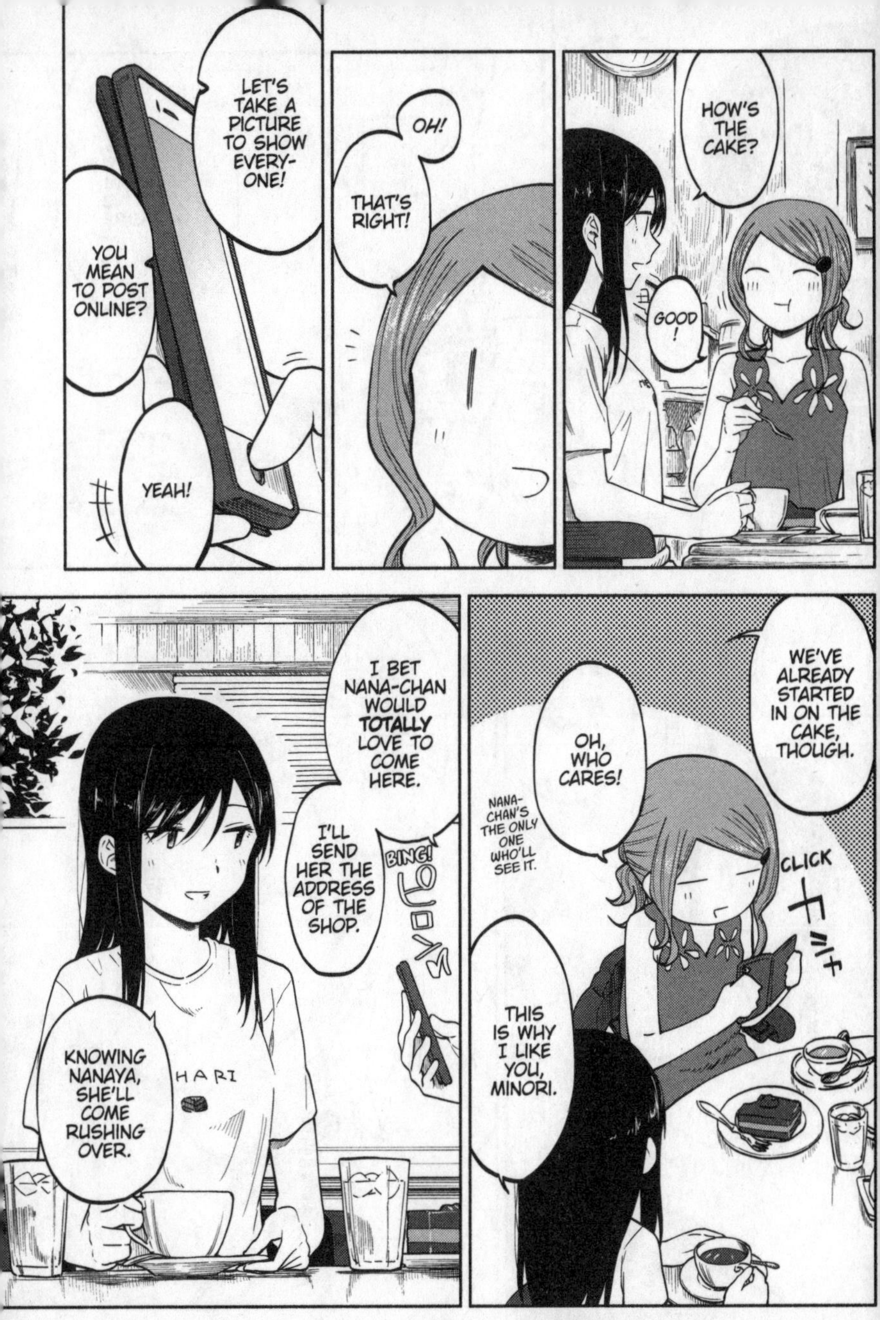
HOW'S THE CAKE?
GOOD!
OH!
THAT'S RIGHT!
LET'S TAKE A PICTURE TO SHOW EVERYONE!
YOU MEAN TO POST ONLINE?
YEAH!
WE'VE ALREADY STARTED IN ON THE CAKE, THOUGH.
OH, WHO CARES!
NANA-CHAN'S THE ONLY ONE WHO'LL SEE IT.
CLICK
THIS IS WHY I LIKE YOU, MINORI.
I BET NANA-CHAN WOULD TOTALLY LOVE TO COME HERE.
I'LL SEND HER THE ADDRESS OF THE SHOP.
BING!
KNOWING NANAYA, SHE'LL COME RUSHING OVER.

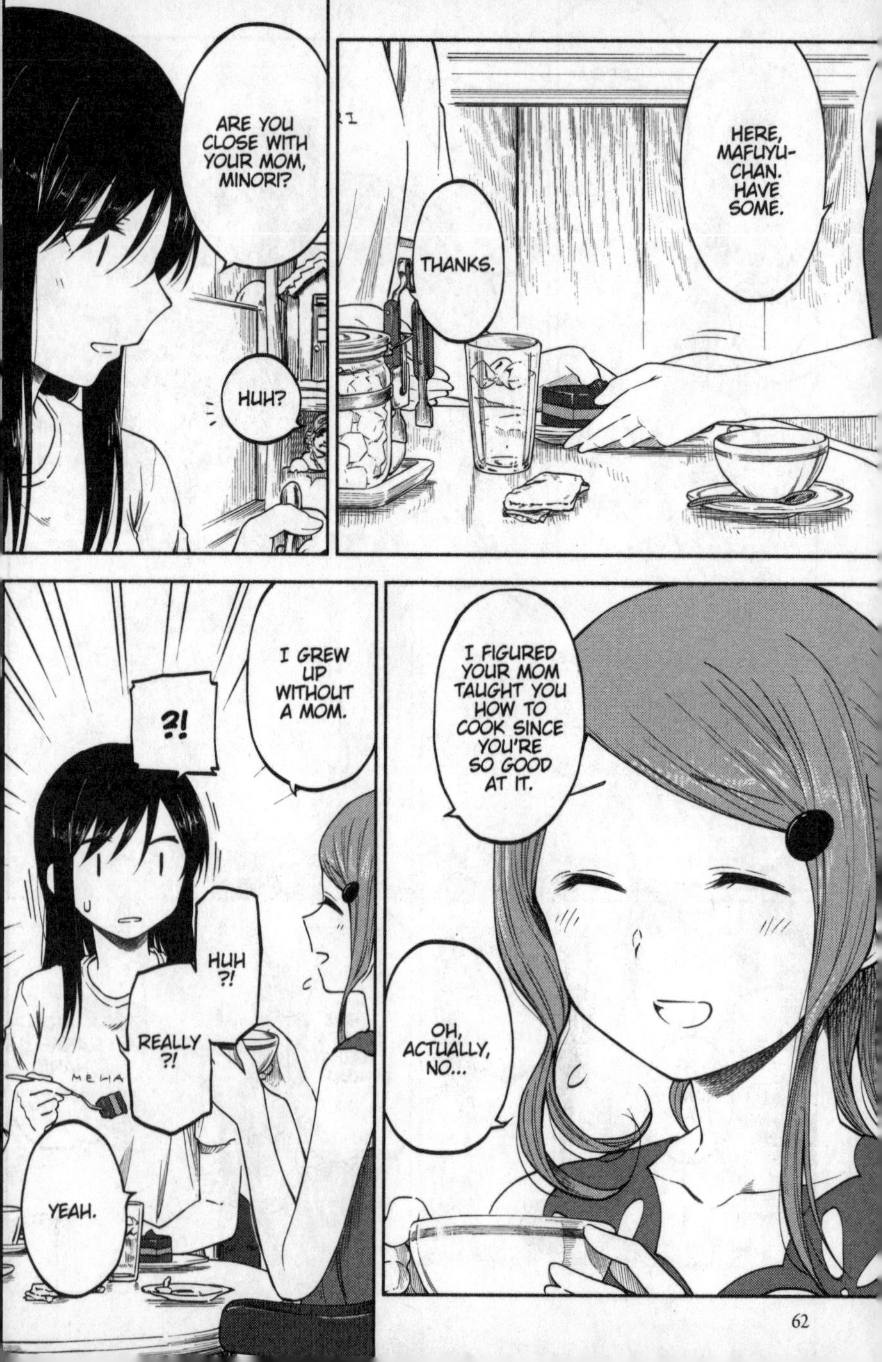
HERE, MAFUYU-CHAN. HAVE SOME.
THANKS.
ARE YOU CLOSE WITH YOUR MOM, MINORI?
HUH?
I FIGURED YOUR MOM TAUGHT YOU HOW TO COOK SINCE YOU'RE SO GOOD AT IT.
OH, ACTUALLY, NO...
I GREW UP WITHOUT A MOM.
?!
HUH ?!
REALLY ?!
YEAH.

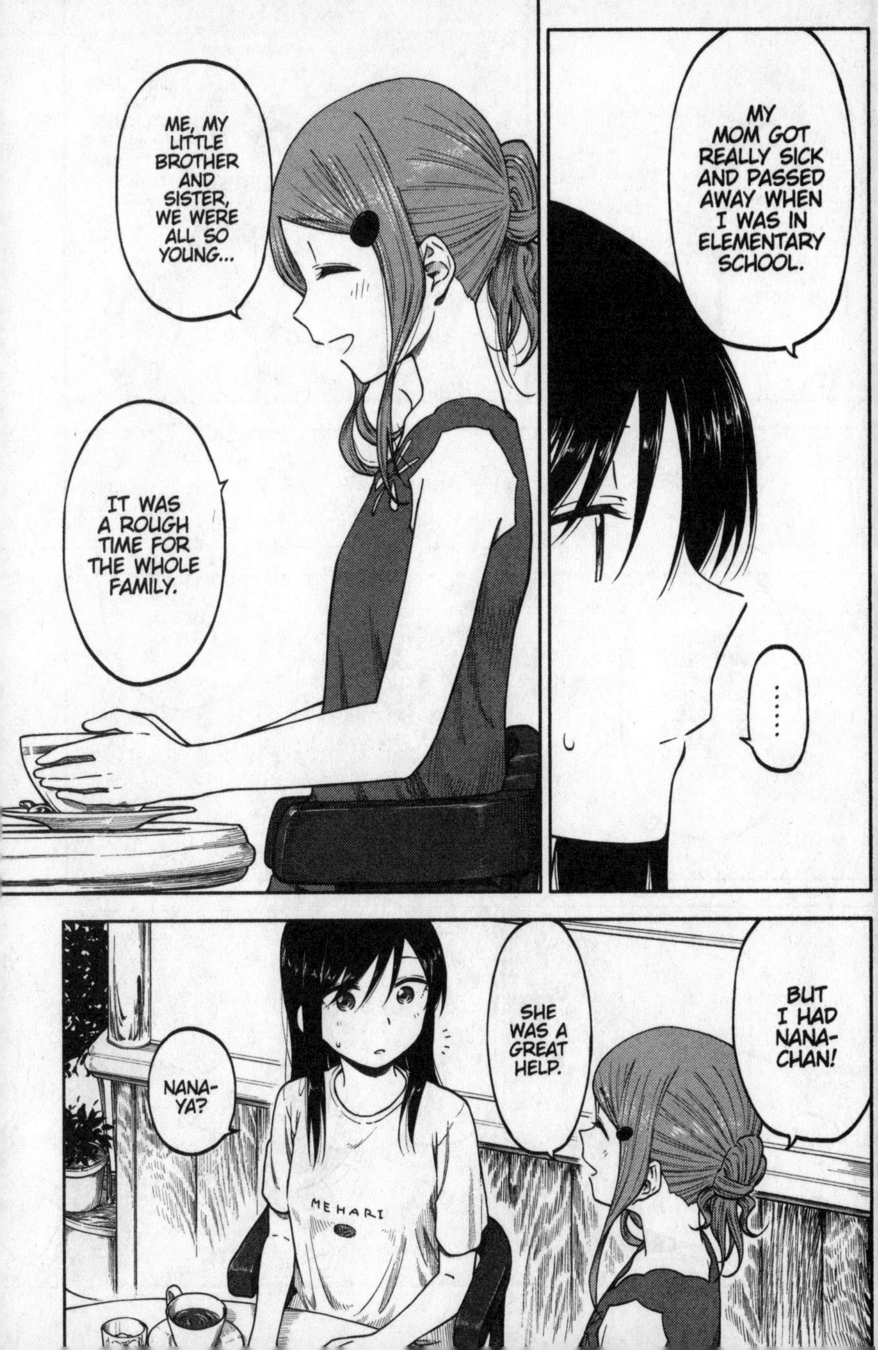
MY MOM GOT REALLY SICK AND PASSED AWAY WHEN I WAS IN ELEMENTARY SCHOOL.
......
ME, MY LITTLE BROTHER AND SISTER, WE WERE ALL SO YOUNG...
IT WAS A ROUGH TIME FOR THE WHOLE FAMILY.
BUT I HAD NANA-CHAN!
SHE WAS A GREAT HELP.
NANA-YA?
MEHARI

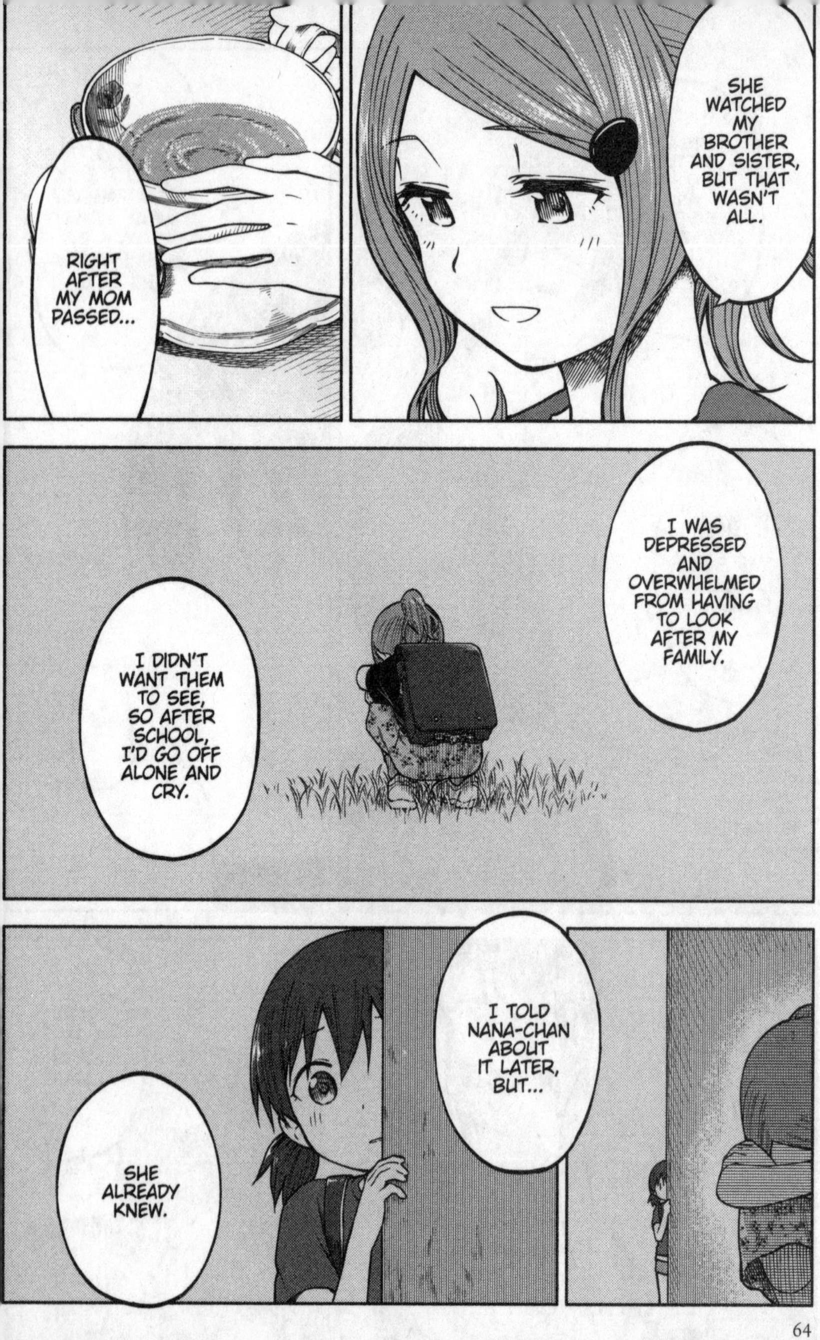
SHE WATCHED MY BROTHER AND SISTER, BUT THAT WASN'T ALL.
RIGHT AFTER MY MOM PASSED...
I WAS DEPRESSED AND OVERWHELMED FROM HAVING TO LOOK AFTER MY FAMILY.
I DIDN'T WANT THEM TO SEE, SO AFTER SCHOOL, I'D GO OFF ALONE AND CRY.
I TOLD NANA-CHAN ABOUT IT LATER, BUT...
SHE ALREADY KNEW.

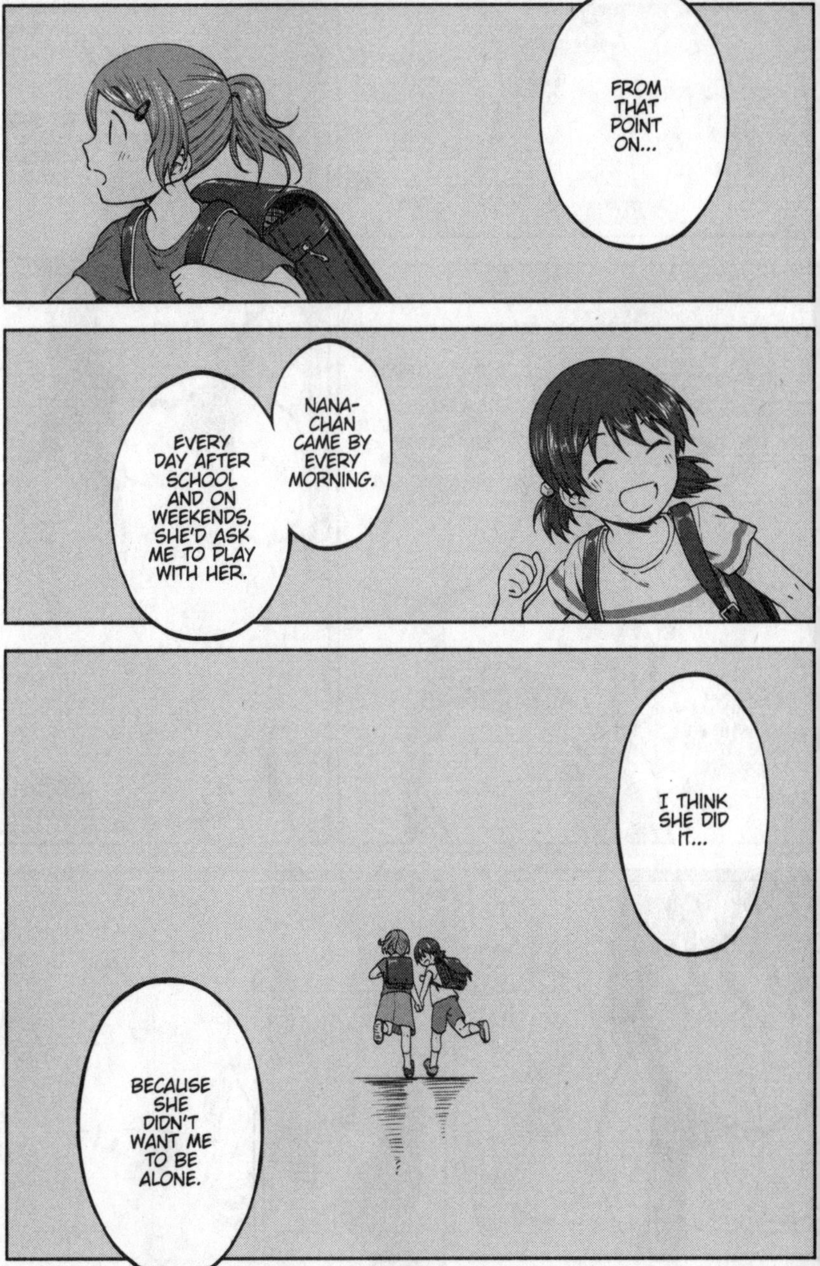
FROM THAT POINT ON...
NANA-CHAN CAME BY EVERY MORNING.
EVERY DAY AFTER SCHOOL AND ON WEEKENDS, SHE'D ASK ME TO PLAY WITH HER.
I THINK SHE DID IT...
BECAUSE SHE DIDN'T WANT ME TO BE ALONE.

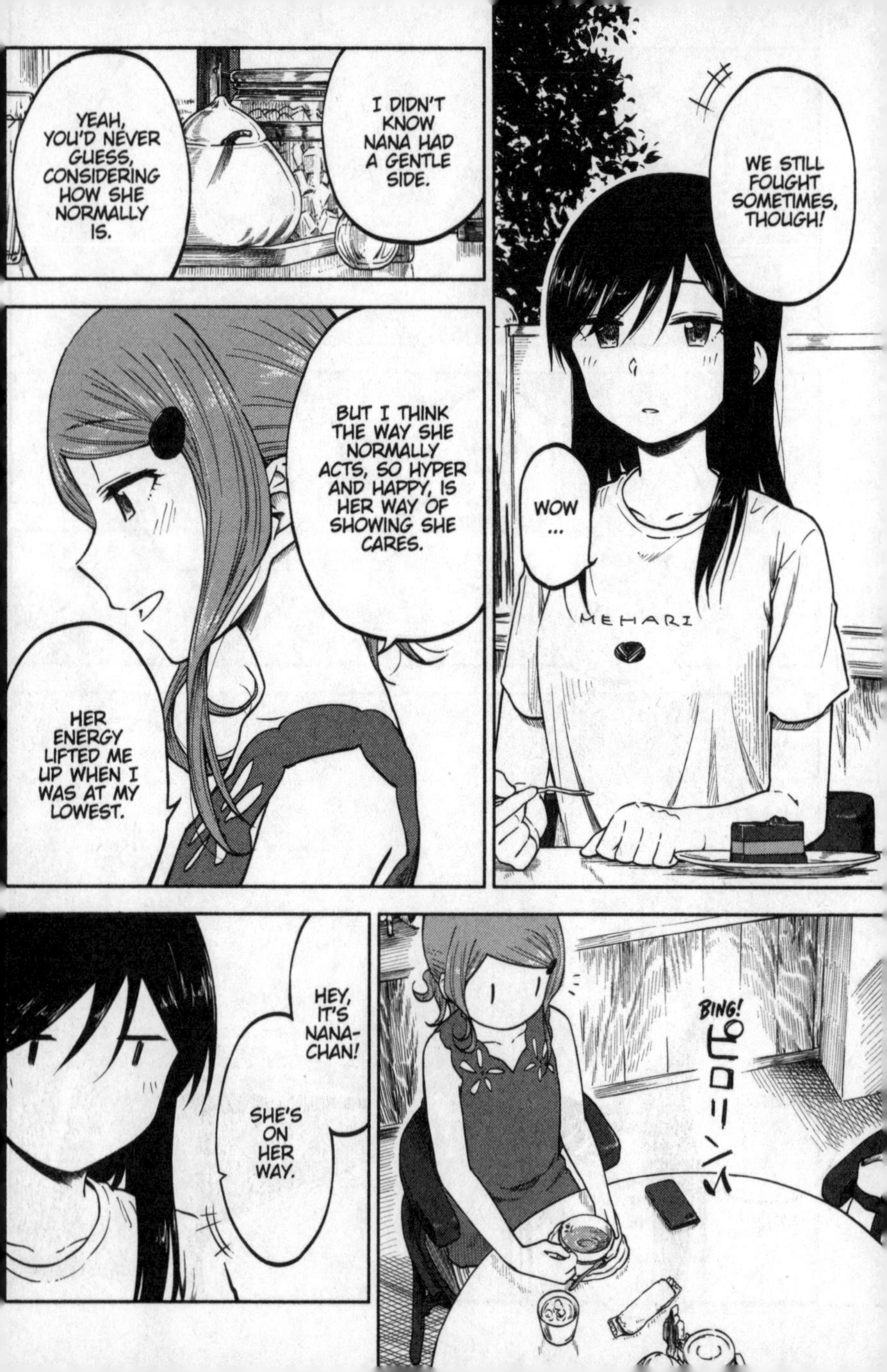
WE STILL FOUGHT SOMETIMES, THOUGH!
WOW ...
MEHARI
I DIDN'T KNOW NANA HAD A GENTLE SIDE.
YEAH, YOU'D NEVER GUESS, CONSIDERING HOW SHE NORMALLY IS.
BUT I THINK THE WAY SHE NORMALLY ACTS, SO HYPER AND HAPPY, IS HER WAY OF SHOWING SHE CARES.
HER ENERGY LIFTED ME UP WHEN I WAS AT MY LOWEST.
BING!
ピロリン♪
HEY, IT'S NANA-CHAN!
SHE'S ON HER WAY.

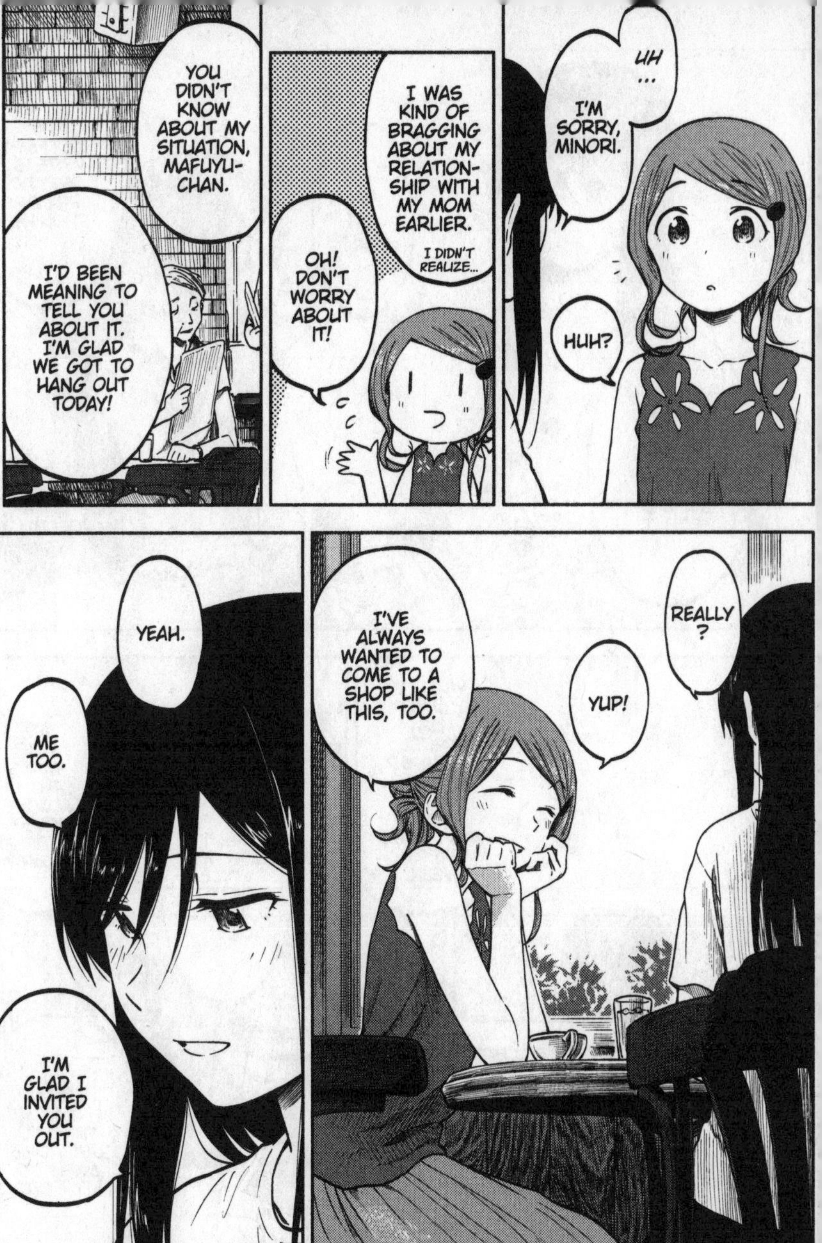
UH ...
I'M SORRY, MINORI.
HUH?
I WAS KIND OF BRAGGING ABOUT MY RELATIONSHIP WITH MY MOM EARLIER.
I DIDN'T REALIZE...
OH! DON'T WORRY ABOUT IT!
YOU DIDN'T KNOW ABOUT MY SITUATION, MAFUYU-CHAN.
I'D BEEN MEANING TO TELL YOU ABOUT IT. I'M GLAD WE GOT TO HANG OUT TODAY!
REALLY?
YUP!
I'VE ALWAYS WANTED TO COME TO A SHOP LIKE THIS, TOO.
YEAH.
ME TOO.
I'M GLAD I INVITED YOU OUT.

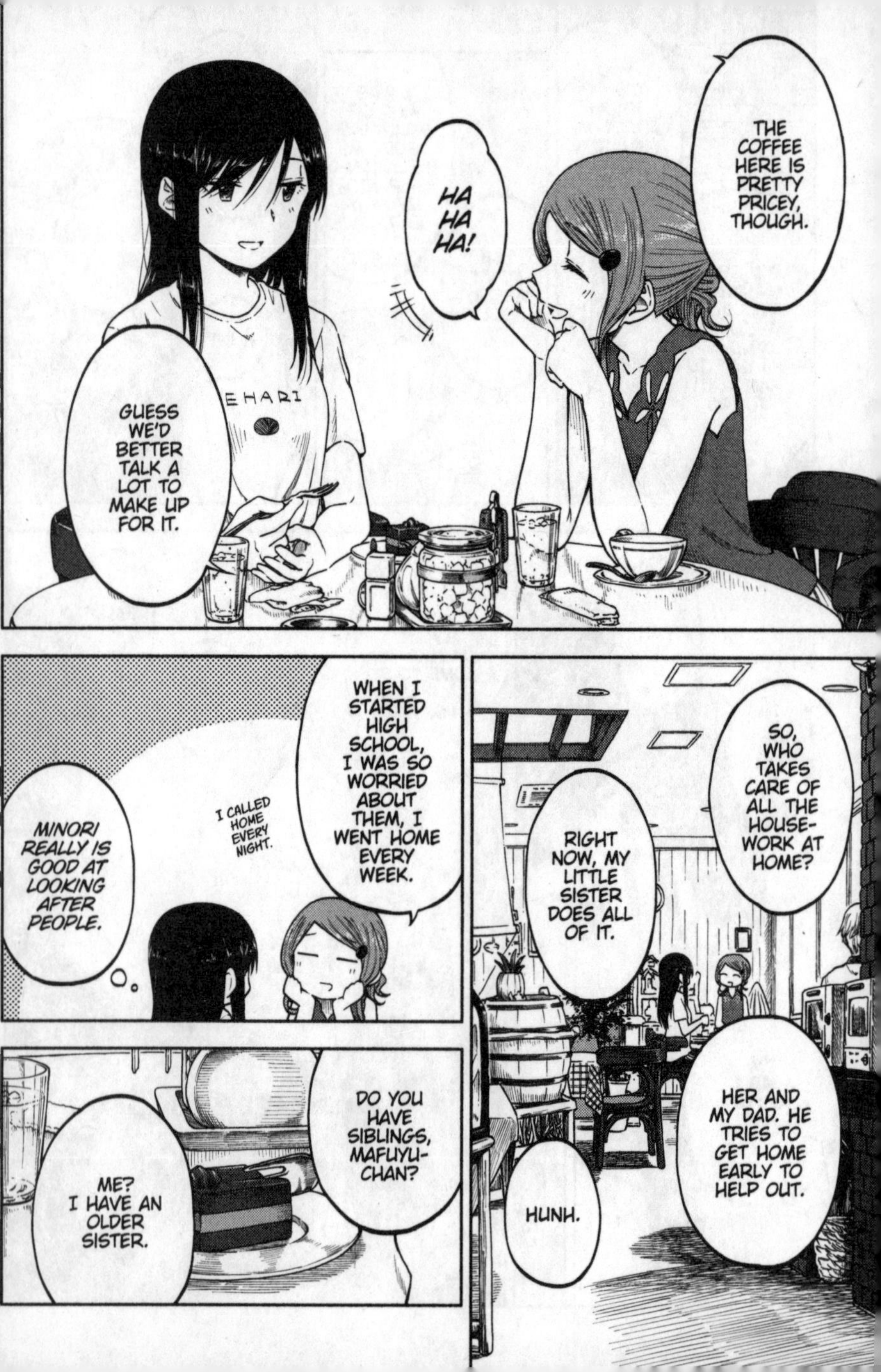
THE COFFEE HERE IS PRETTY PRICEY, THOUGH.
HA HA HA!
GUESS WE'D BETTER TALK A LOT TO MAKE UP FOR IT.
SO, WHO TAKES CARE OF ALL THE HOUSE-WORK AT HOME?
RIGHT NOW, MY LITTLE SISTER DOES ALL OF IT.
HER AND MY DAD. HE TRIES TO GET HOME EARLY TO HELP OUT.
HUNH.
WHEN I STARTED HIGH SCHOOL, I WAS SO WORRIED ABOUT THEM, I WENT HOME EVERY WEEK.
I CALLED HOME EVERY NIGHT.
MINORI REALLY IS GOOD AT LOOKING AFTER PEOPLE.
DO YOU HAVE SIBLINGS, MAFUYU-CHAN?
ME? I HAVE AN OLDER SISTER.

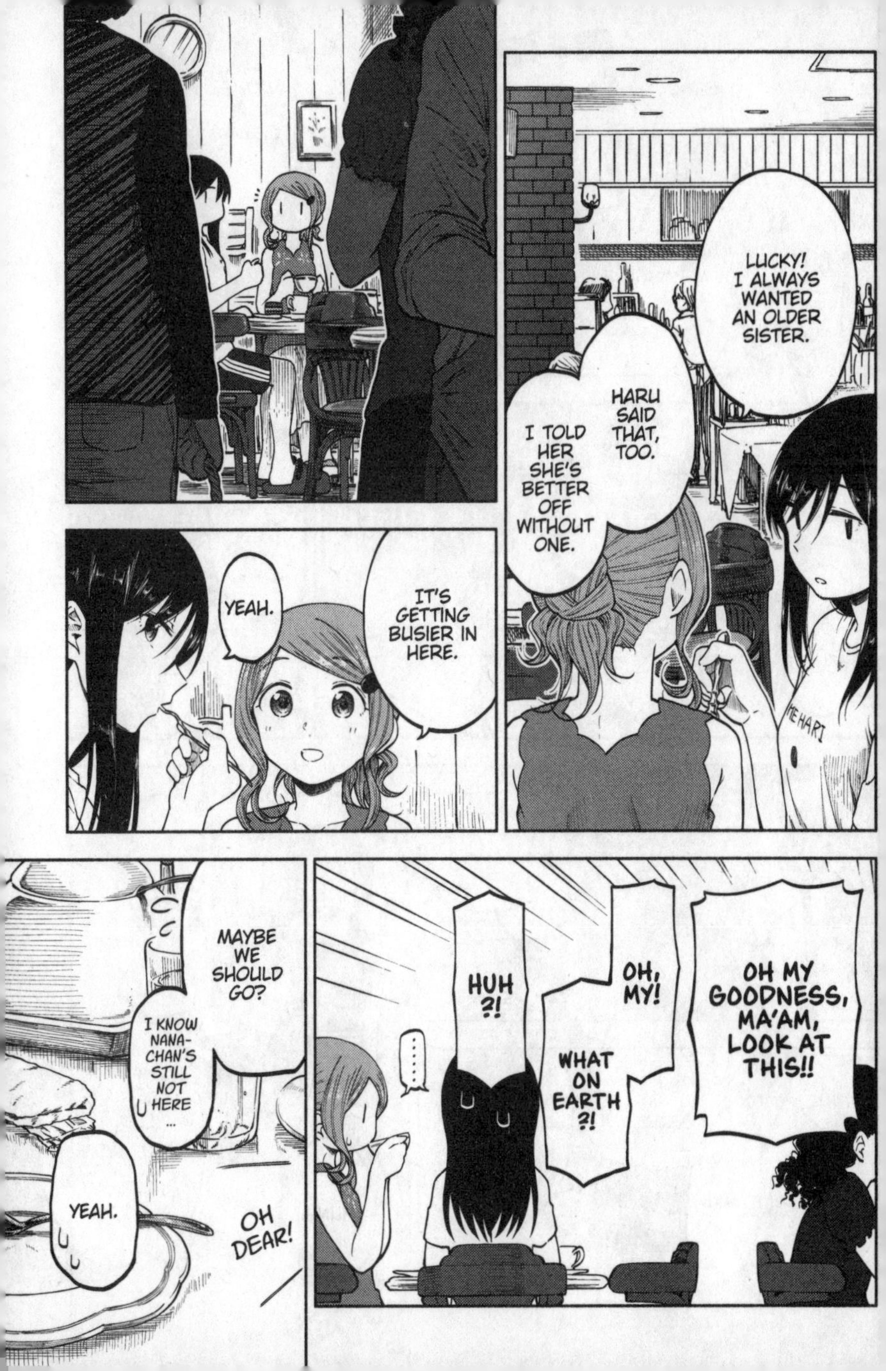
LUCKY! I ALWAYS WANTED AN OLDER SISTER.
HARU SAID THAT, TOO.
I TOLD HER SHE'S BETTER OFF WITHOUT ONE.
MEHARI
IT'S GETTING BUSIER IN HERE.
YEAH.
OH MY GOODNESS, MA'AM, LOOK AT THIS!!
OH, MY!
WHAT ON EARTH?!
HUH?!
……
MAYBE WE SHOULD GO?
I KNOW NANA-CHAN'S STILL NOT HERE...
YEAH.
OH DEAR!

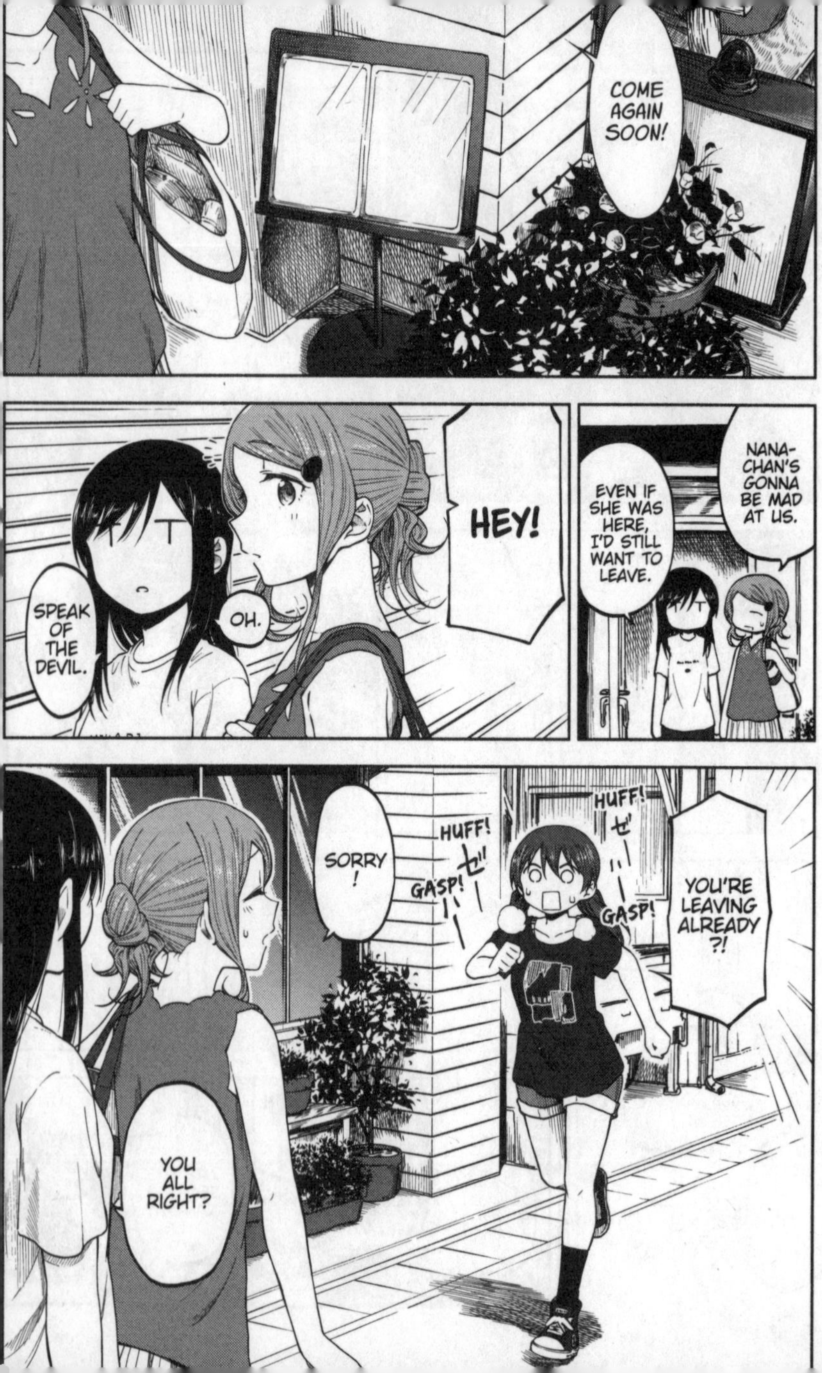
COME AGAIN SOON!
NANA-CHAN'S GONNA BE MAD AT US.
EVEN IF SHE WAS HERE, I'D STILL WANT TO LEAVE.
HEY!
OH.
SPEAK OF THE DEVIL.
YOU'RE LEAVING ALREADY ?!
HUFF! ゼ
GASP! ハ
HUFF! ゼ
GASP! ハ
SORRY!
YOU ALL RIGHT?

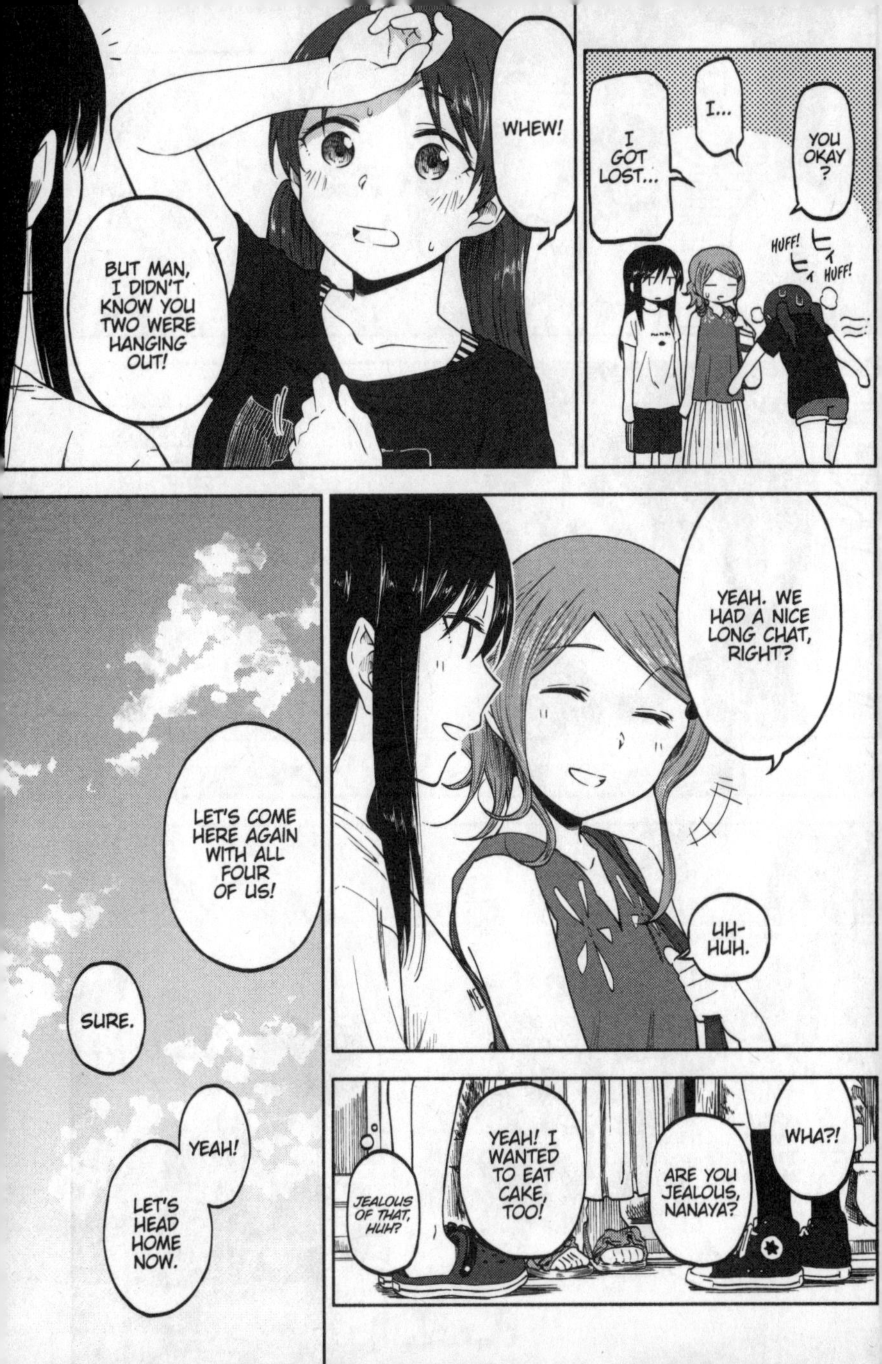
YOU OKAY?
I...
I GOT LOST...
HUFF! ヒィ
ヒィ HUFF!
WHEW!
BUT MAN, I DIDN'T KNOW YOU TWO WERE HANGING OUT!
YEAH. WE HAD A NICE LONG CHAT, RIGHT?
UH-HUH.
WHA?!
ARE YOU JEALOUS, NANAYA?
YEAH! I WANTED TO EAT CAKE, TOO!
JEALOUS OF THAT, HUH?
LET'S COME HERE AGAIN WITH ALL FOUR OF US!
SURE.
YEAH!
LET'S HEAD HOME NOW.

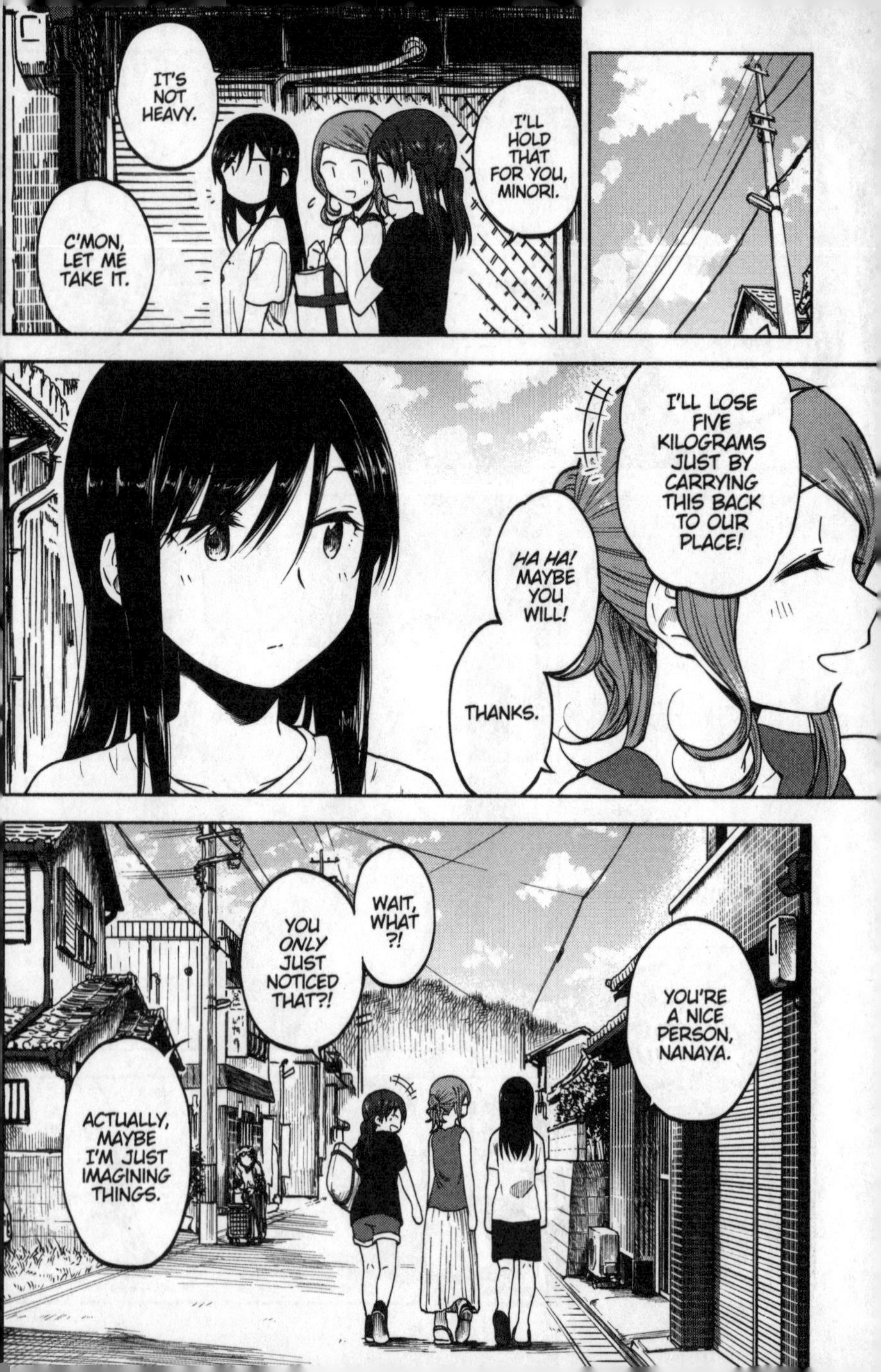
I'LL HOLD THAT FOR YOU, MINORI.
IT'S NOT HEAVY.
C'MON, LET ME TAKE IT.
I'LL LOSE FIVE KILOGRAMS JUST BY CARRYING THIS BACK TO OUR PLACE!
HA HA! MAYBE YOU WILL!
THANKS.
YOU'RE A NICE PERSON, NANAYA.
WAIT, WHAT?!
YOU ONLY JUST NOTICED THAT?!
ACTUALLY, MAYBE I'M JUST IMAGINING THINGS.

Our Wonderful Days

story & art by Kei Hamuro

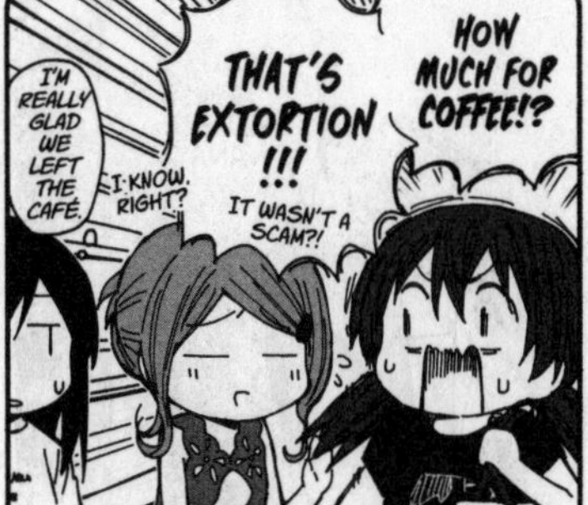
HOW MUCH FOR COFFEE!?
THAT'S EXTORTION !!!
IT WASN'T A SCAM?!
I·KNOW. RIGHT?
I'M REALLY GLAD WE LEFT THE CAFÉ.

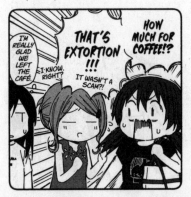

Our *Wonderful* *Days* Tsurezure Biyori

Chapter 10
Mature Taste

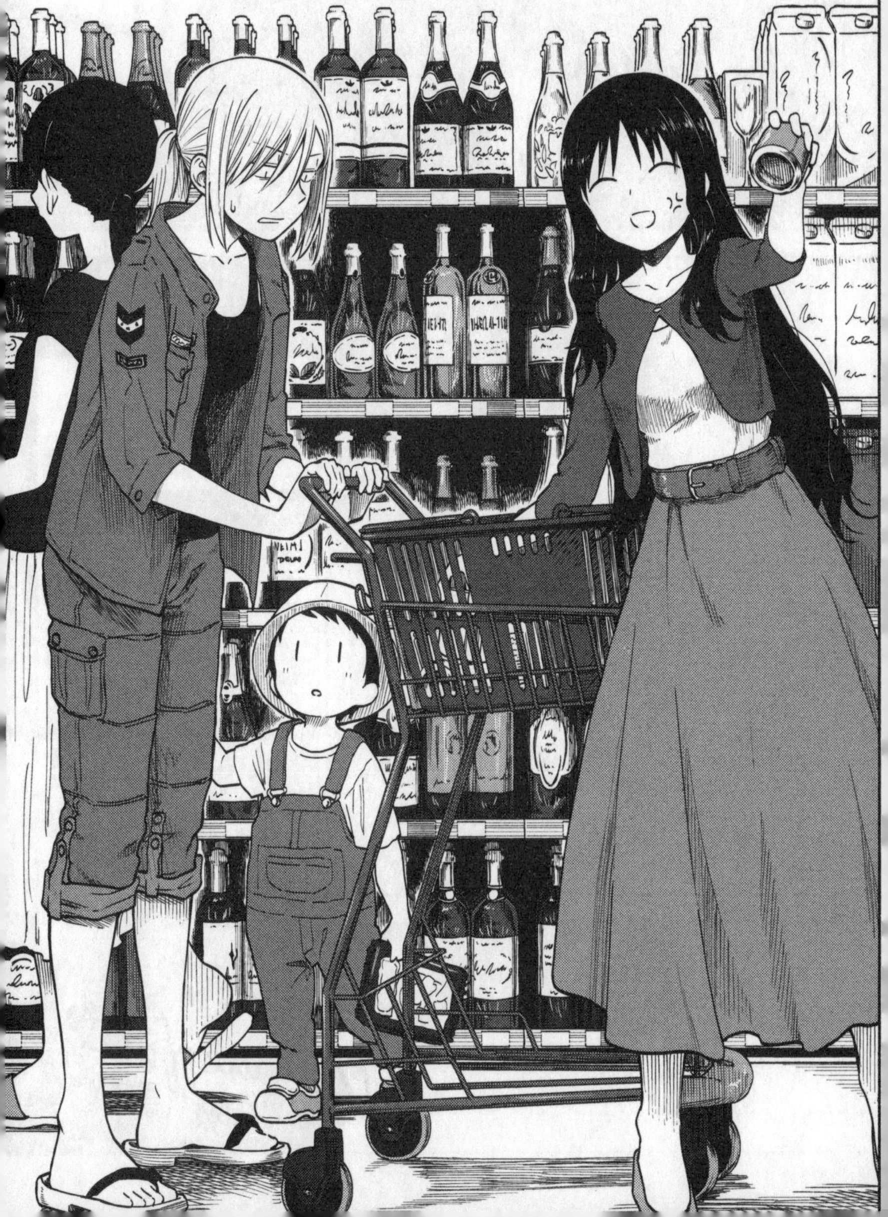

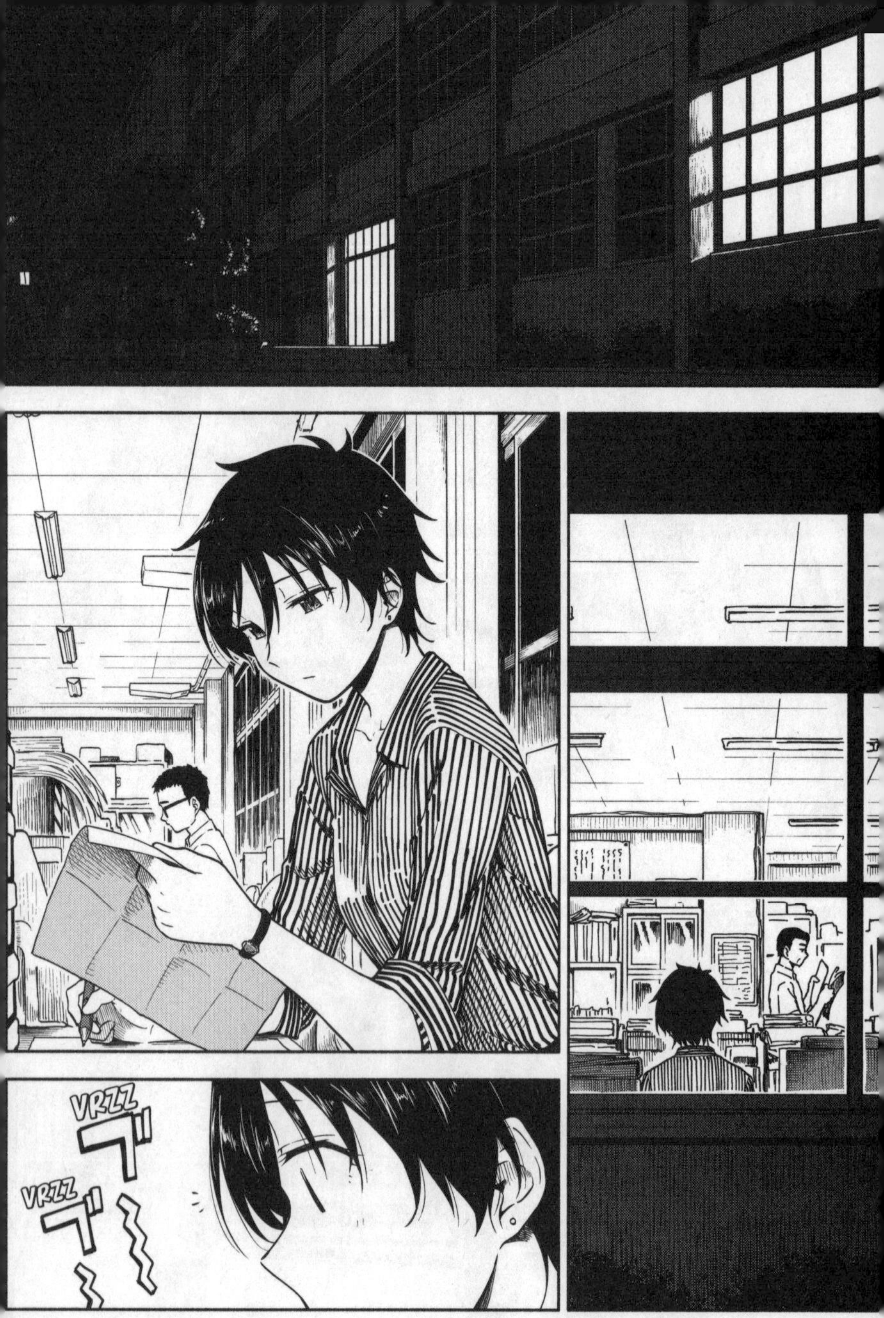
VRZZ
ブ
VRZZ
ブ

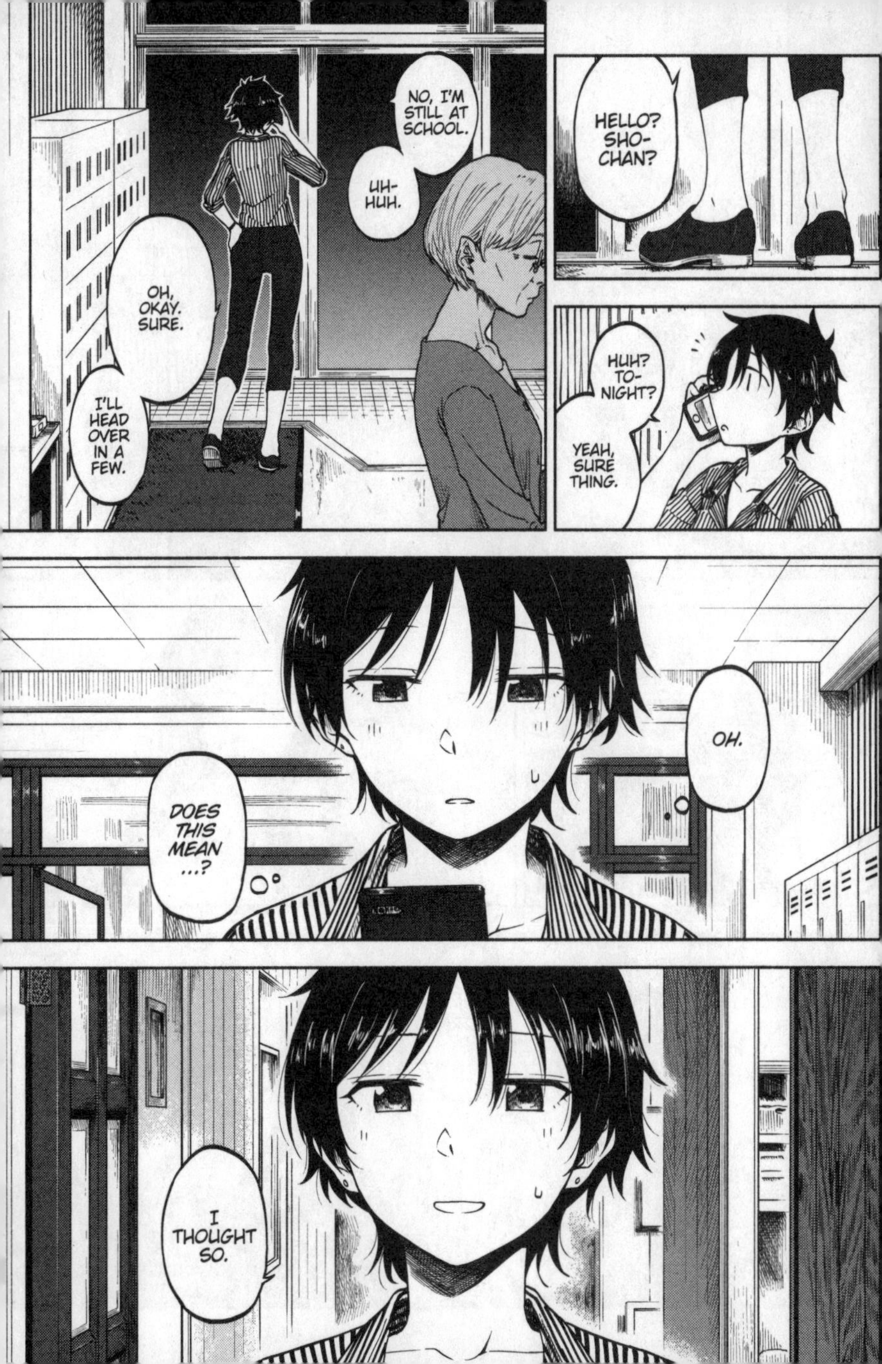
HELLO? SHO-CHAN?
HUH? TO-NIGHT?
YEAH, SURE THING.
NO, I'M STILL AT SCHOOL.
UH-HUH.
OH, OKAY. SURE.
I'LL HEAD OVER IN A FEW.
OH.
DOES THIS MEAN ...?
I THOUGHT SO.

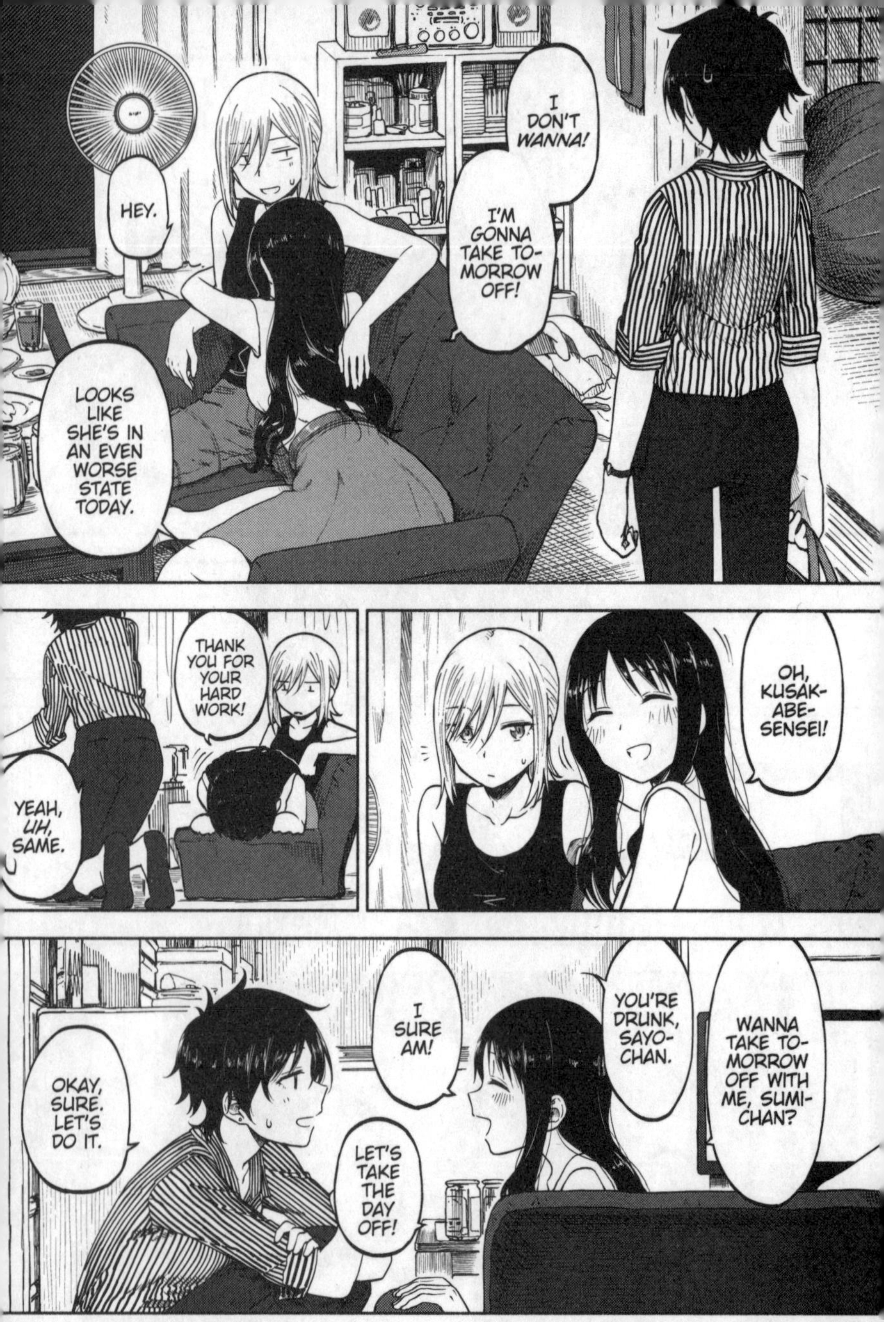
I DON'T *WANNA!*
I'M GONNA TAKE TO-MORROW OFF!
HEY.
LOOKS LIKE SHE'S IN AN EVEN WORSE STATE TODAY.
OH, KUSAK-ABE-SENSEI!
THANK YOU FOR YOUR HARD WORK!
YEAH, *UH,* SAME.
WANNA TAKE TO-MORROW OFF WITH ME, SUMI-CHAN?
YOU'RE DRUNK, SAYO-CHAN.
I SURE AM!
LET'S TAKE THE DAY OFF!
OKAY, SURE. LET'S DO IT.

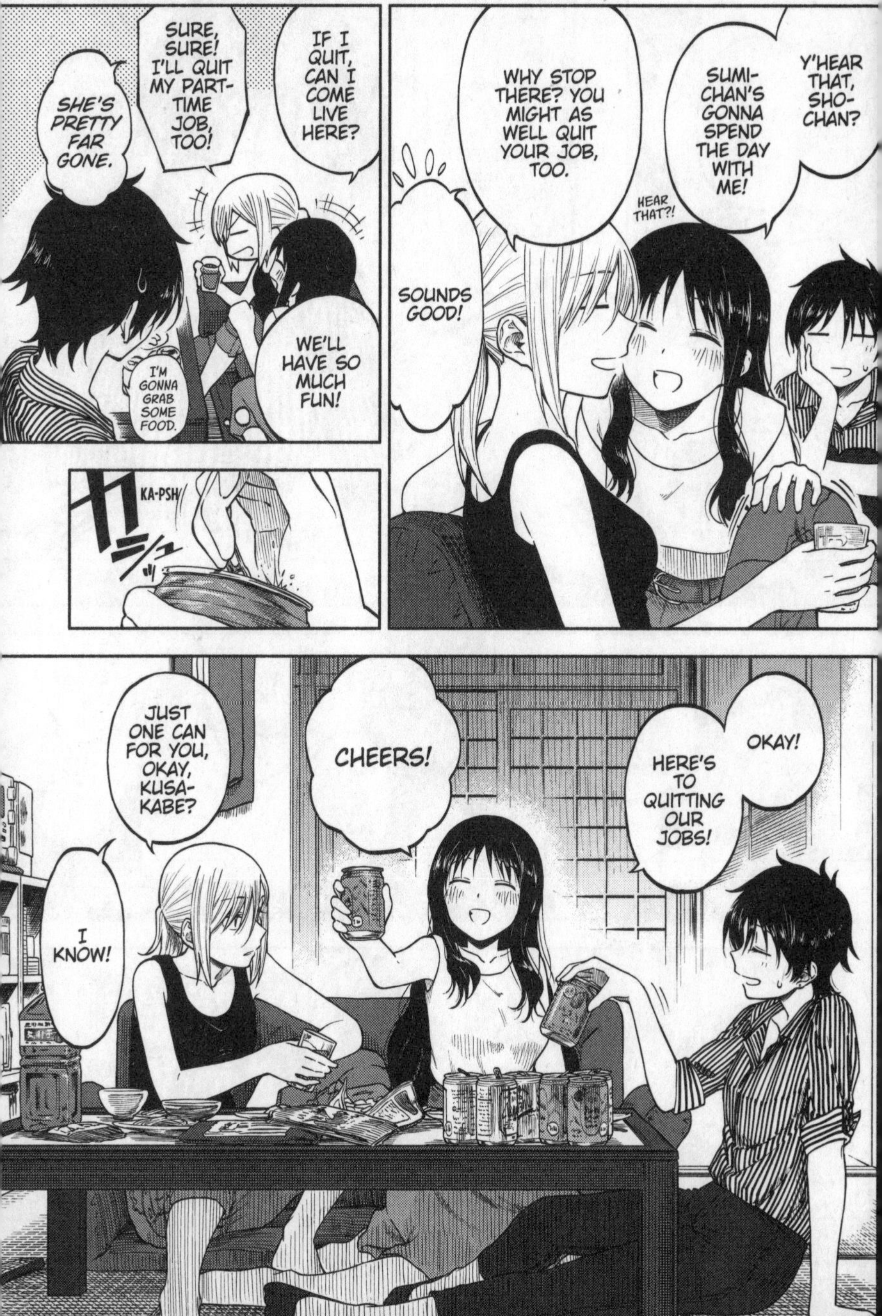
Y'HEAR THAT, SHO-CHAN?
SUMI-CHAN'S GONNA SPEND THE DAY WITH ME!
HEAR THAT?!
WHY STOP THERE? YOU MIGHT AS WELL QUIT YOUR JOB, TOO.
SOUNDS GOOD!
IF I QUIT, CAN I COME LIVE HERE?
SURE, SURE! I'LL QUIT MY PART-TIME JOB, TOO!
SHE'S PRETTY FAR GONE.
WE'LL HAVE SO MUCH FUN!
I'M GONNA GRAB SOME FOOD.
KA-PSH
OKAY!
HERE'S TO QUITTING OUR JOBS!
CHEERS!
JUST ONE CAN FOR YOU, OKAY, KUSA-KABE?
I KNOW!

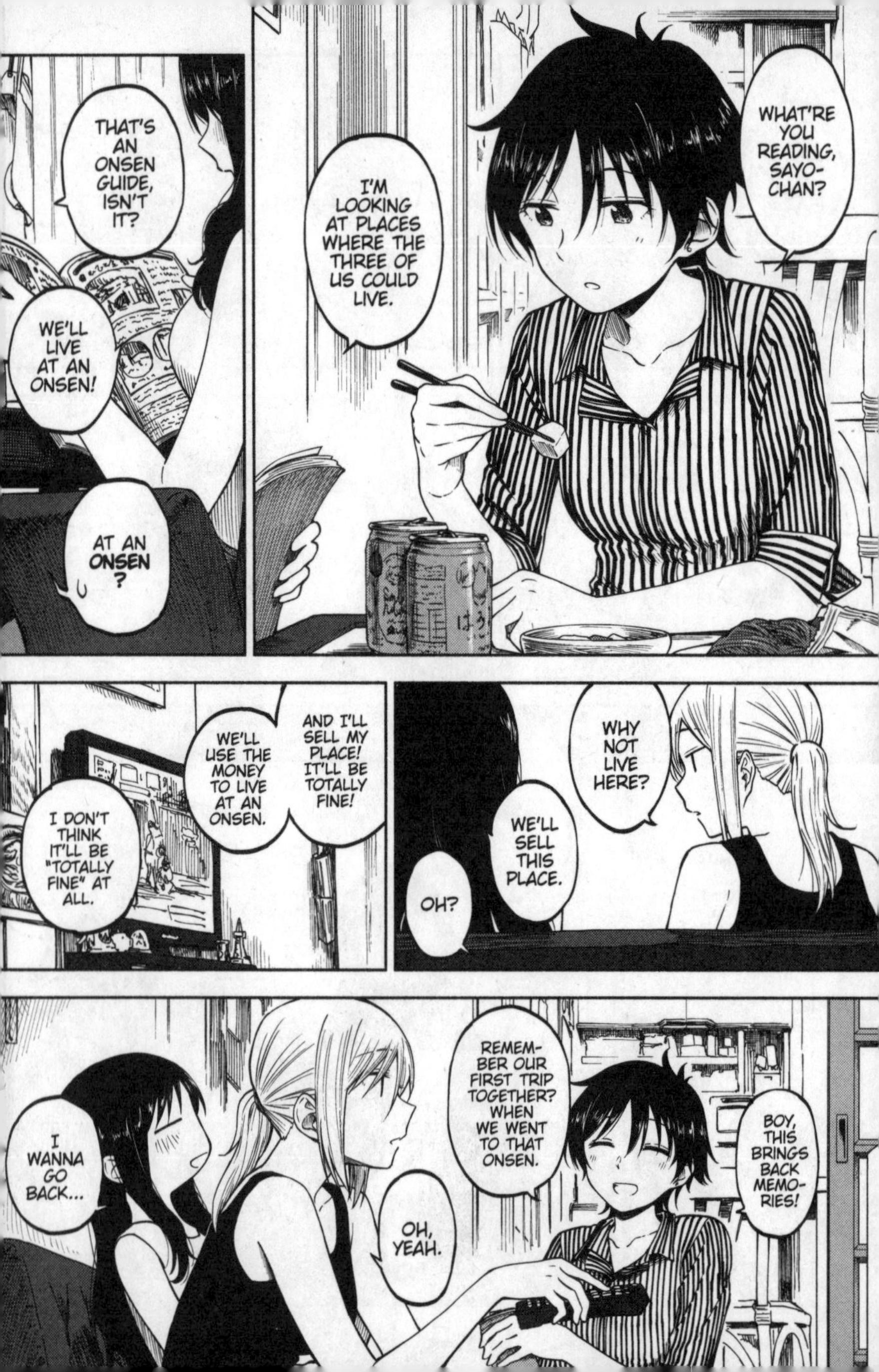
WHAT'RE YOU READING, SAYO-CHAN?
I'M LOOKING AT PLACES WHERE THE THREE OF US COULD LIVE.
THAT'S AN ONSEN GUIDE, ISN'T IT?
WE'LL LIVE AT AN ONSEN!
AT AN ONSEN?
WHY NOT LIVE HERE?
WE'LL SELL THIS PLACE.
OH?
AND I'LL SELL MY PLACE! IT'LL BE TOTALLY FINE!
WE'LL USE THE MONEY TO LIVE AT AN ONSEN.
I DON'T THINK IT'LL BE "TOTALLY FINE" AT ALL.
BOY, THIS BRINGS BACK MEMO-RIES!
REMEM-BER OUR FIRST TRIP TOGETHER? WHEN WE WENT TO THAT ONSEN.
OH, YEAH.
I WANNA GO BACK...

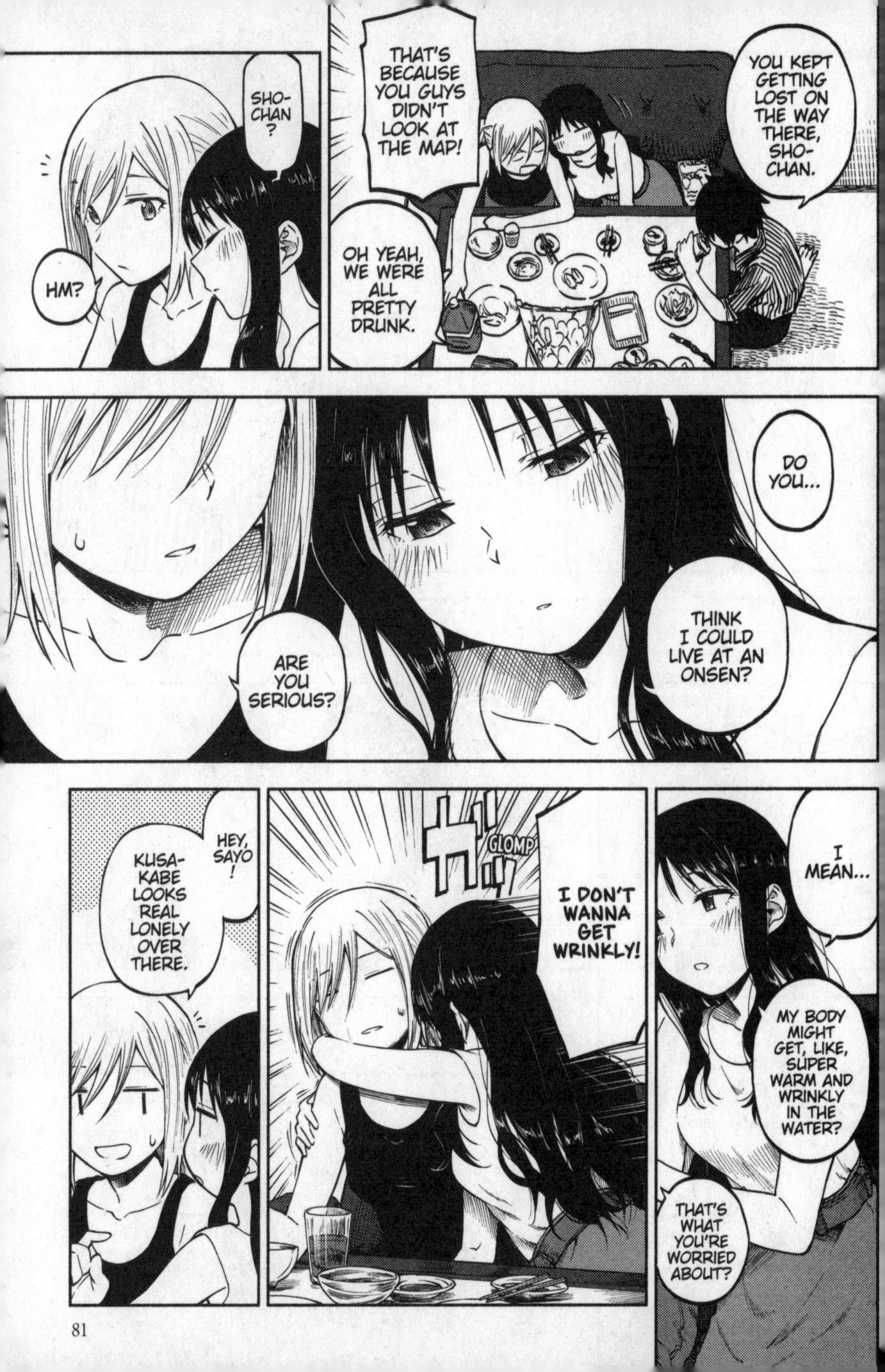
YOU KEPT GETTING LOST ON THE WAY THERE, SHO-CHAN.
THAT'S BECAUSE YOU GUYS DIDN'T LOOK AT THE MAP!
OH YEAH, WE WERE ALL PRETTY DRUNK.
SHO-CHAN?
HM?
DO YOU...
THINK I COULD LIVE AT AN ONSEN?
ARE YOU SERIOUS?
I MEAN...
MY BODY MIGHT GET, LIKE, SUPER WARM AND WRINKLY IN THE WATER?
THAT'S WHAT YOU'RE WORRIED ABOUT?
GLOMP
I DON'T WANNA GET WRINKLY!
HEY, SAYO!
KUSA-KABE LOOKS REAL LONELY OVER THERE.

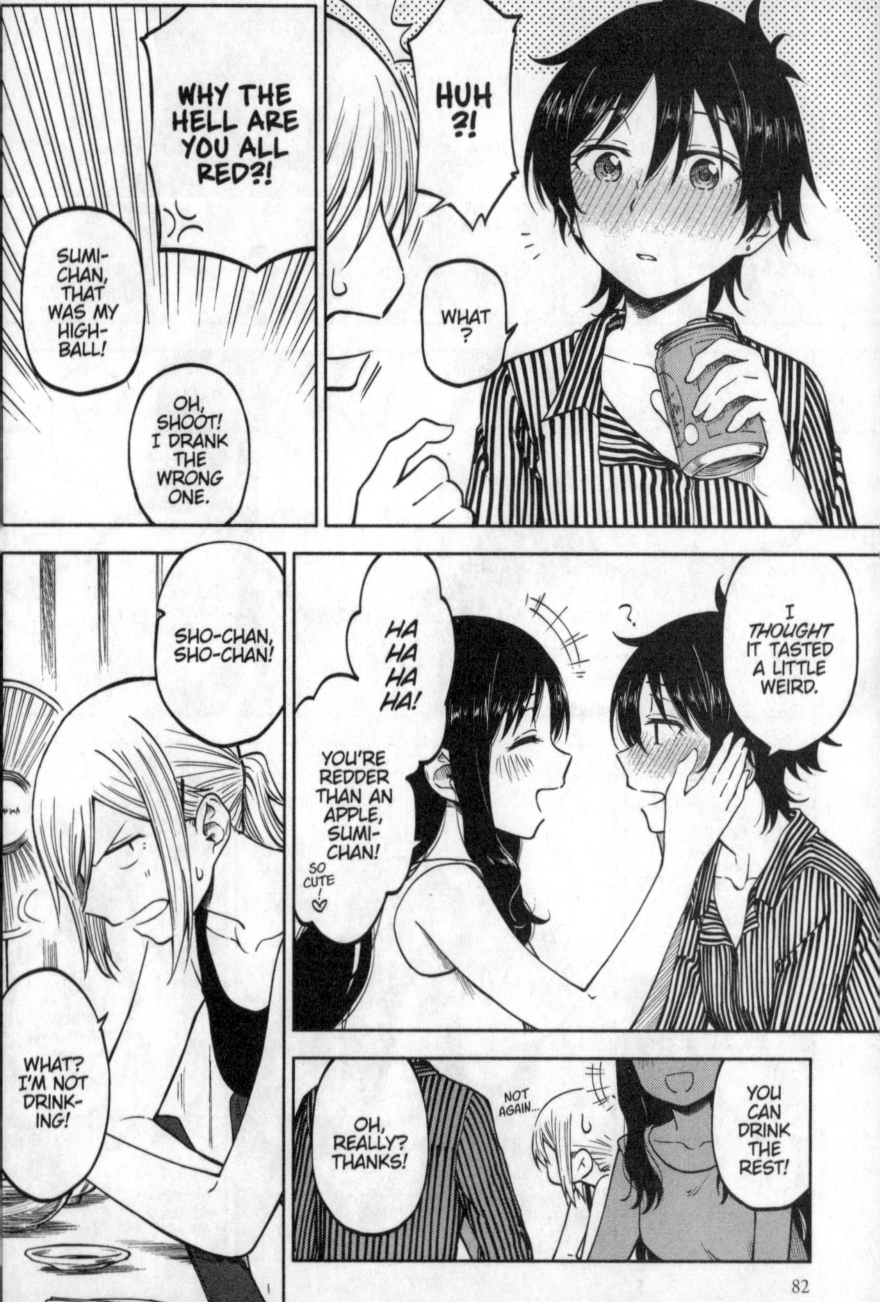
HUH?!
WHAT?
WHY THE HELL ARE YOU ALL RED?!
SUMI-CHAN, THAT WAS MY HIGH-BALL!
OH, SHOOT! I DRANK THE WRONG ONE.
I THOUGHT IT TASTED A LITTLE WEIRD.
HA HA HA HA!
YOU'RE REDDER THAN AN APPLE, SUMI-CHAN!
SO CUTE
YOU CAN DRINK THE REST!
NOT AGAIN...
OH, REALLY? THANKS!
SHO-CHAN, SHO-CHAN!
WHAT? I'M NOT DRINK-ING!

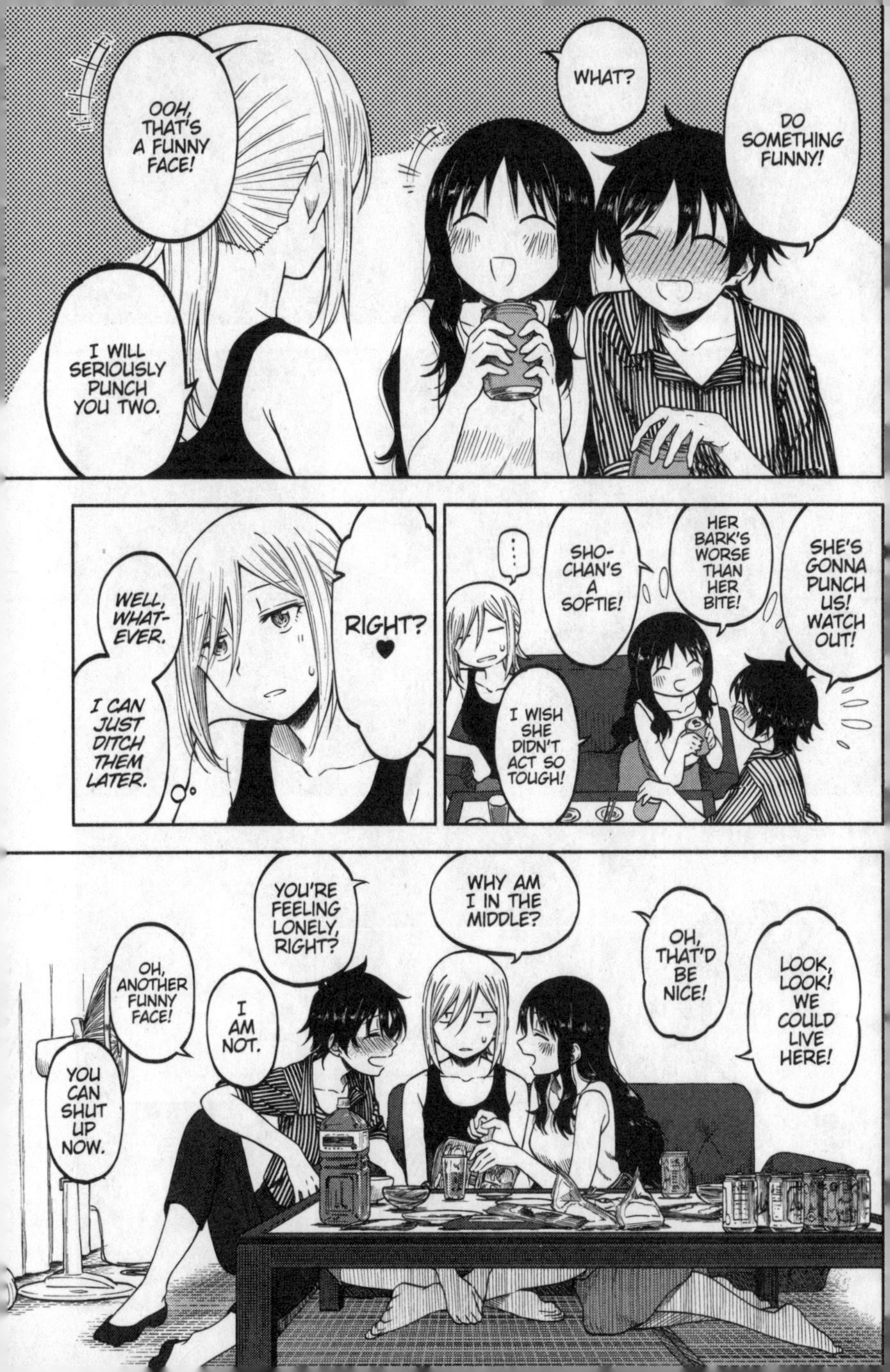
DO SOMETHING FUNNY!
WHAT?
OOH, THAT'S A FUNNY FACE!
I WILL SERIOUSLY PUNCH YOU TWO.
SHE'S GONNA PUNCH US! WATCH OUT!
HER BARK'S WORSE THAN HER BITE!
SHO-CHAN'S A SOFTIE!
...
I WISH SHE DIDN'T ACT SO TOUGH!
RIGHT? ♥
WELL, WHAT-EVER.
I CAN JUST DITCH THEM LATER.
LOOK, LOOK! WE COULD LIVE HERE!
OH, THAT'D BE NICE!
WHY AM I IN THE MIDDLE?
YOU'RE FEELING LONELY, RIGHT?
I AM NOT.
OH, ANOTHER FUNNY FACE!
YOU CAN SHUT UP NOW.

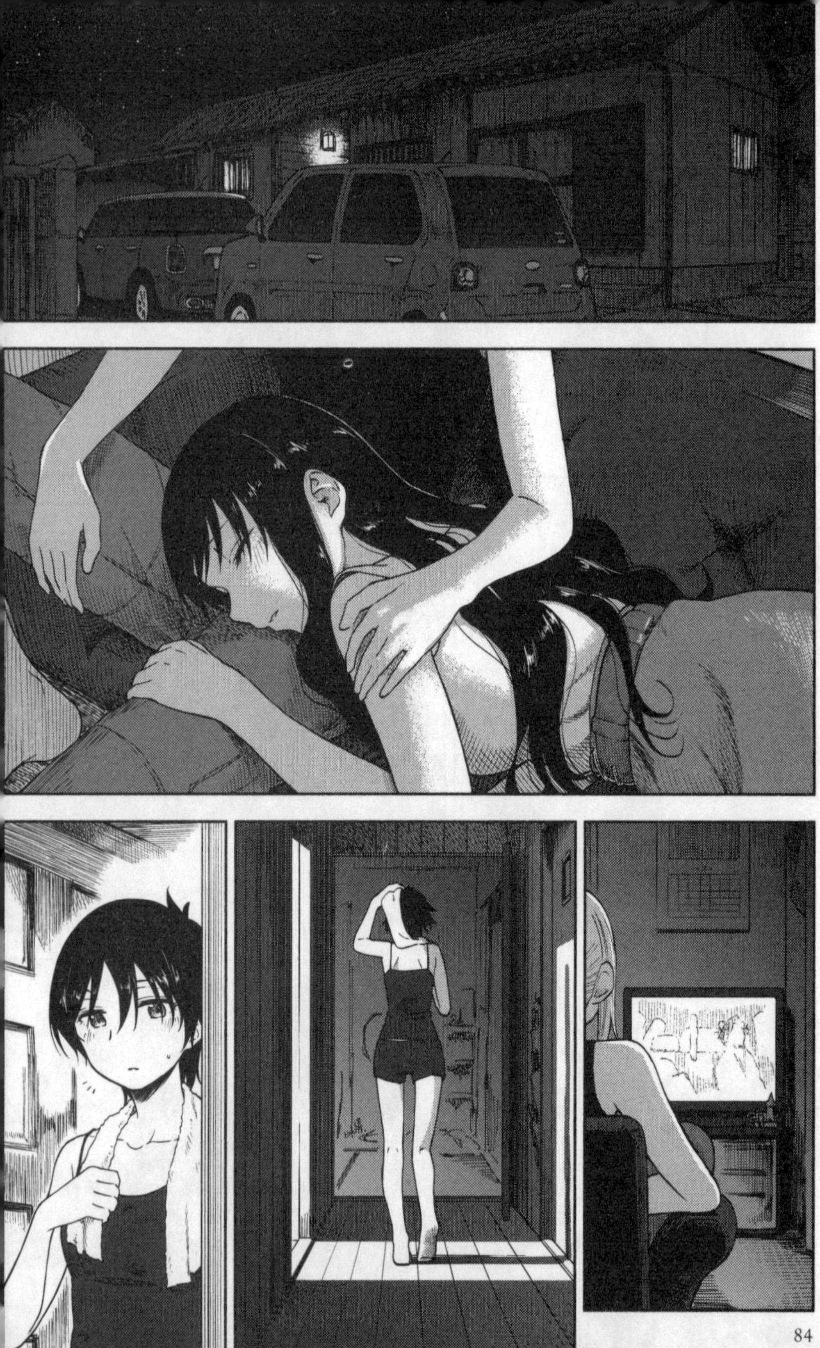

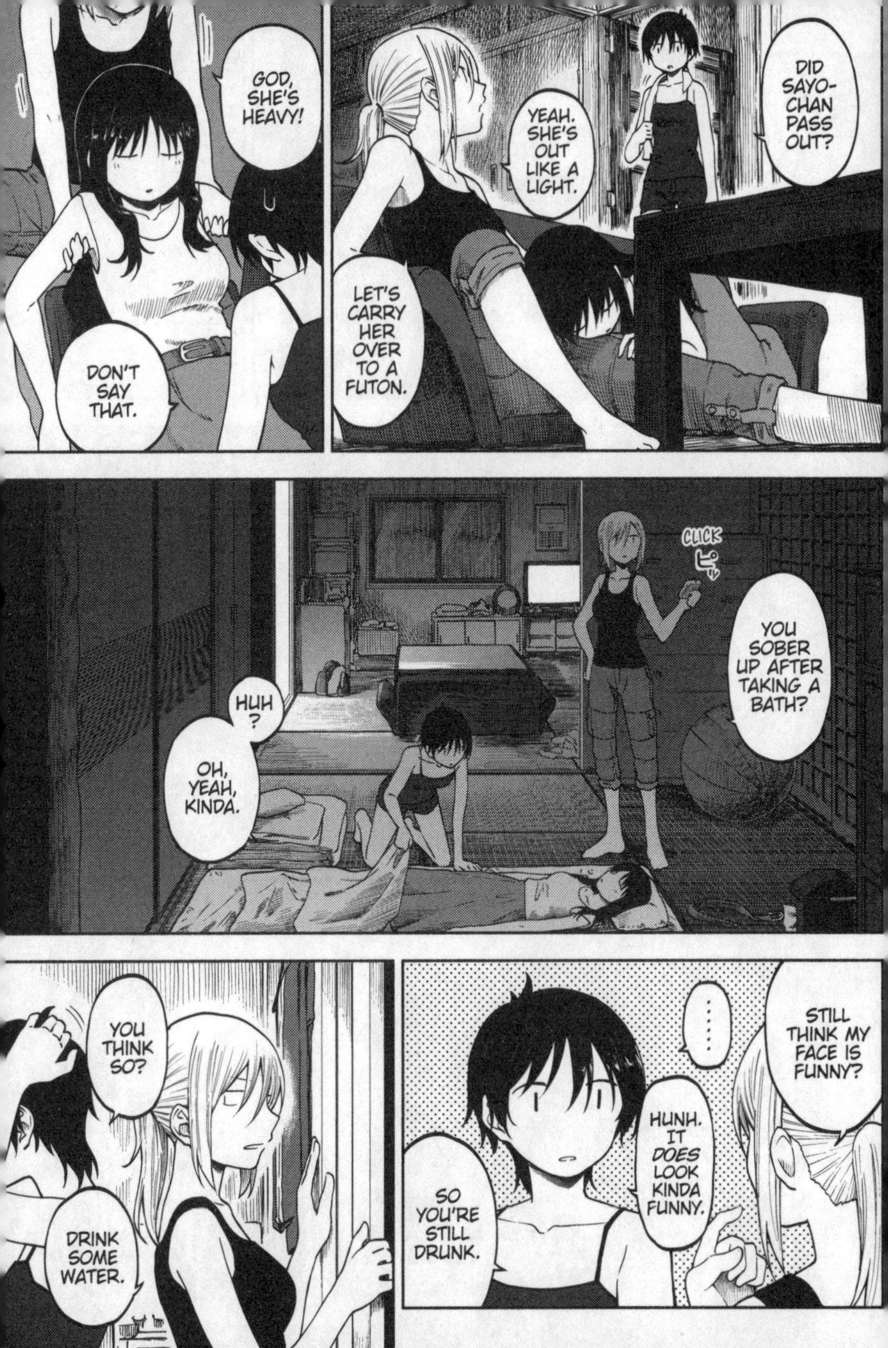
DID SAYO-CHAN PASS OUT?
YEAH. SHE'S OUT LIKE A LIGHT.
LET'S CARRY HER OVER TO A FUTON.
GOD, SHE'S HEAVY!
DON'T SAY THAT.
CLICK
ピッ
YOU SOBER UP AFTER TAKING A BATH?
HUH?
OH, YEAH, KINDA.
STILL THINK MY FACE IS FUNNY?
......
HUNH. IT DOES LOOK KINDA FUNNY.
SO YOU'RE STILL DRUNK.
YOU THINK SO?
DRINK SOME WATER.

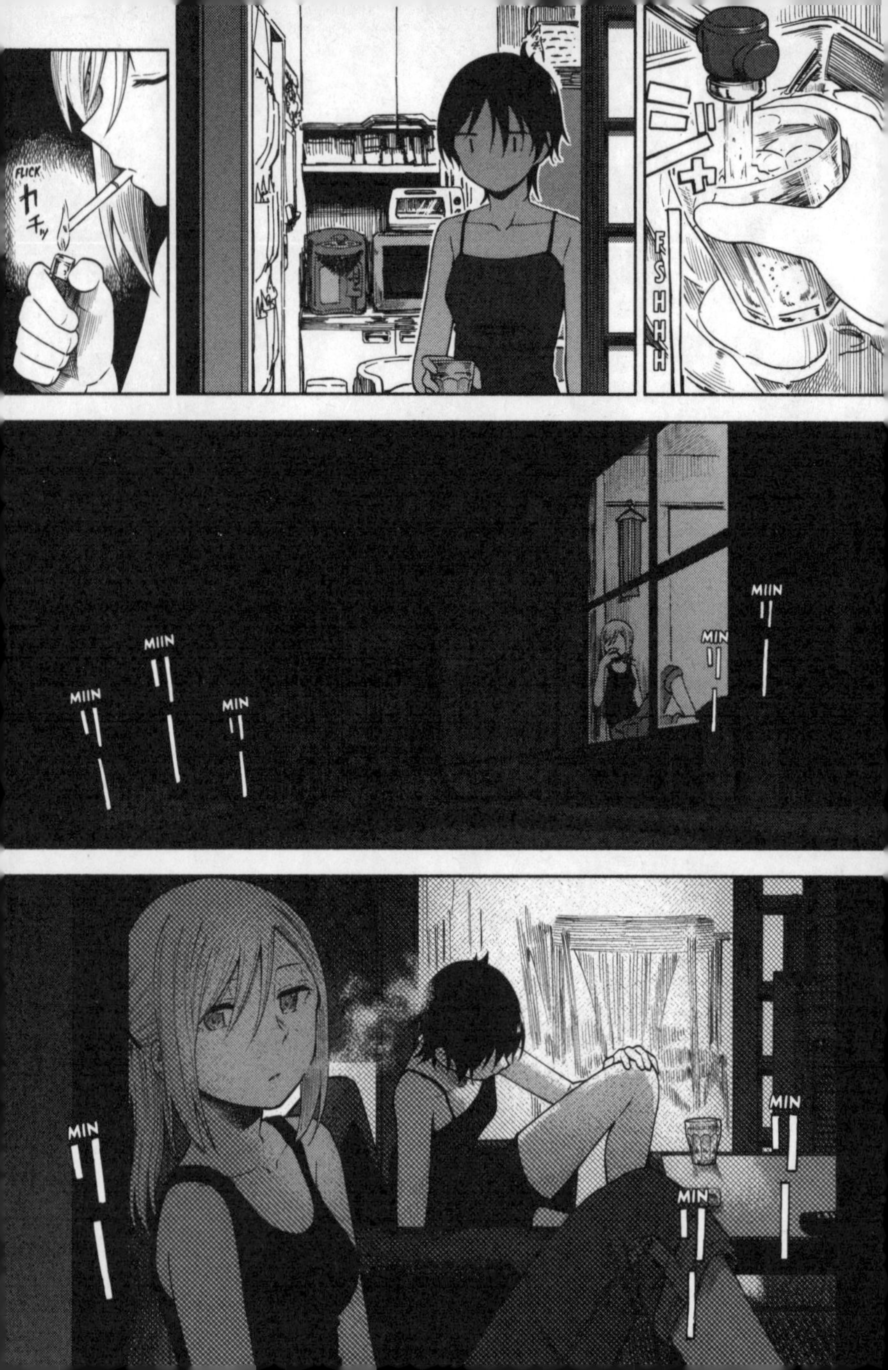
FSHHH
FLICK
カチッ
MIIN
MIN
MIN
MIIN
MIIN
MIN
MIN
MIN

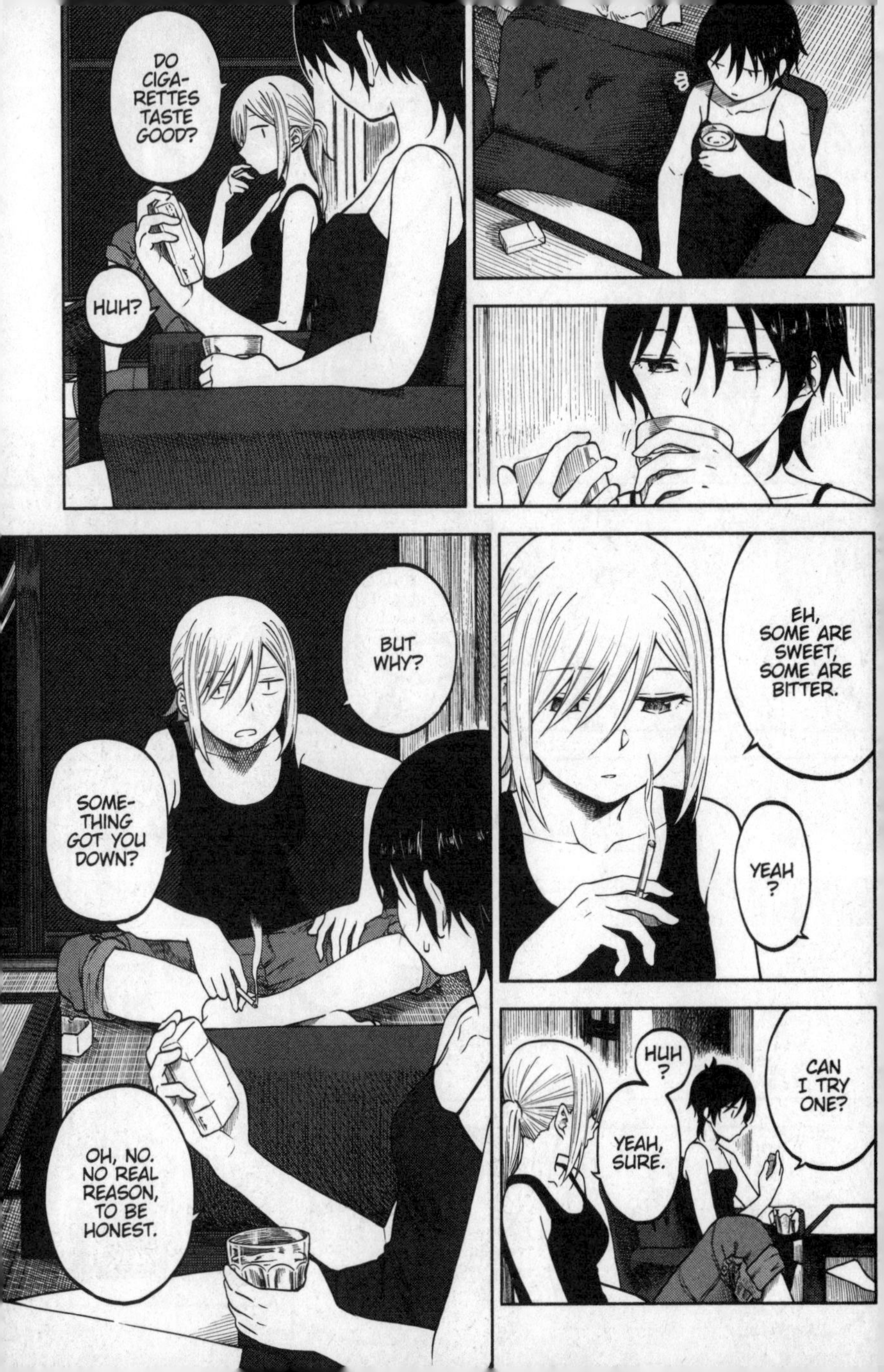
DO CIGA-RETTES TASTE GOOD?
HUH?
EH, SOME ARE SWEET, SOME ARE BITTER.
YEAH?
CAN I TRY ONE?
HUH?
YEAH, SURE.
BUT WHY?
SOME-THING GOT YOU DOWN?
OH, NO. NO REAL REASON, TO BE HONEST.

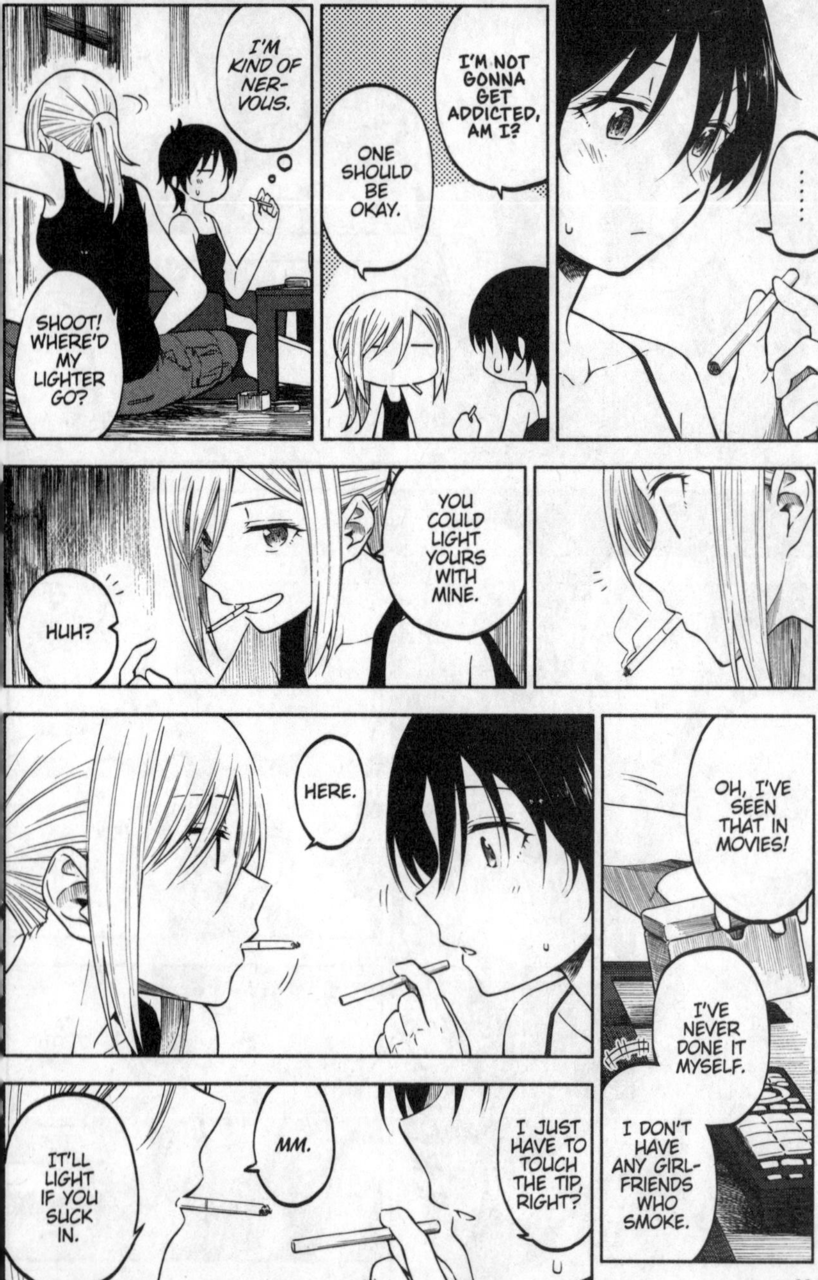
……
I'M NOT GONNA GET ADDICTED, AM I?
ONE SHOULD BE OKAY.
I'M KIND OF NER-VOUS.
SHOOT! WHERE'D MY LIGHTER GO?
YOU COULD LIGHT YOURS WITH MINE.
HUH?
OH, I'VE SEEN THAT IN MOVIES!
I'VE NEVER DONE IT MYSELF.
I DON'T HAVE ANY GIRL-FRIENDS WHO SMOKE.
HERE.
I JUST HAVE TO TOUCH THE TIP, RIGHT?
MM.
IT'LL LIGHT IF YOU SUCK IN.

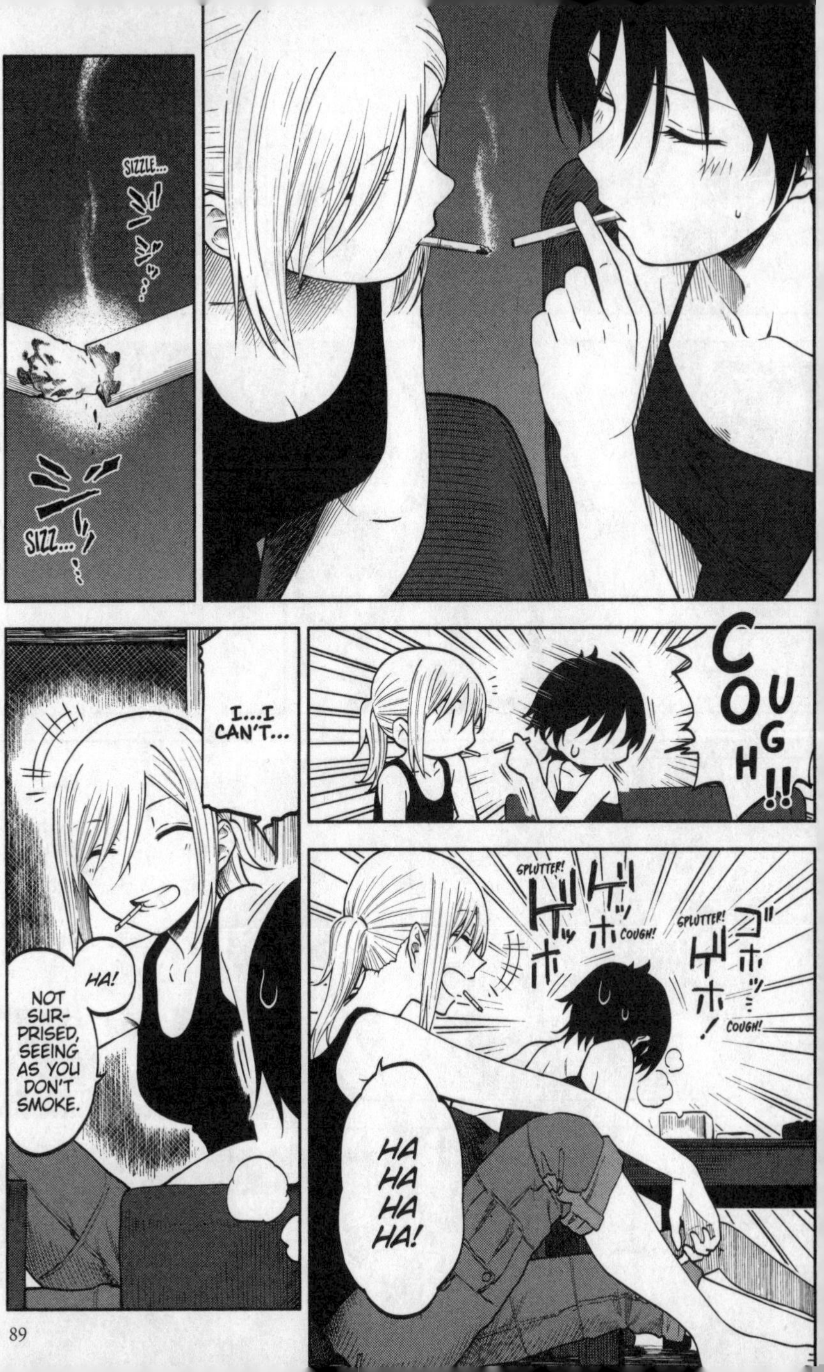
SIZZLE...
SIZZ...
COUGH!!
SPLUTTER!
COUGH!
SPLUTTER!
COUGH!
HA HA HA HA HA!
I...I CAN'T...
HA!
NOT SURPRISED, SEEING AS YOU DON'T SMOKE.

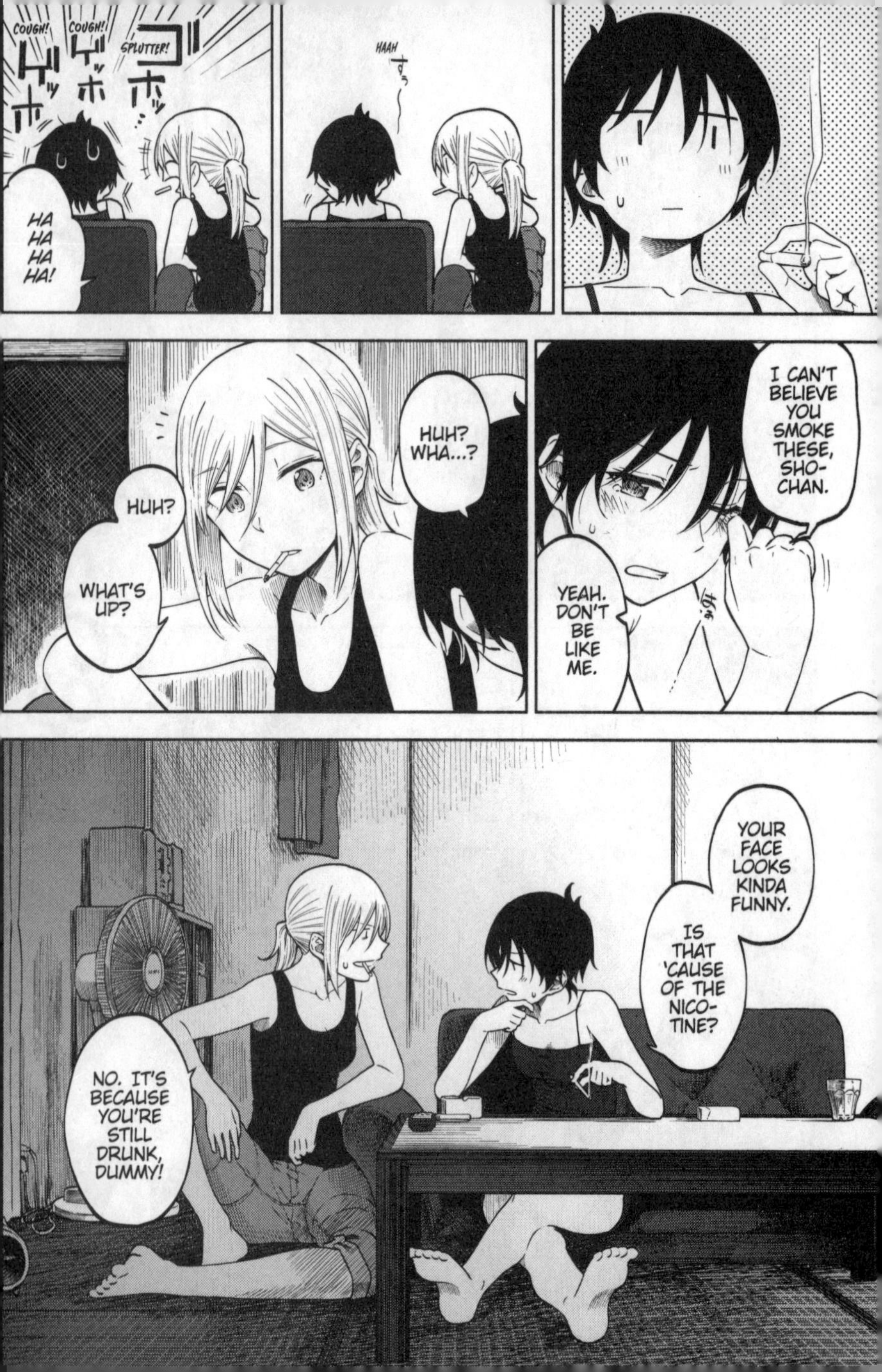
HAAH
COUGH!
COUGH!
SPLUTTER!
HA HA HA HA!
I CAN'T BELIEVE YOU SMOKE THESE, SHO-CHAN.
YEAH. DON'T BE LIKE ME.
HUH? WHA...?
HUH?
WHAT'S UP?
YOUR FACE LOOKS KINDA FUNNY.
IS THAT 'CAUSE OF THE NICOTINE?
NO. IT'S BECAUSE YOU'RE STILL DRUNK, DUMMY!

Our Wonderful Days
story & art by Kei Hamuro

Our Wonderful Days
Days Tsurezure Biyori

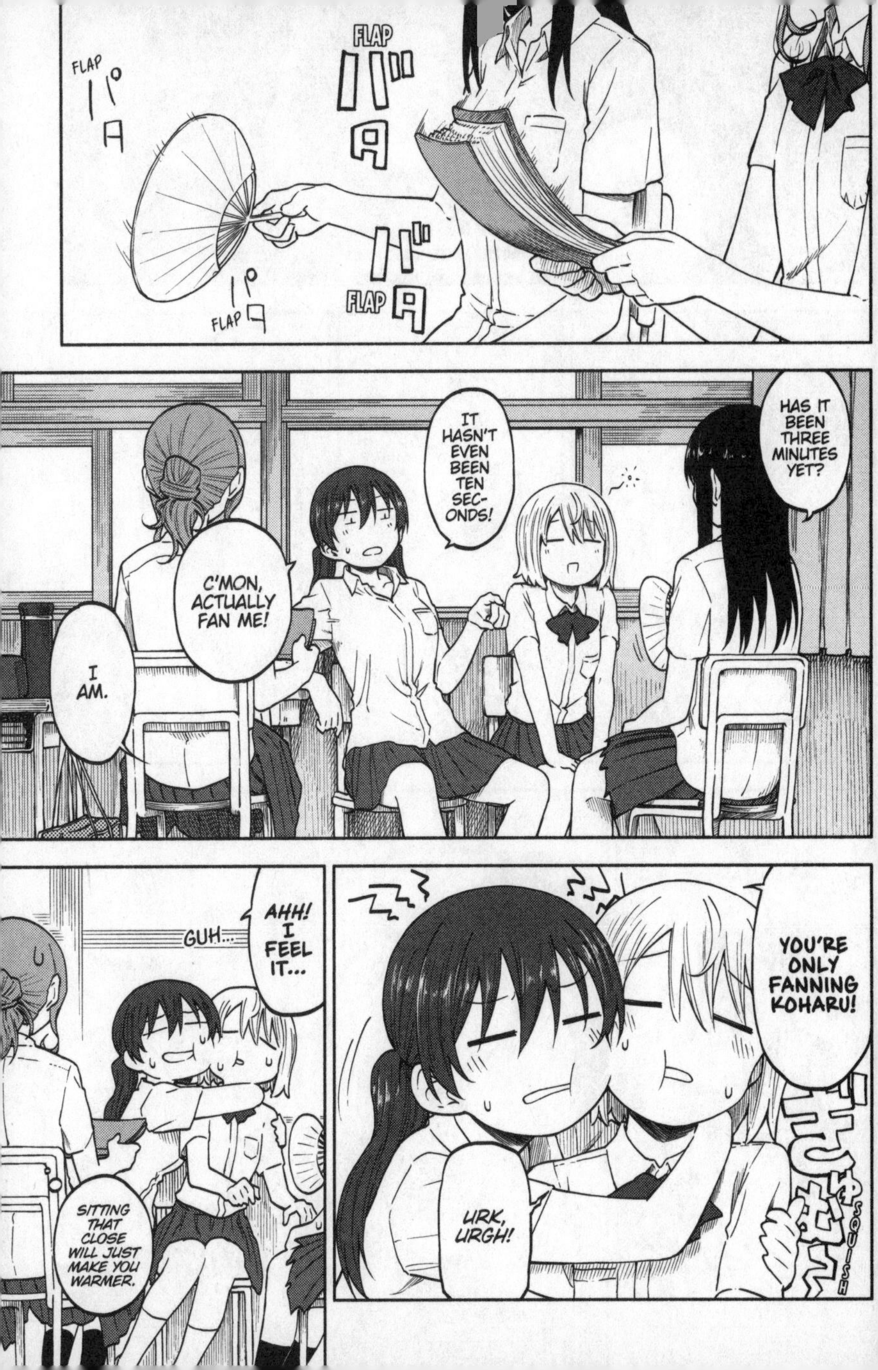
FLAP
バタ
FLAP
バタ
FLAP
パタ
FLAP
パタ
HAS IT BEEN THREE MINUTES YET?
IT HASN'T EVEN BEEN TEN SEC-ONDS!
C'MON, ACTUALLY FAN ME!
I AM.
YOU'RE ONLY FANNING KOHARU!
SQUISH
URK, URGH!
AHH! I FEEL IT...
GUH...
SITTING THAT CLOSE WILL JUST MAKE YOU WARMER.

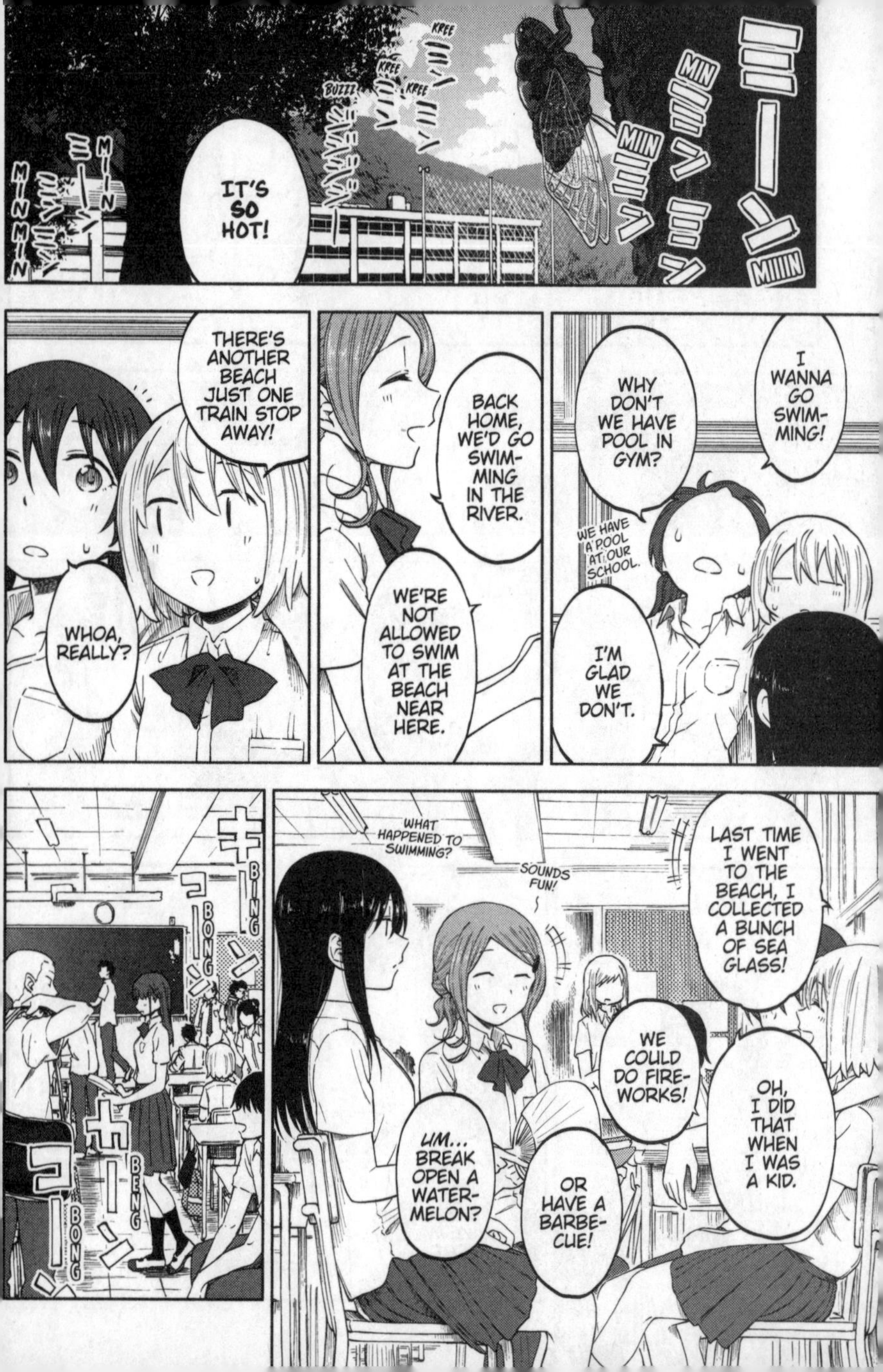
MIIIN
MIN
MIN
KREE
KREE
KREE
BUZZZ
IT'S SO HOT!
MI-IN
MIN-MIN
I WANNA GO SWIMMING!
WHY DON'T WE HAVE POOL IN GYM?
WE HAVE A POOL AT OUR SCHOOL.
I'M GLAD WE DON'T.
BACK HOME, WE'D GO SWIMMING IN THE RIVER.
WE'RE NOT ALLOWED TO SWIM AT THE BEACH NEAR HERE.
THERE'S ANOTHER BEACH JUST ONE TRAIN STOP AWAY!
WHOA, REALLY?
LAST TIME I WENT TO THE BEACH, I COLLECTED A BUNCH OF SEA GLASS!
SOUNDS FUN!
WHAT HAPPENED TO SWIMMING?
OH, I DID THAT WHEN I WAS A KID.
WE COULD DO FIREWORKS!
OR HAVE A BARBECUE!
UM... BREAK OPEN A WATERMELON?
BING
BONG
BENG
BONG

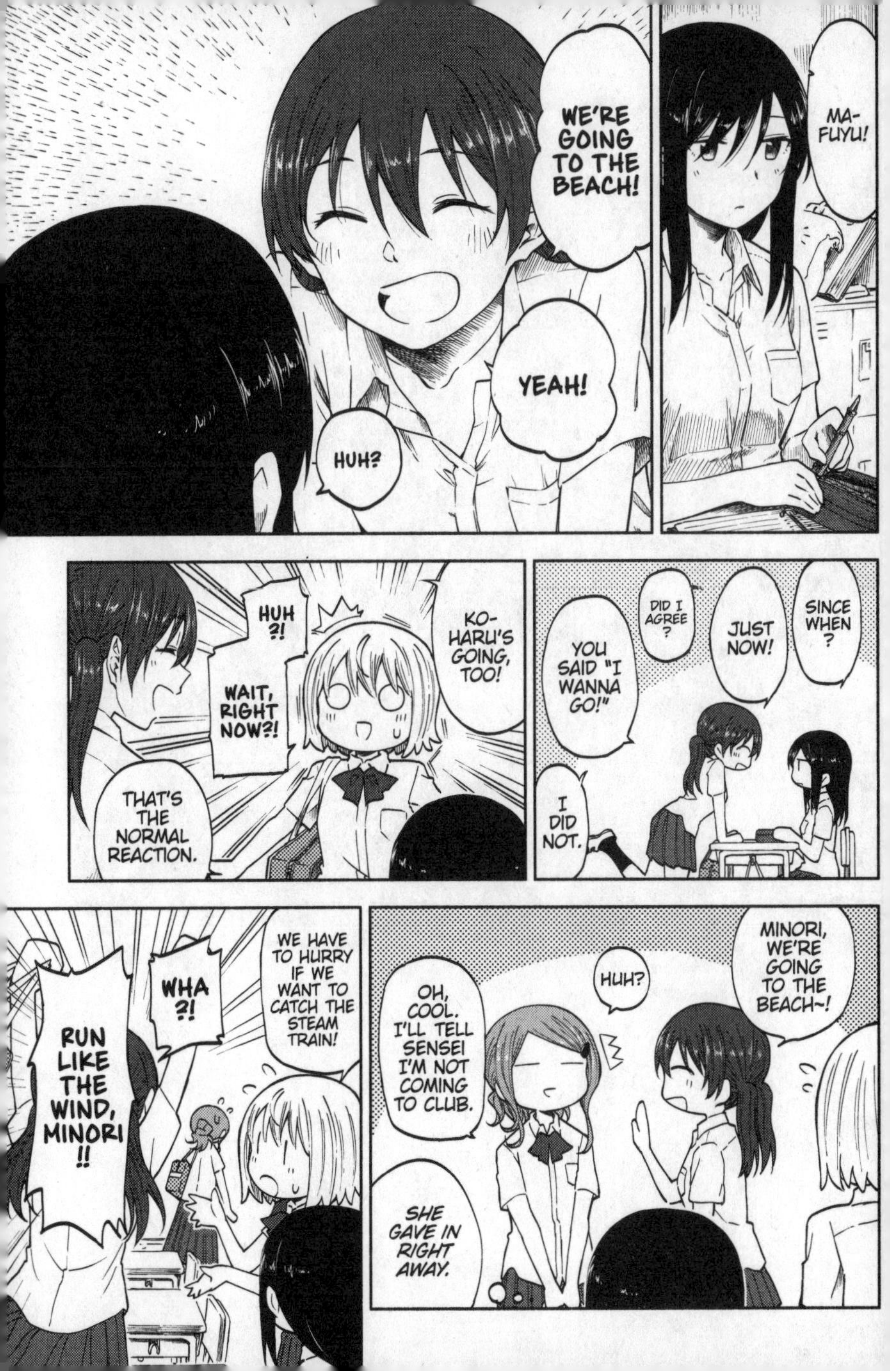
MA-FUYU!
WE'RE GOING TO THE BEACH!
YEAH!
HUH?
SINCE WHEN?
JUST NOW!
DID I AGREE?
YOU SAID "I WANNA GO!"
I DID NOT.
KO-HARU'S GOING, TOO!
HUH?!
WAIT, RIGHT NOW?!
THAT'S THE NORMAL REACTION.
MINORI, WE'RE GOING TO THE BEACH~!
HUH?
OH, COOL. I'LL TELL SENSEI I'M NOT COMING TO CLUB.
SHE GAVE IN RIGHT AWAY.
WE HAVE TO HURRY IF WE WANT TO CATCH THE STEAM TRAIN!
WHA?!
RUN LIKE THE WIND, MINORI!!

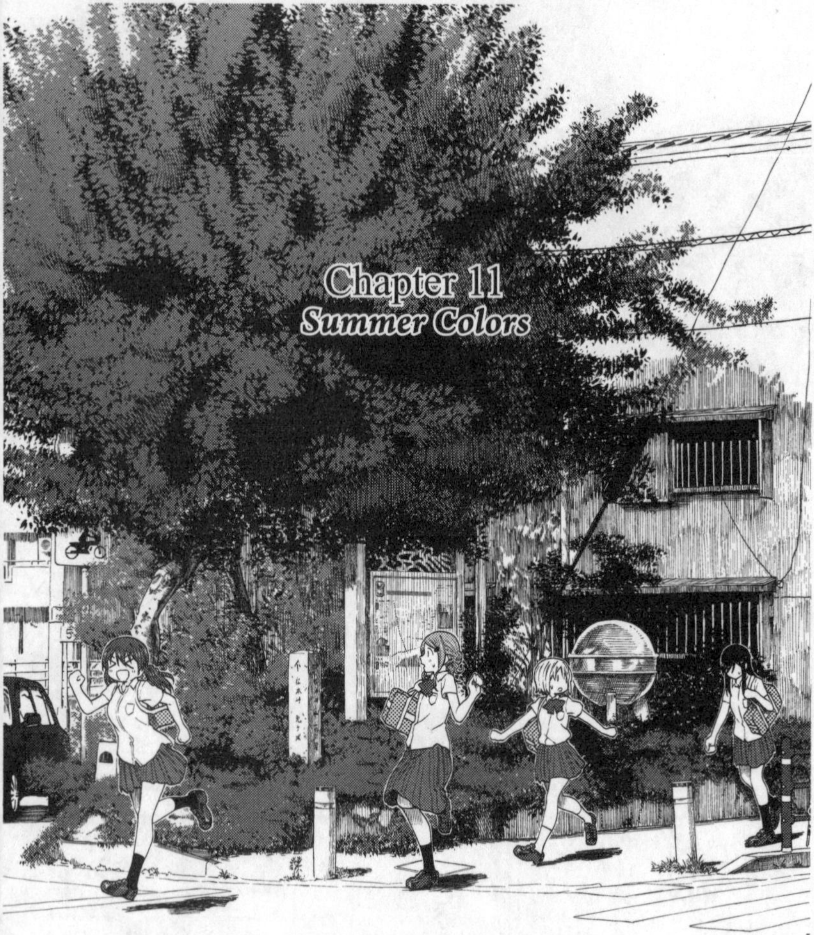
Chapter 11
Summer Colors

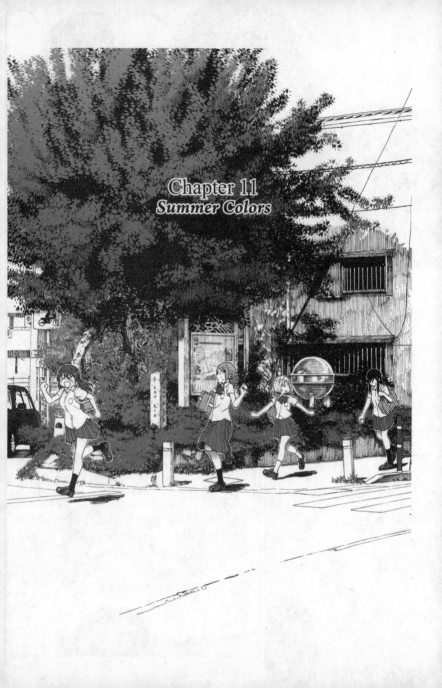

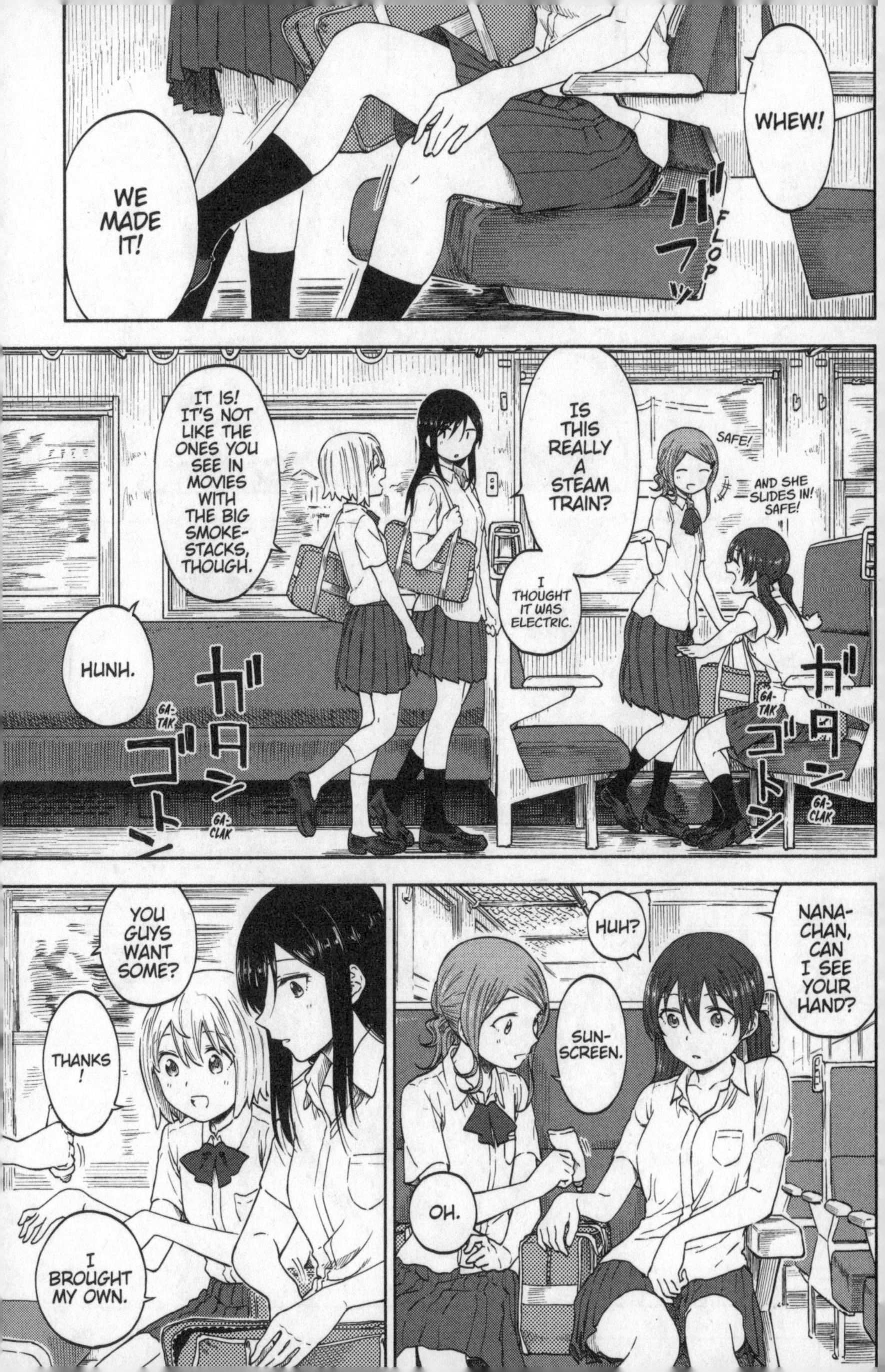
WHEW!
バフッ
FLOP!
WE MADE IT!
SAFE!
AND SHE SLIDES IN! SAFE!
IS THIS REALLY A STEAM TRAIN?
I THOUGHT IT WAS ELECTRIC.
IT IS! IT'S NOT LIKE THE ONES YOU SEE IN MOVIES WITH THE BIG SMOKE-STACKS, THOUGH.
ガタンゴトン
GA-TAK GA-CLAK
HUNH.
ガタンゴトン
GA-TAK GA-CLAK
NANA-CHAN, CAN I SEE YOUR HAND?
HUH?
SUN-SCREEN.
OH.
YOU GUYS WANT SOME?
THANKS!
I BROUGHT MY OWN.

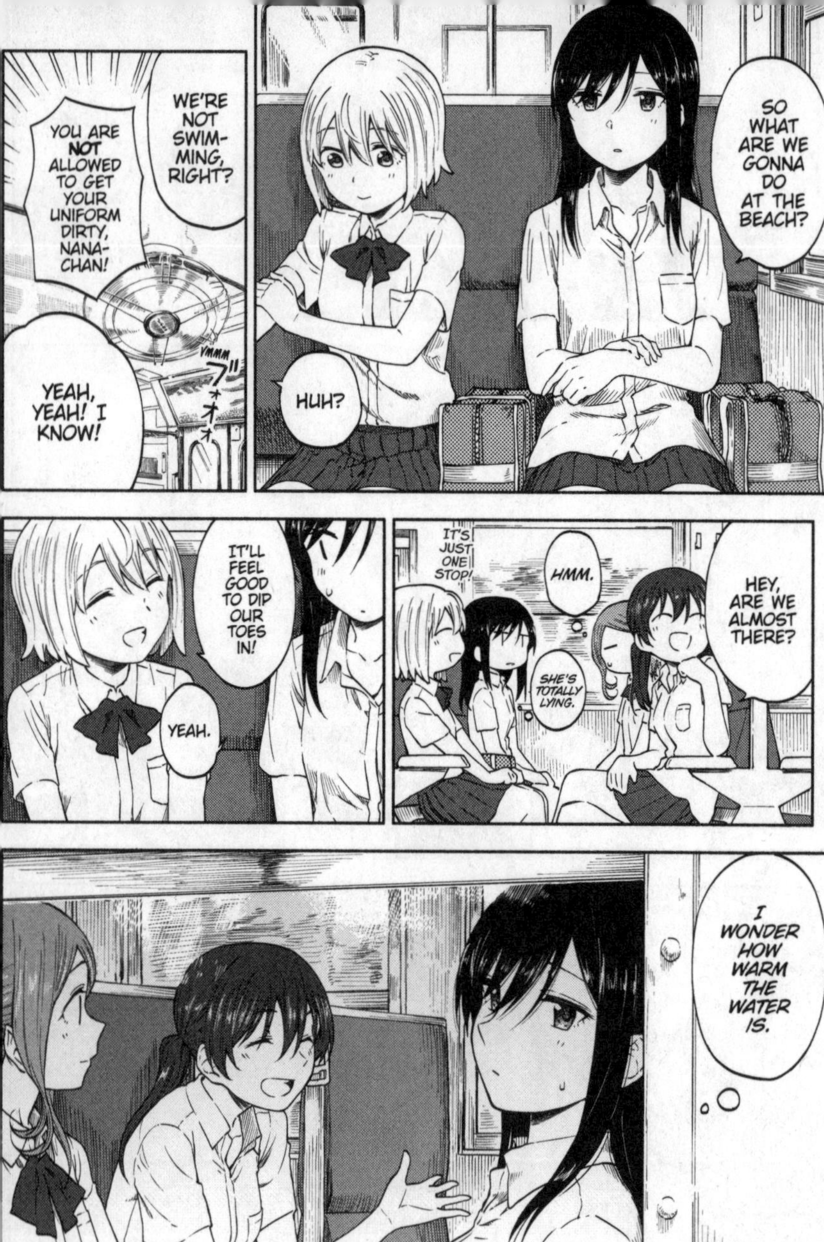
SO WHAT ARE WE GONNA DO AT THE BEACH?
HUH?
WE'RE NOT SWIMMING, RIGHT?
YOU ARE NOT ALLOWED TO GET YOUR UNIFORM DIRTY, NANA-CHAN!
VMMM
YEAH, YEAH! I KNOW!
HEY, ARE WE ALMOST THERE?
HMM.
IT'S JUST ONE STOP!
SHE'S TOTALLY LYING.
IT'LL FEEL GOOD TO DIP OUR TOES IN!
YEAH.
I WONDER HOW WARM THE WATER IS.

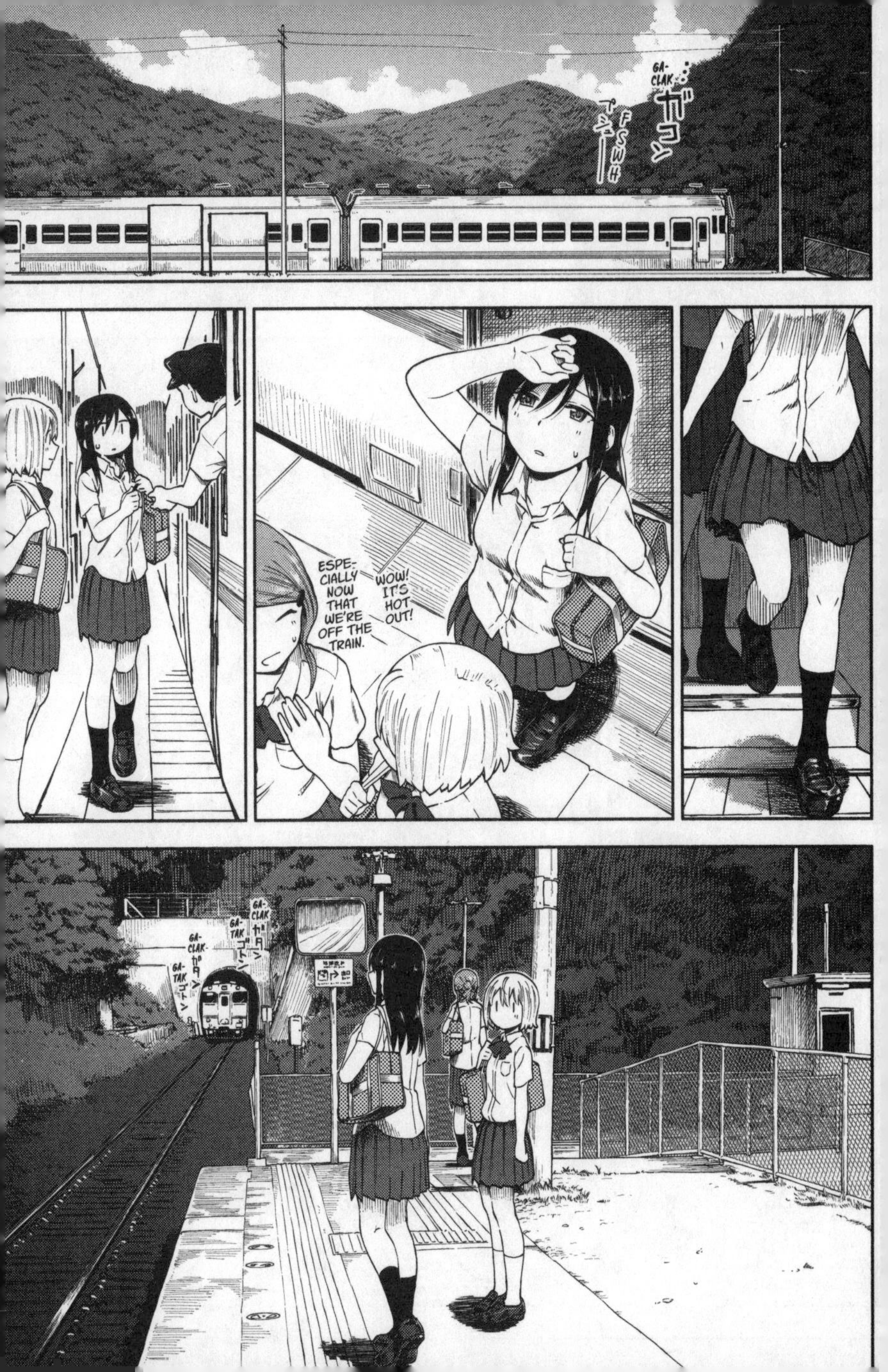
GA-CLAK
ガコン
FSWH
プシュー
WOW! IT'S HOT OUT!
ESPECIALLY NOW THAT WE'RE OFF THE TRAIN.
GA-CLAK
ガタン
GA-TAK
ゴトン
GA-CLAK
ガタン
GA-TAK
ゴトン

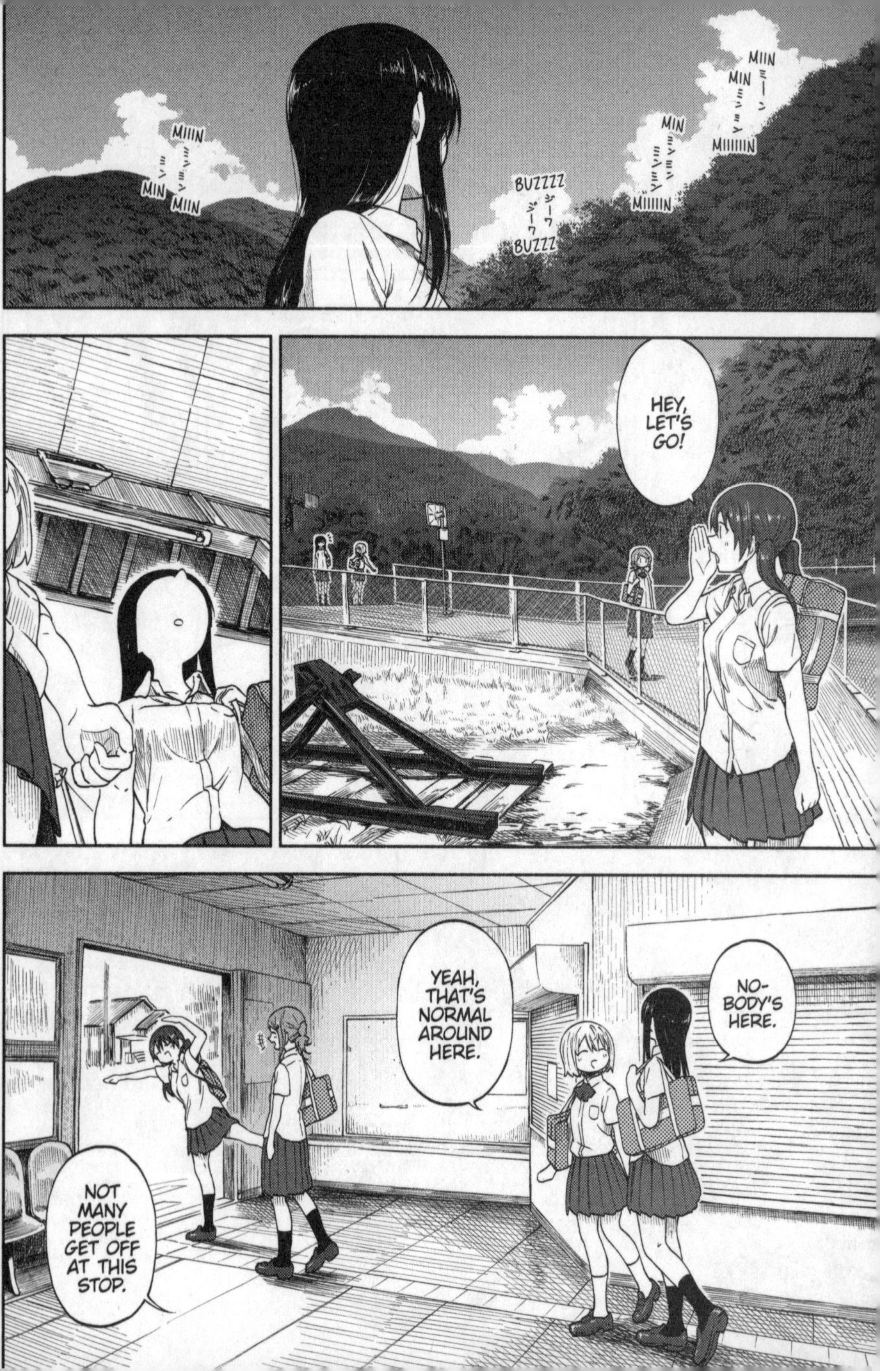
MIIN ミーン
MIN ミンミン
MIIIIIN
MIN ミンミン
ミンミン MIIIIN
BUZZZZ ジーワ
ジーワ BUZZZ
MIIN ミンミン
ミン MIN MIIN
HEY, LET'S GO!
NO-BODY'S HERE.
YEAH, THAT'S NORMAL AROUND HERE.
NOT MANY PEOPLE GET OFF AT THIS STOP.

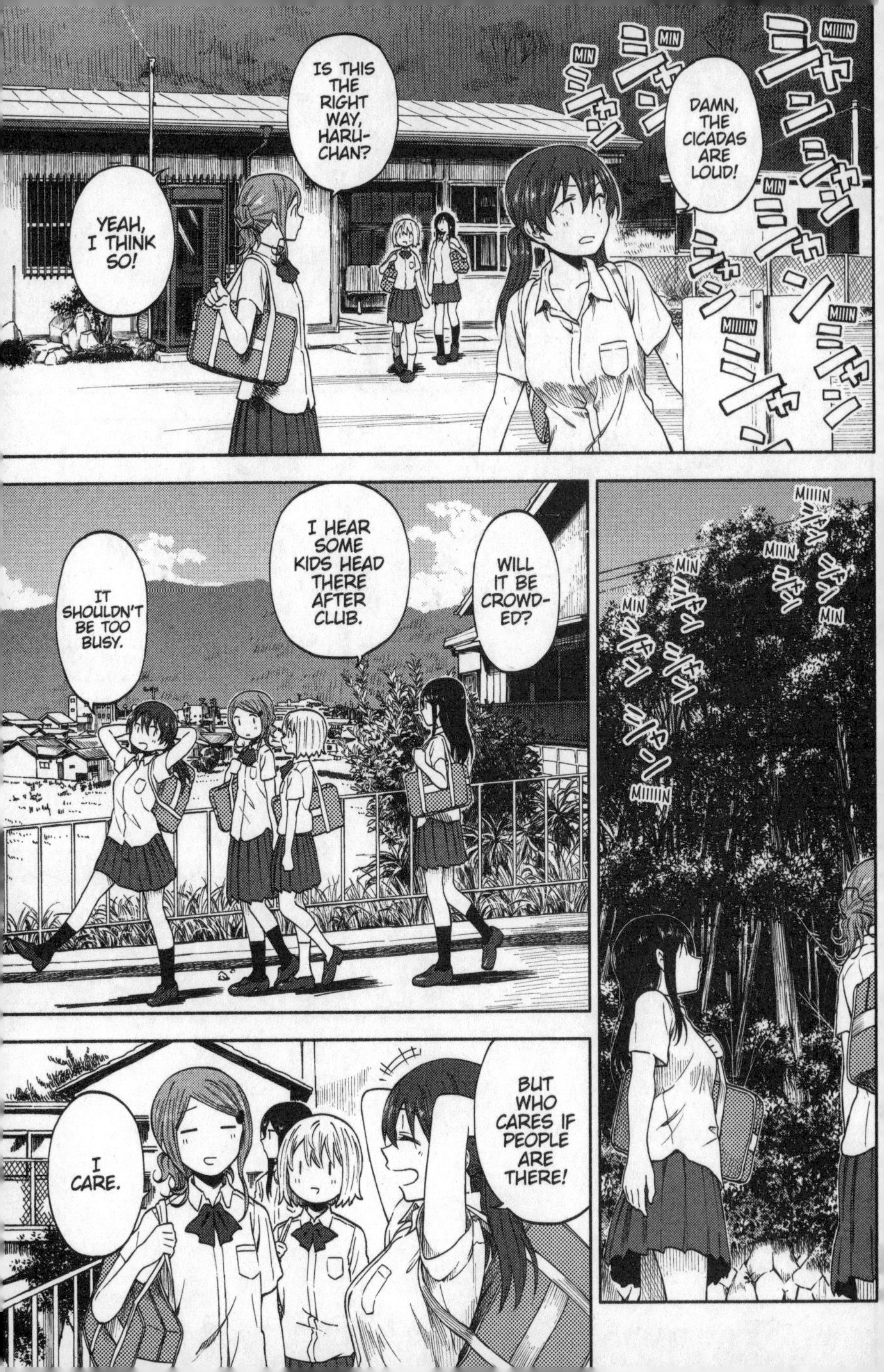
MIIIN
MIN
MIN
DAMN, THE CICADAS ARE LOUD!
MIN
MIIIN
MIIIIN
IS THIS THE RIGHT WAY, HARU-CHAN?
YEAH, I THINK SO!
MIIIN
MIIIN
MIN
MIN
MIN
MIIIIN
WILL IT BE CROWDED?
I HEAR SOME KIDS HEAD THERE AFTER CLUB.
IT SHOULDN'T BE TOO BUSY.
BUT WHO CARES IF PEOPLE ARE THERE!
I CARE.

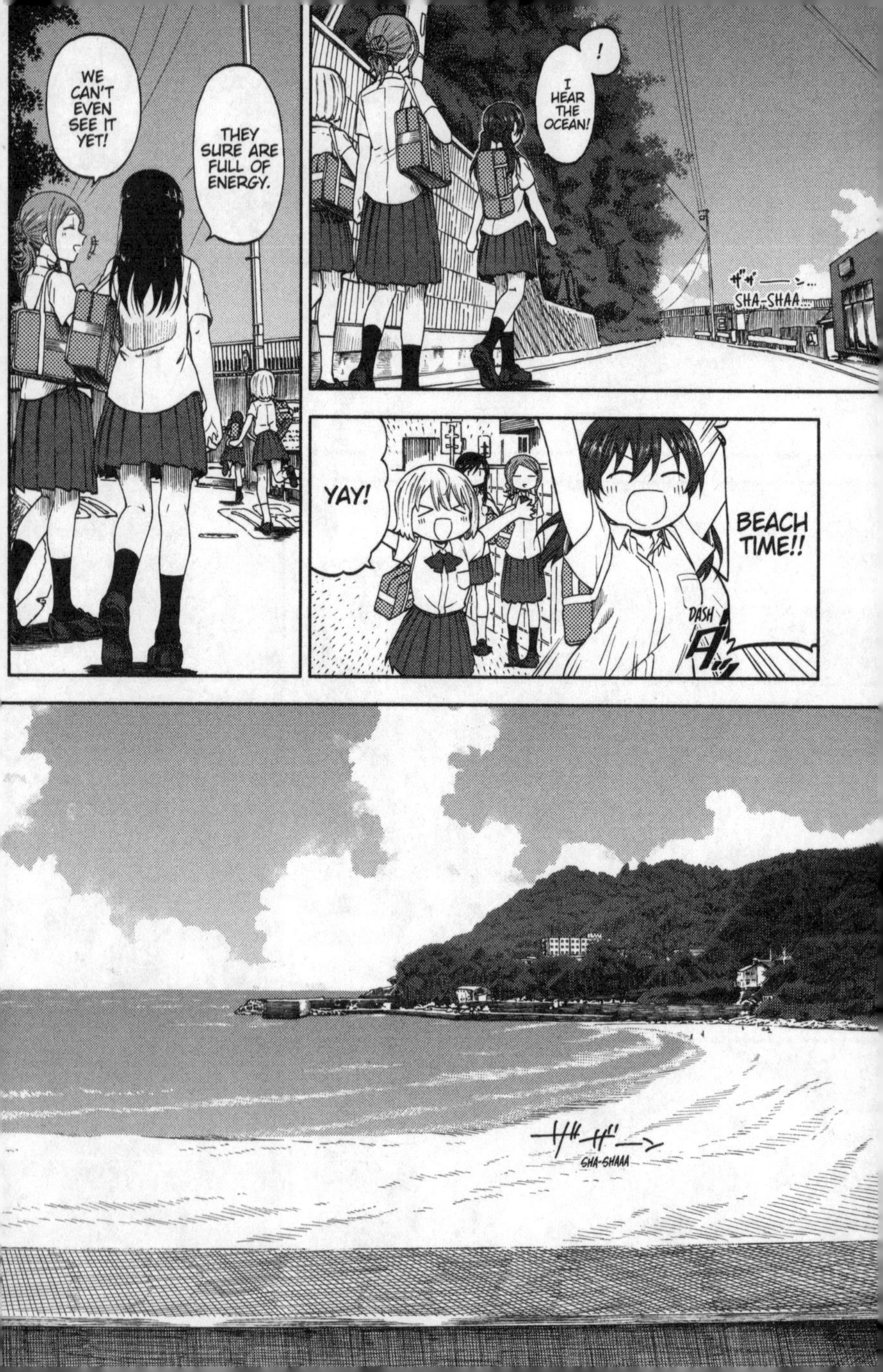
!
I HEAR THE OCEAN!
ザザーーン…
SHA-SHAA...
BEACH TIME!!
DASH
YAY!
THEY SURE ARE FULL OF ENERGY.
WE CAN'T EVEN SEE IT YET!
ザザーン
SHA-SHAAA

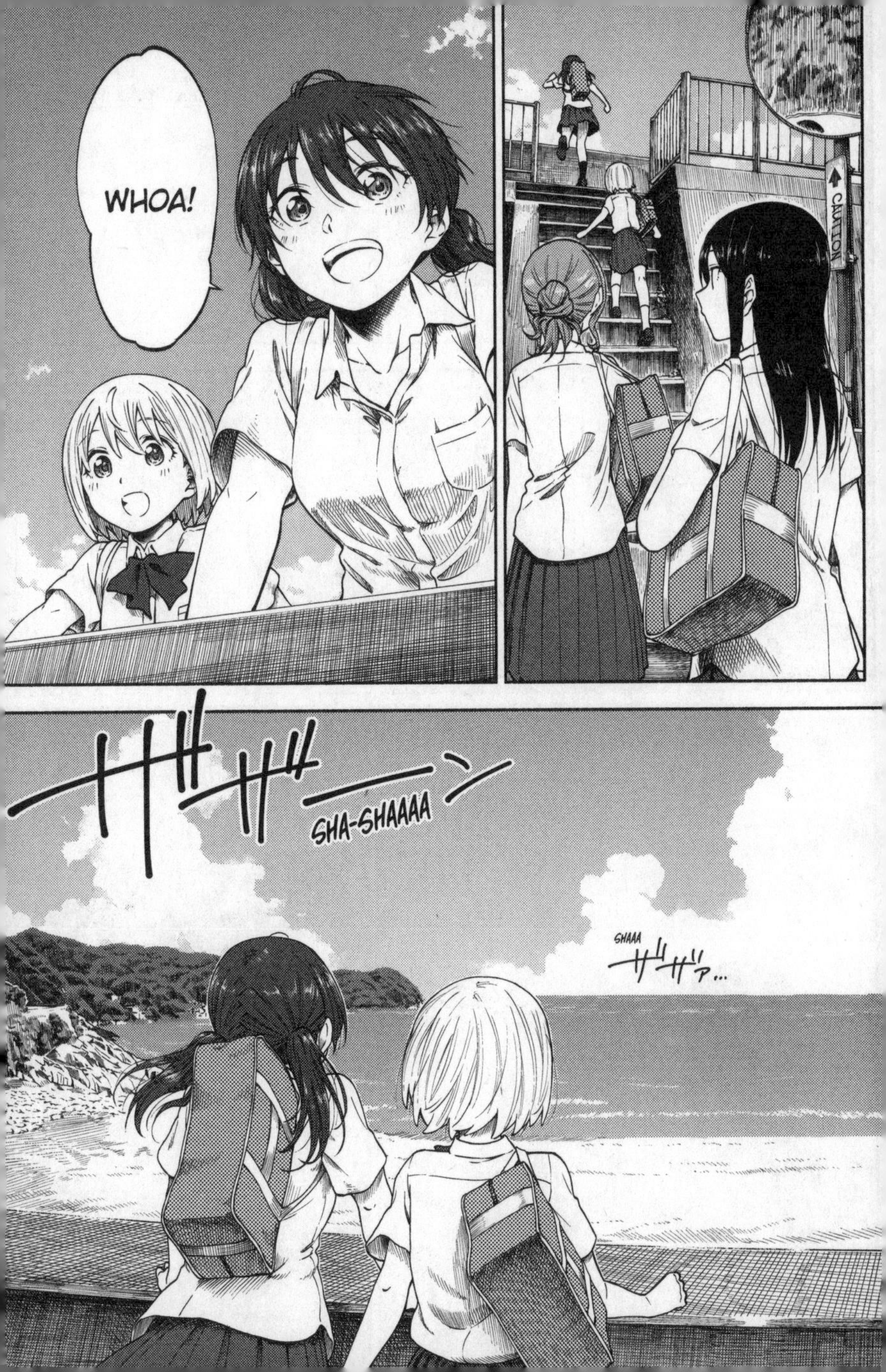
CAUTION
WHOA!
ザザーン
SHA-SHAAAA
SHAAA
ザザァ…

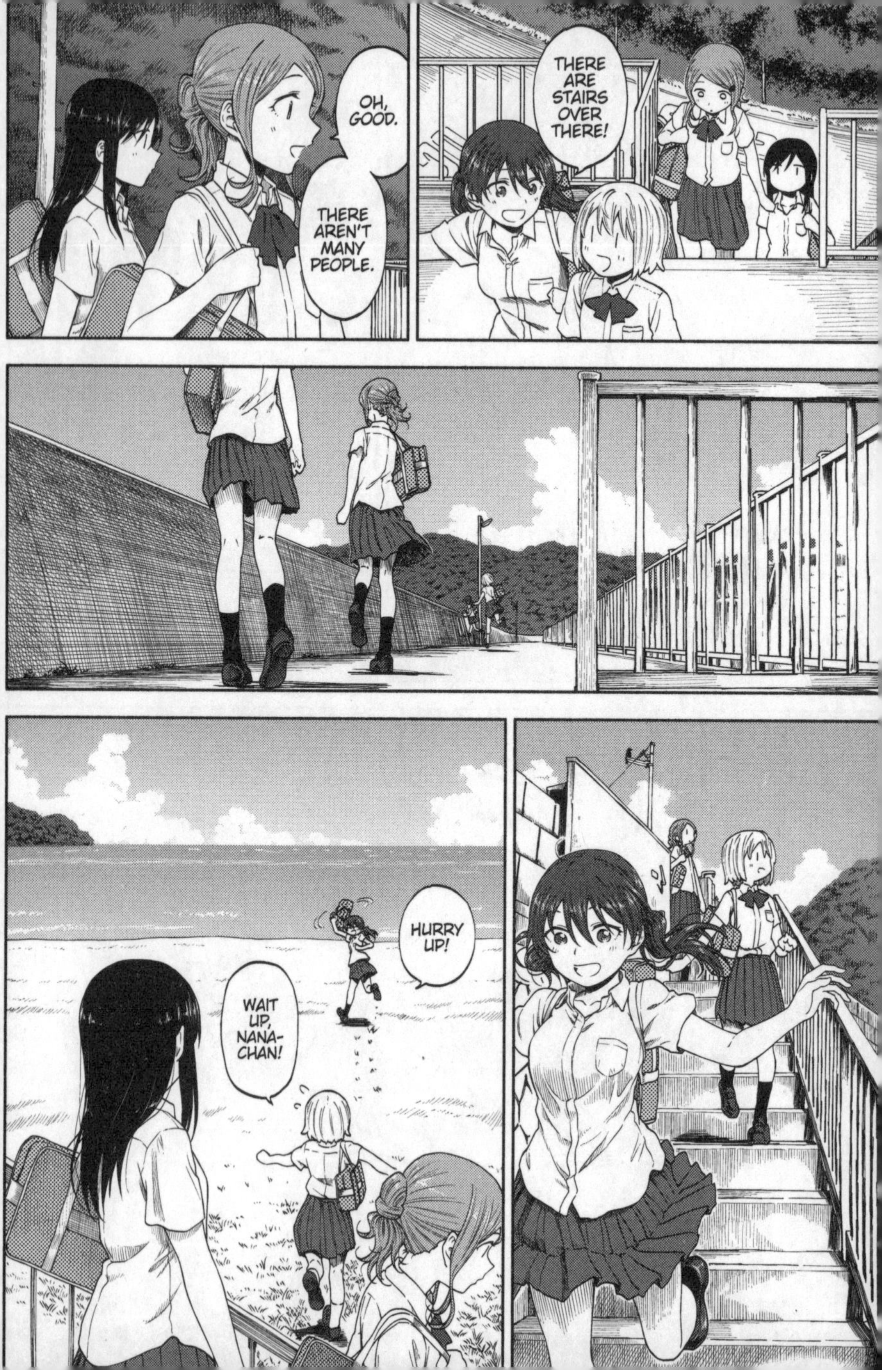
THERE ARE STAIRS OVER THERE!
OH, GOOD.
THERE AREN'T MANY PEOPLE.
HURRY UP!
WAIT UP, NANA-CHAN!

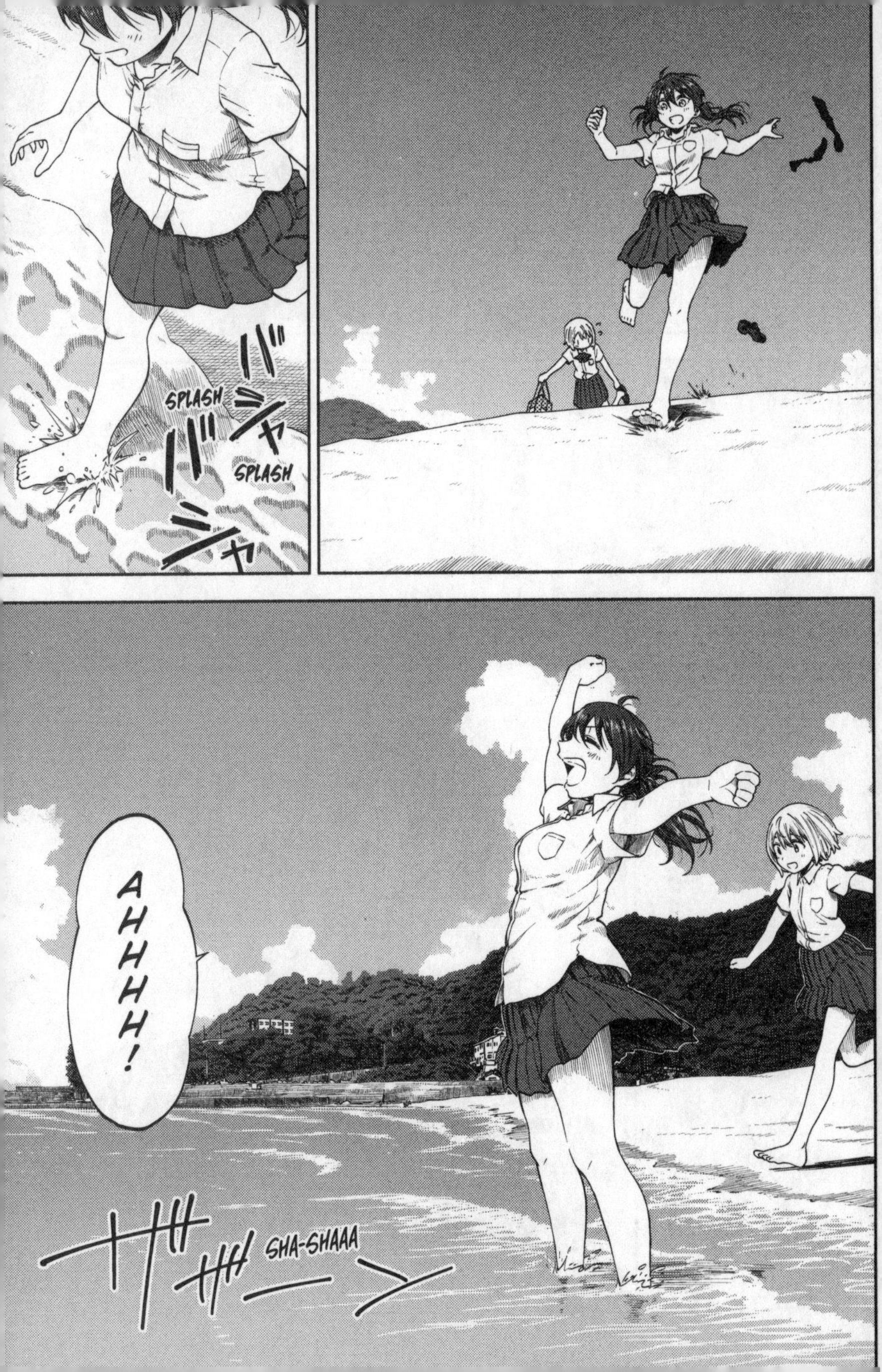
バシャ
SPLASH
バシャ
SPLASH
AHHHHH!
ザザーン
SHA-SHAAA

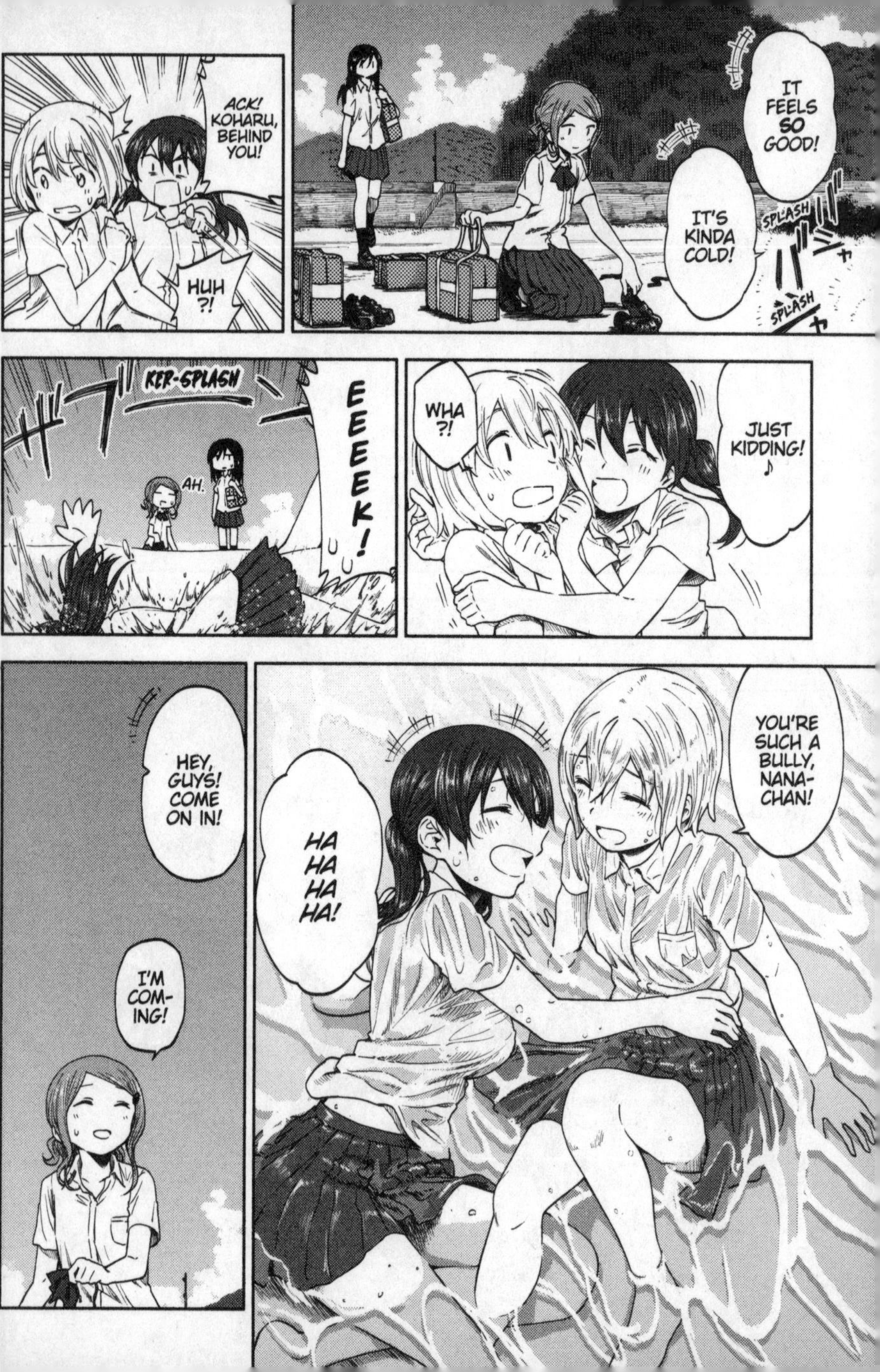
IT FEELS SO GOOD!
IT'S KINDA COLD!
SPLASH
SPLASH
ACK! KOHARU, BEHIND YOU!
HUH ?!
JUST KIDDING! ♪
WHA ?!
KER-SPLASH
EEEEEK!
AH.
YOU'RE SUCH A BULLY, NANA-CHAN!
HA HA HA HA HA!
HEY, GUYS! COME ON IN!
I'M COMING!

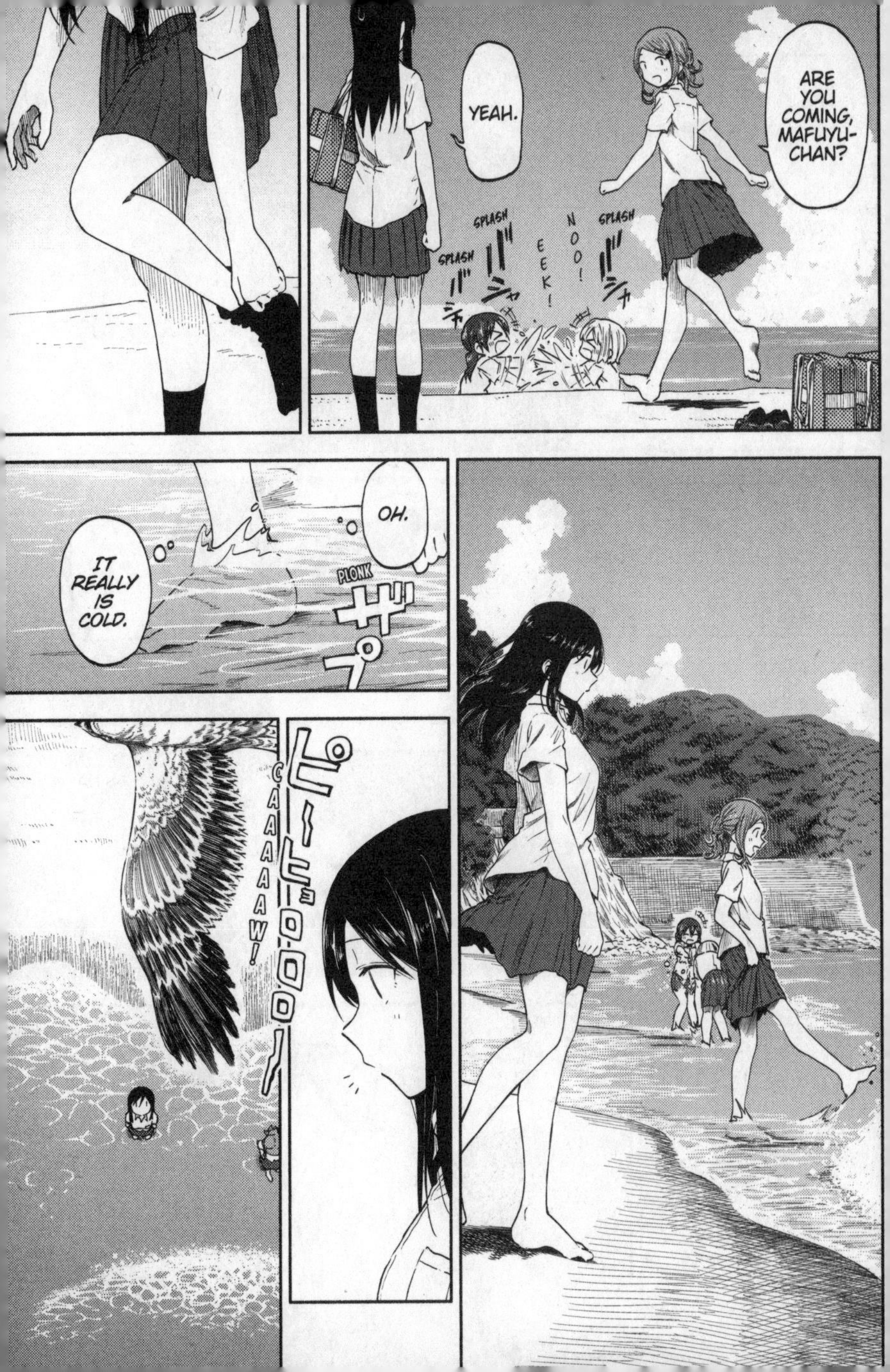

ARE YOU COMING, MAFUYU-CHAN?
YEAH.
SPLASH
NOO!
EEK!
SPLASH
SPLASH
OH.
IT REALLY IS COLD.
PLONK
ザプ
ピーヒョロロロー
CAAAAAAAW!

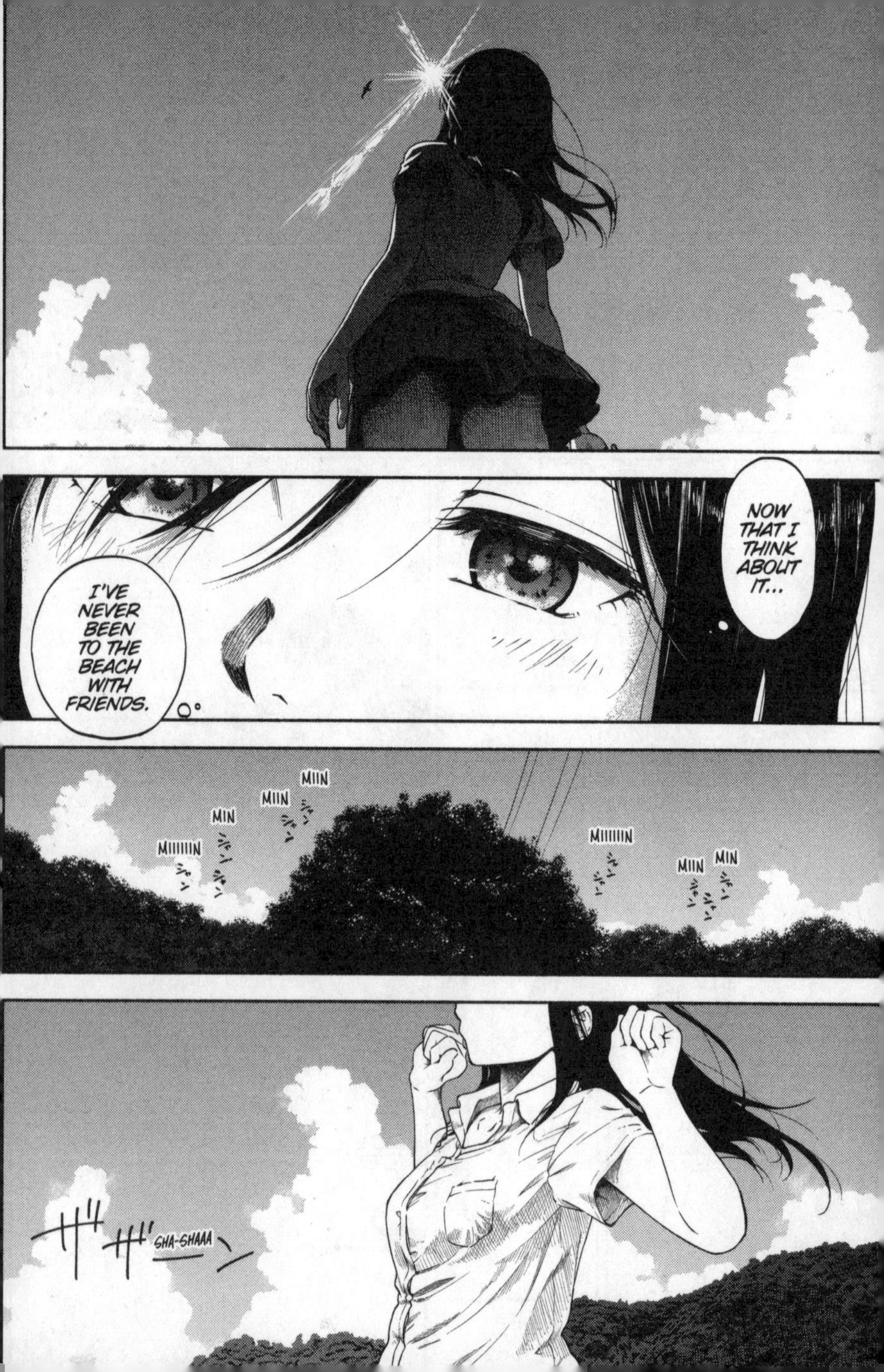
NOW THAT I THINK ABOUT IT...
I'VE NEVER BEEN TO THE BEACH WITH FRIENDS.
MIN
MIIN
MIIIIIIN
MIIN
MIIN
MIN
MIIIIIIN
SHA-SHAAA

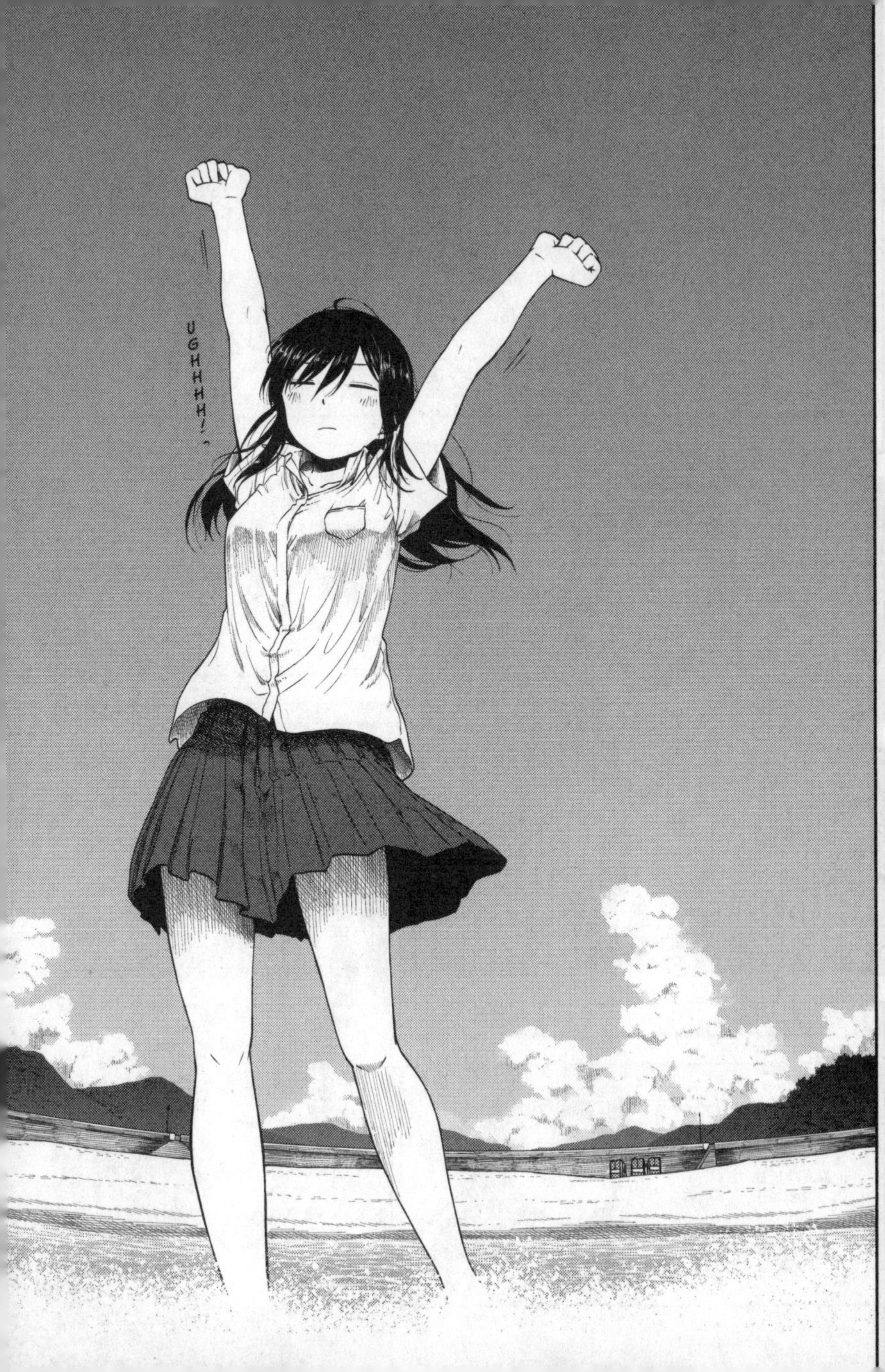
UGHHHH!

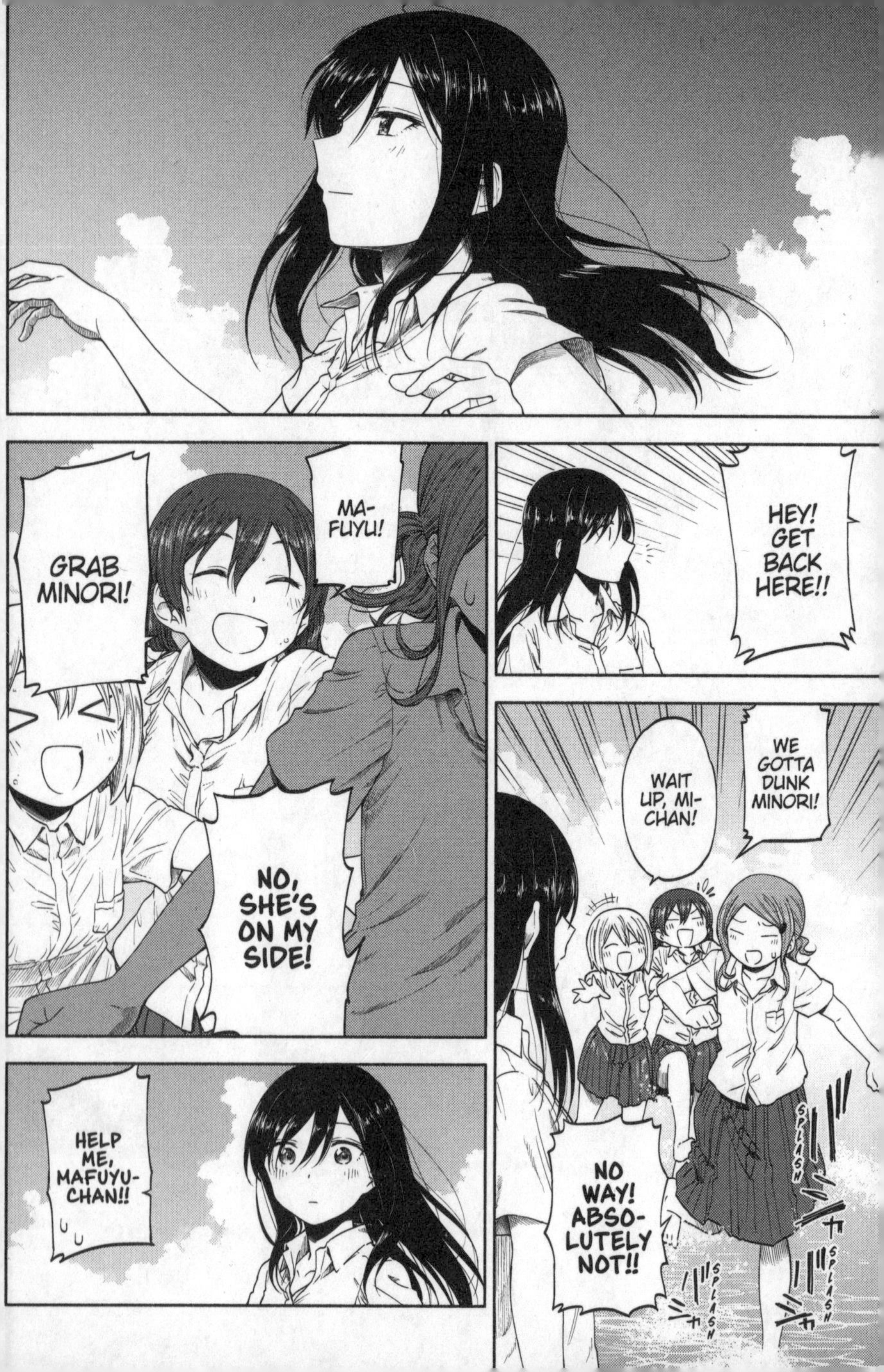
HEY! GET BACK HERE!!
MA-FUYU!
GRAB MINORI!
NO, SHE'S ON MY SIDE!
WE GOTTA DUNK MINORI!
WAIT UP, MI-CHAN!
NO WAY! ABSOLUTELY NOT!!
SPLASH
SPLASH
SPLASH
SPLASH
HELP ME, MAFUYU-CHAN!!

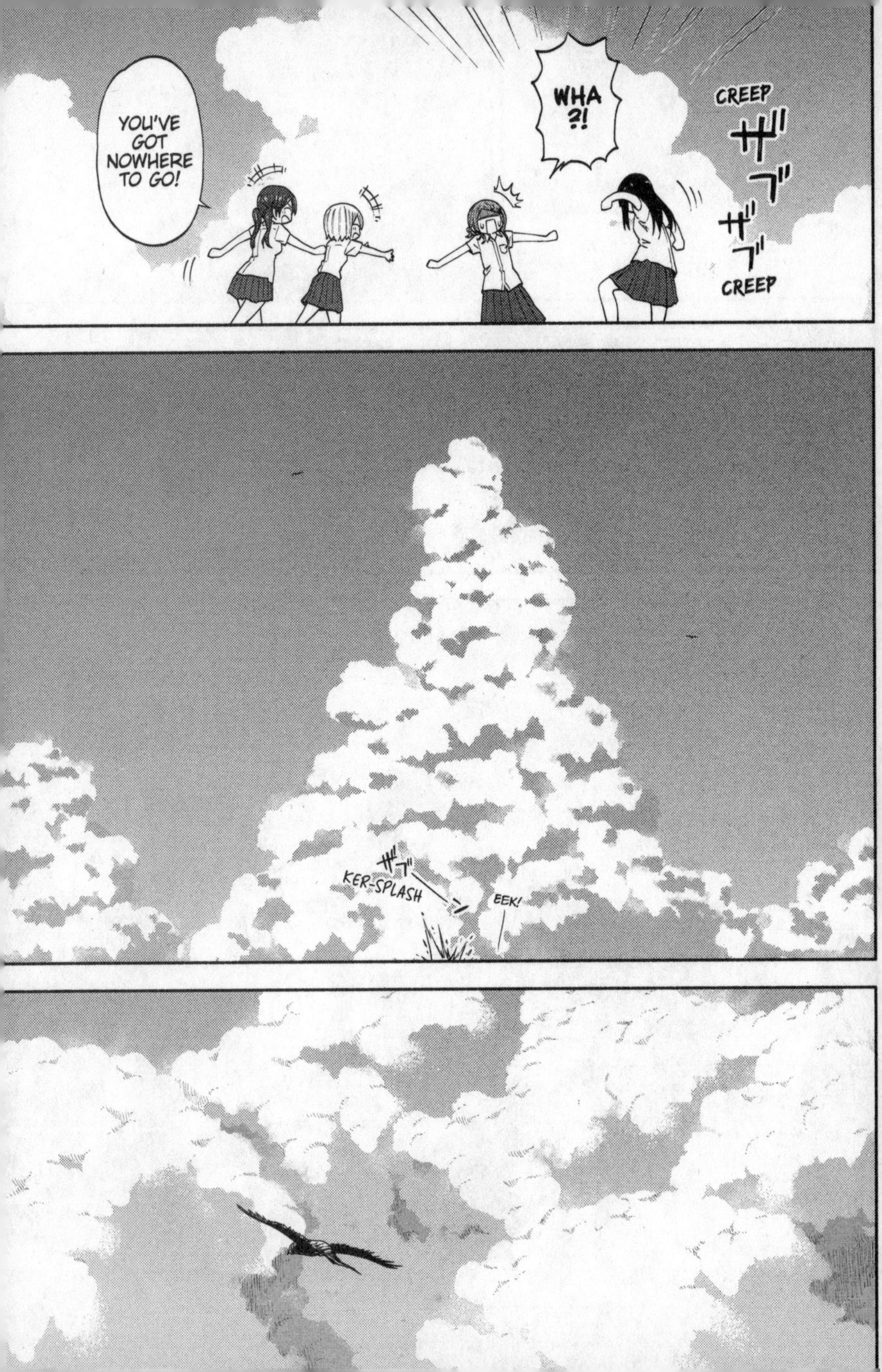
CREEP
ザブ
ザブ
CREEP
WHA ?!
YOU'VE GOT NOWHERE TO GO!
EEK!
ザブ
KER-SPLASH

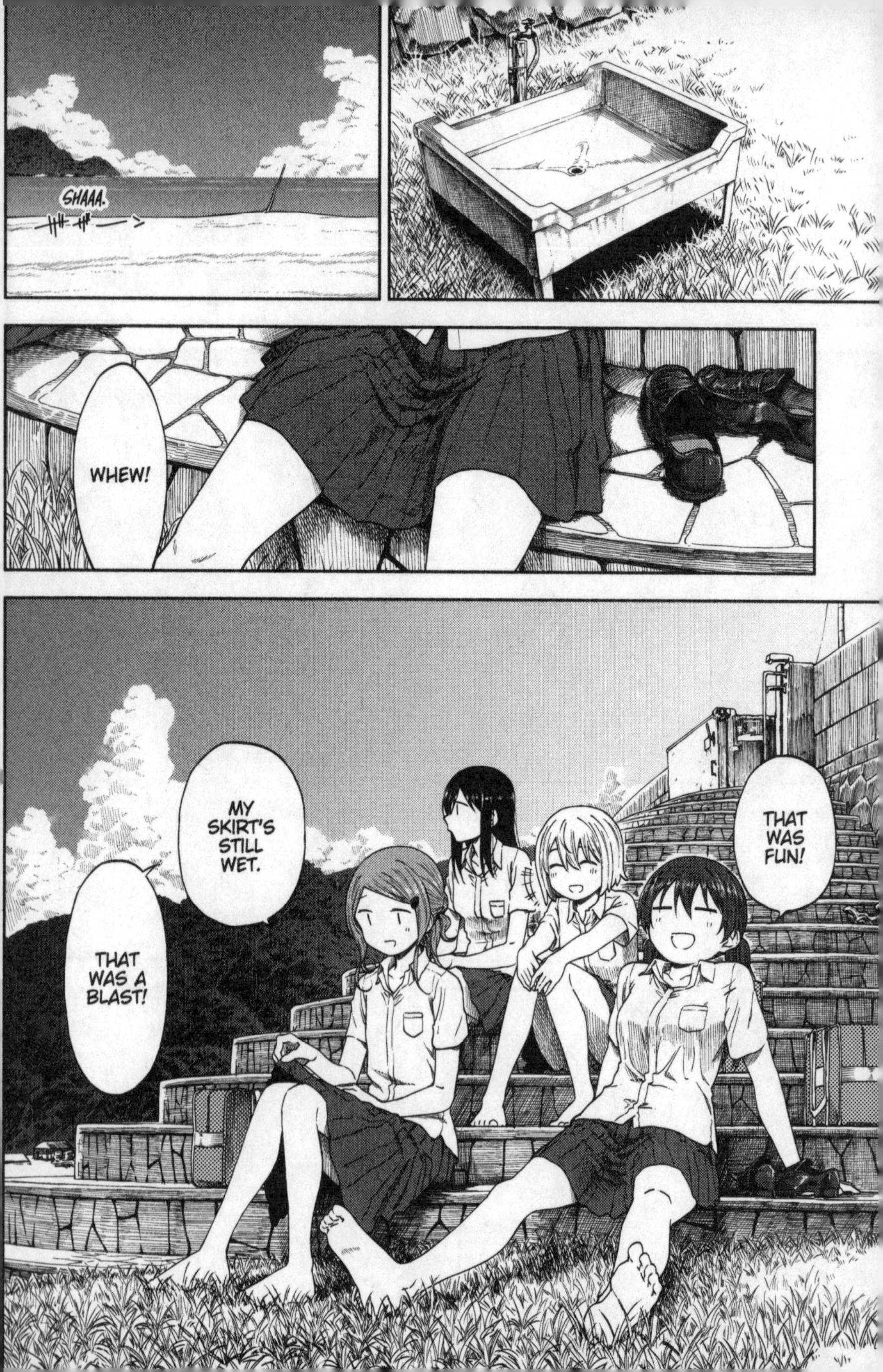
SHAAA.
WHEW!
THAT WAS FUN!
MY SKIRT'S STILL WET.
THAT WAS A BLAST!

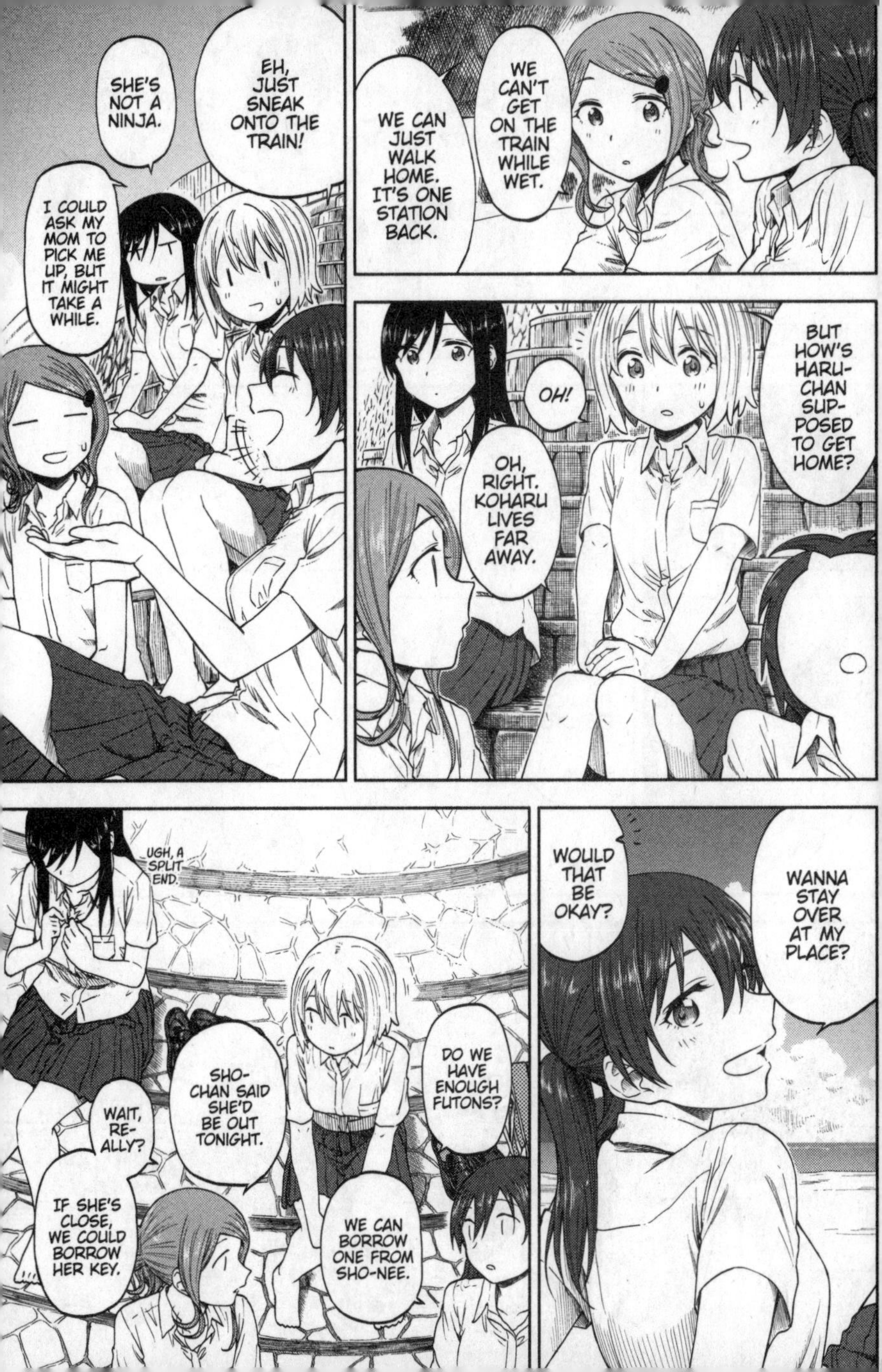
WE CAN'T GET ON THE TRAIN WHILE WET.
WE CAN JUST WALK HOME. IT'S ONE STATION BACK.
BUT HOW'S HARU-CHAN SUP-POSED TO GET HOME?
OH!
OH, RIGHT. KOHARU LIVES FAR AWAY.
EH, JUST SNEAK ONTO THE TRAIN!
SHE'S NOT A NINJA.
I COULD ASK MY MOM TO PICK ME UP, BUT IT MIGHT TAKE A WHILE.
WANNA STAY OVER AT MY PLACE?
WOULD THAT BE OKAY?
UGH, A SPLIT END.
DO WE HAVE ENOUGH FUTONS?
WE CAN BORROW ONE FROM SHO-NEE.
SHO-CHAN SAID SHE'D BE OUT TONIGHT.
WAIT, RE-ALLY?
IF SHE'S CLOSE, WE COULD BORROW HER KEY.

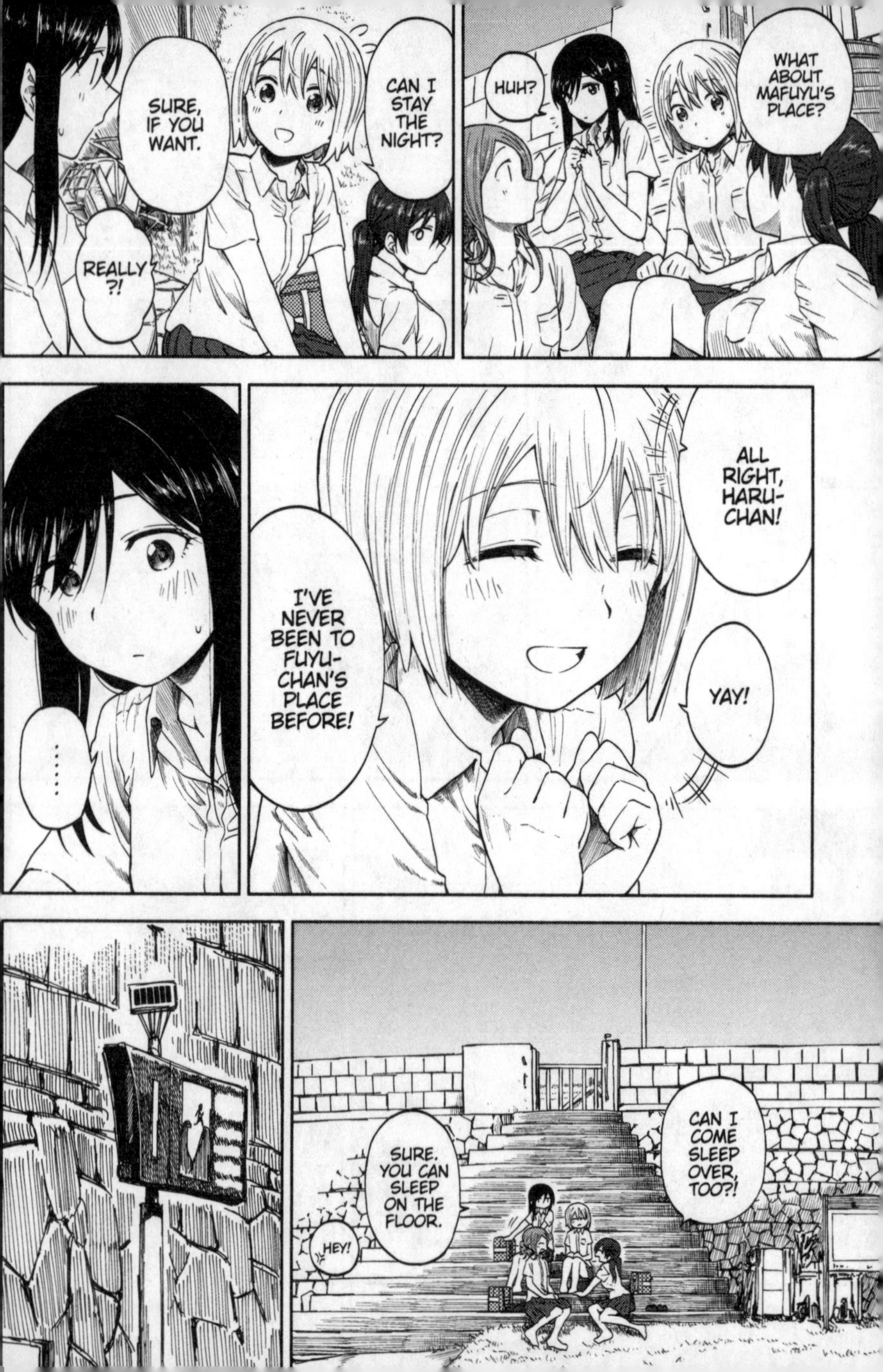
WHAT ABOUT MAFUYU'S PLACE?
HUH?
CAN I STAY THE NIGHT?
SURE, IF YOU WANT.
REALLY?!
ALL RIGHT, HARU-CHAN!
YAY!
I'VE NEVER BEEN TO FUYU-CHAN'S PLACE BEFORE!
......
CAN I COME SLEEP OVER, TOO?!
SURE. YOU CAN SLEEP ON THE FLOOR.
HEY!

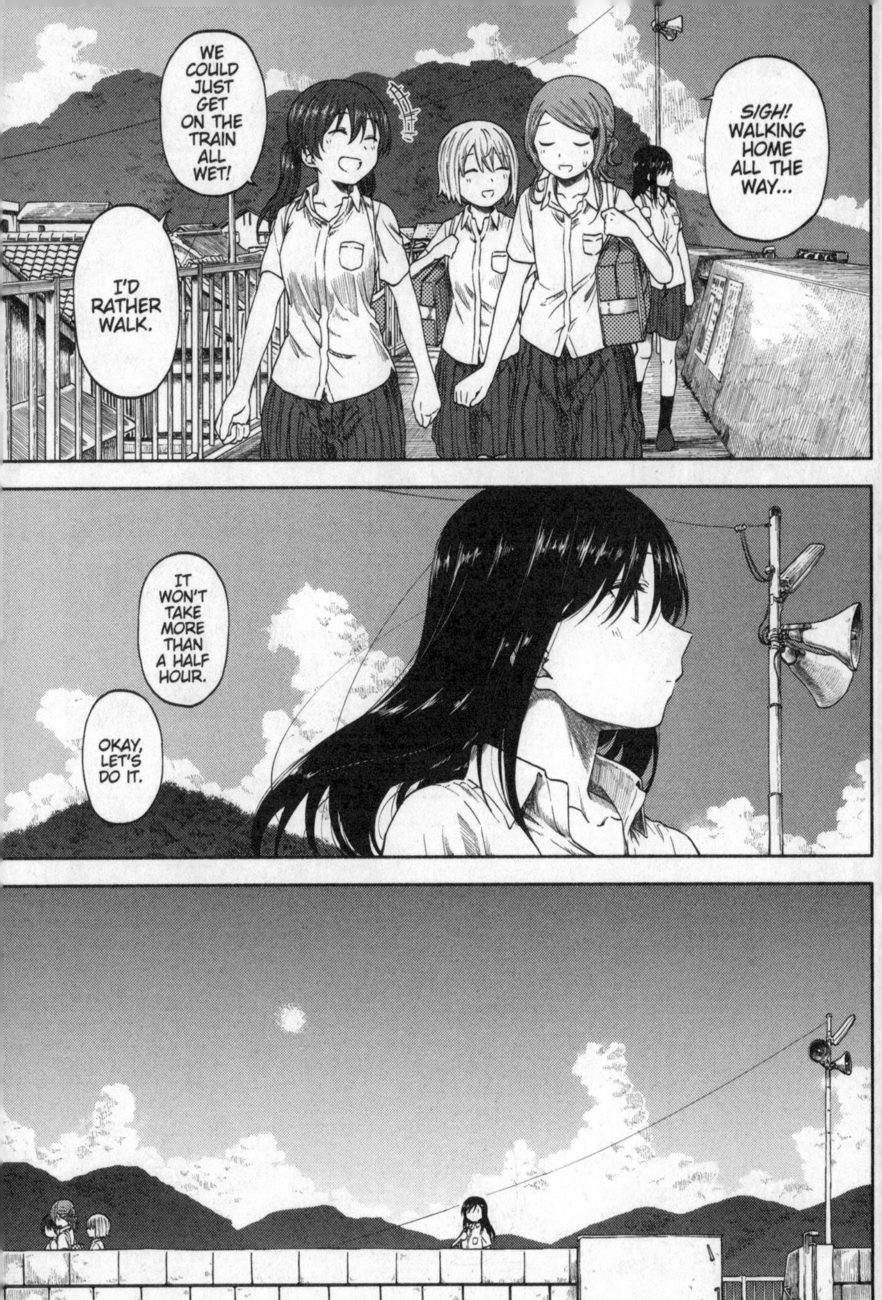
SIGH! WALKING HOME ALL THE WAY...
WE COULD JUST GET ON THE TRAIN ALL WET!
I'D RATHER WALK.
IT WON'T TAKE MORE THAN A HALF HOUR.
OKAY, LET'S DO IT.

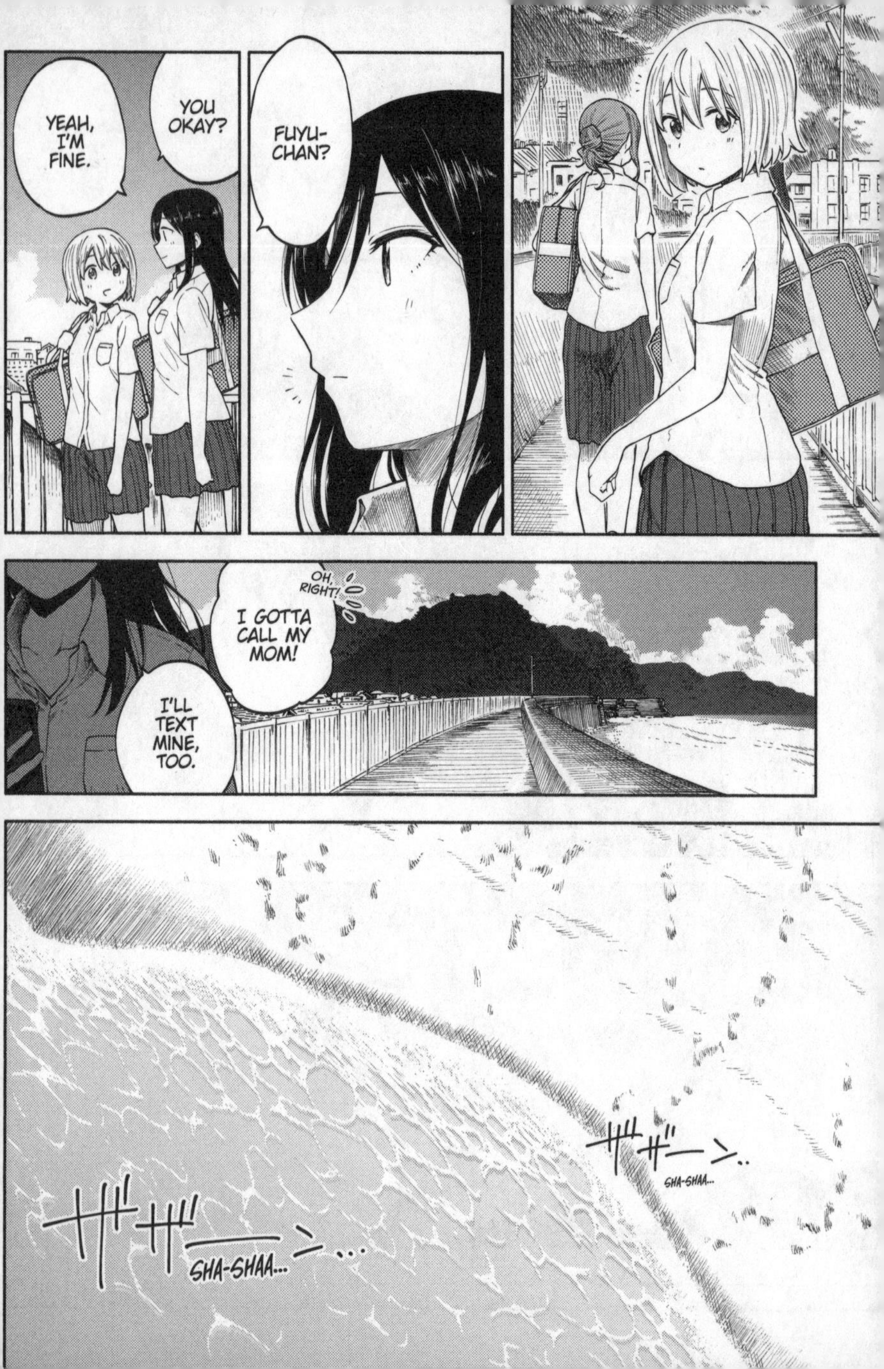
FUYU-
CHAN?
YOU
OKAY?
YEAH,
I'M
FINE.
OH,
RIGHT!
I GOTTA
CALL MY
MOM!
I'LL
TEXT
MINE,
TOO.
ザザーン..
SHA-SHAA...
ザザーーン...
SHA-SHAA...

Our Wonderful Days

story & art by Kei Hamuro

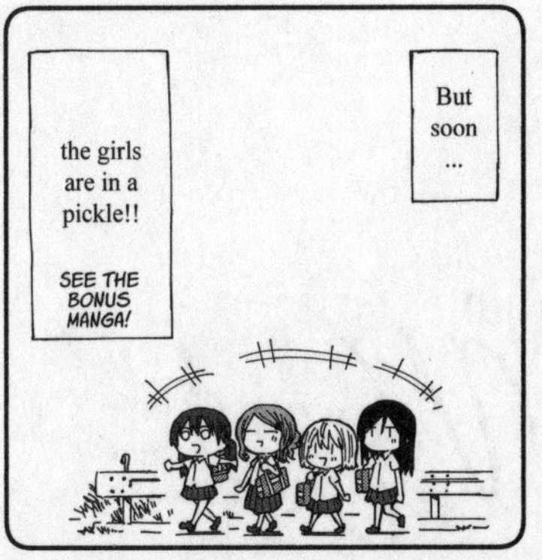
But soon ...
the girls are in a pickle!!
SEE THE BONUS MANGA!

Our *Wonderful* **Days** Tsurezure Biyori

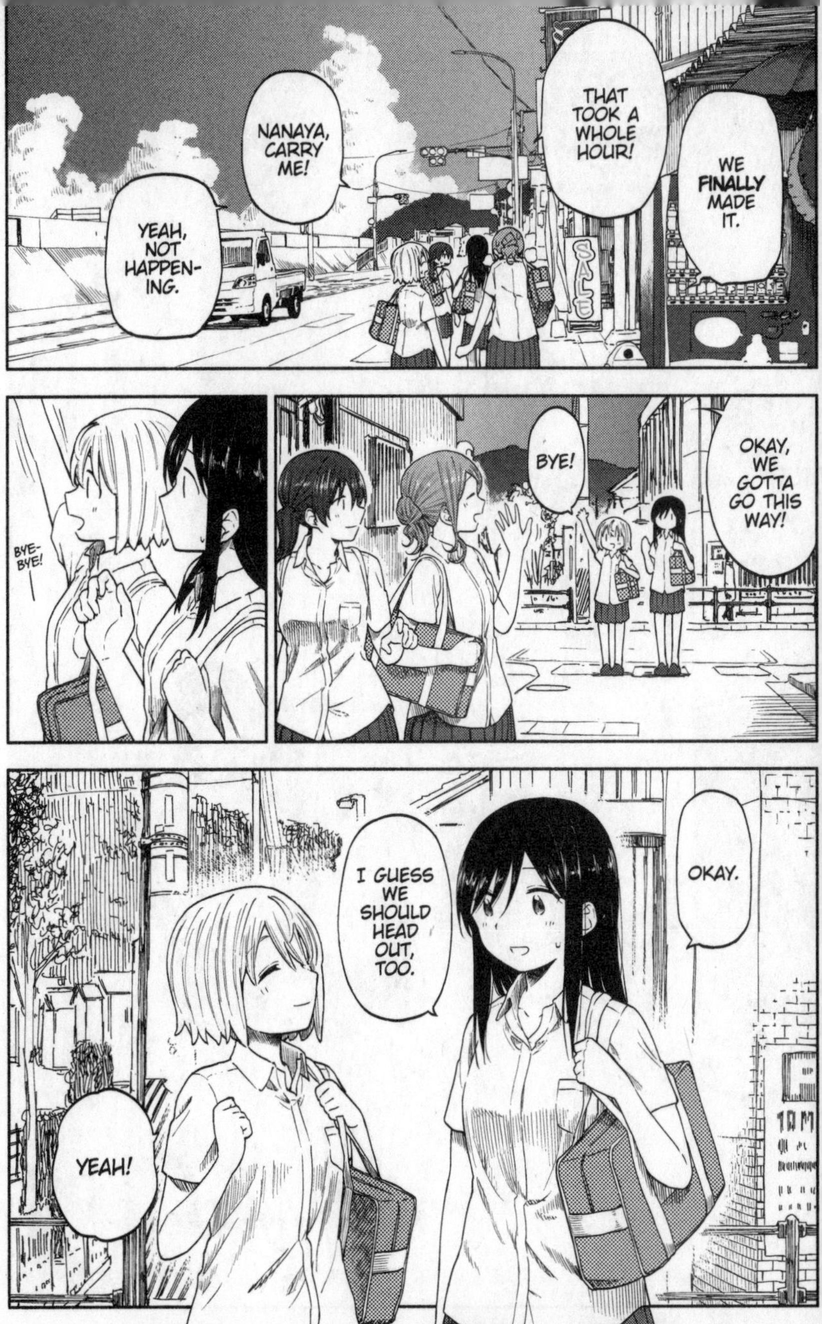
WE FINALLY MADE IT.
THAT TOOK A WHOLE HOUR!
NANAYA, CARRY ME!
YEAH, NOT HAPPENING.
OKAY, WE GOTTA GO THIS WAY!
BYE!
BYE-BYE!
OKAY.
I GUESS WE SHOULD HEAD OUT, TOO.
YEAH!

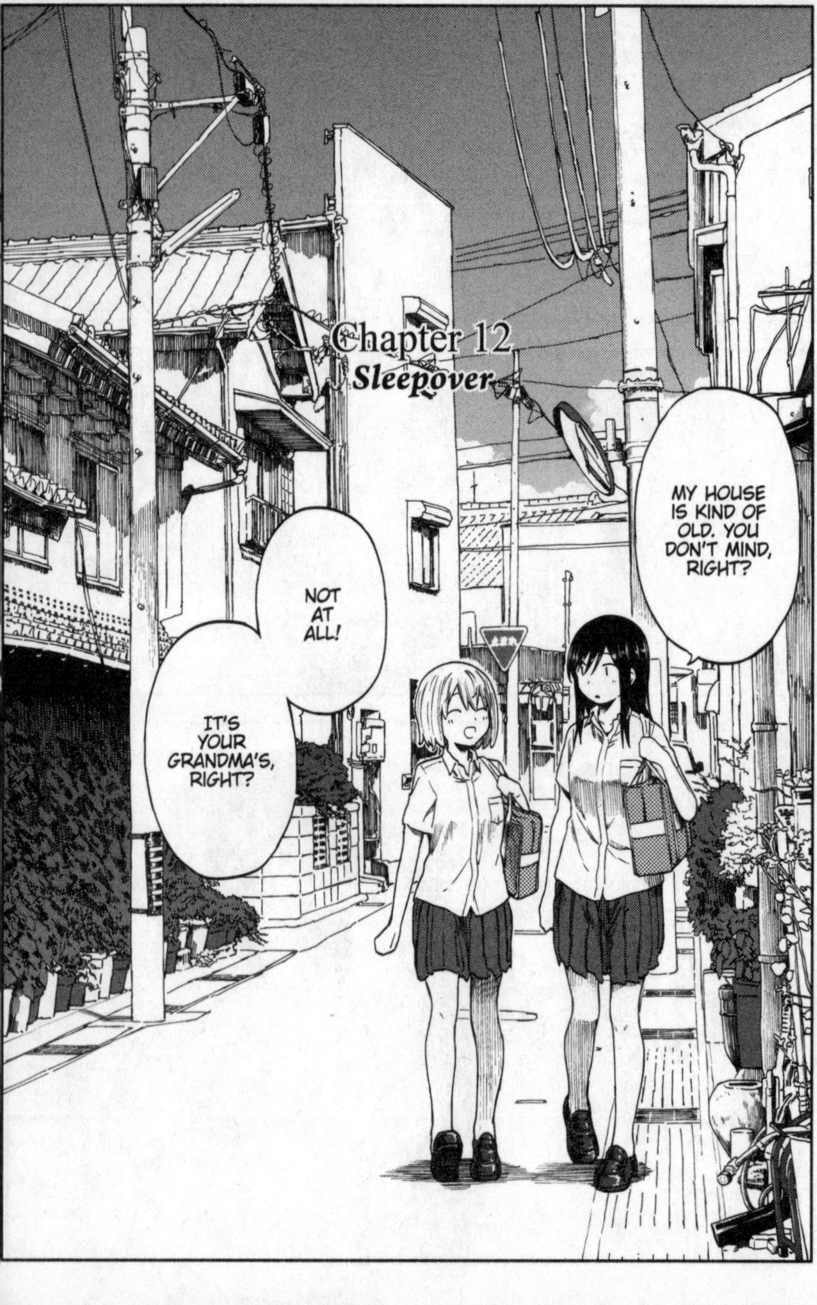
Chapter 12
Sleepover
MY HOUSE IS KIND OF OLD. YOU DON'T MIND, RIGHT?
NOT AT ALL!
IT'S YOUR GRANDMA'S, RIGHT?

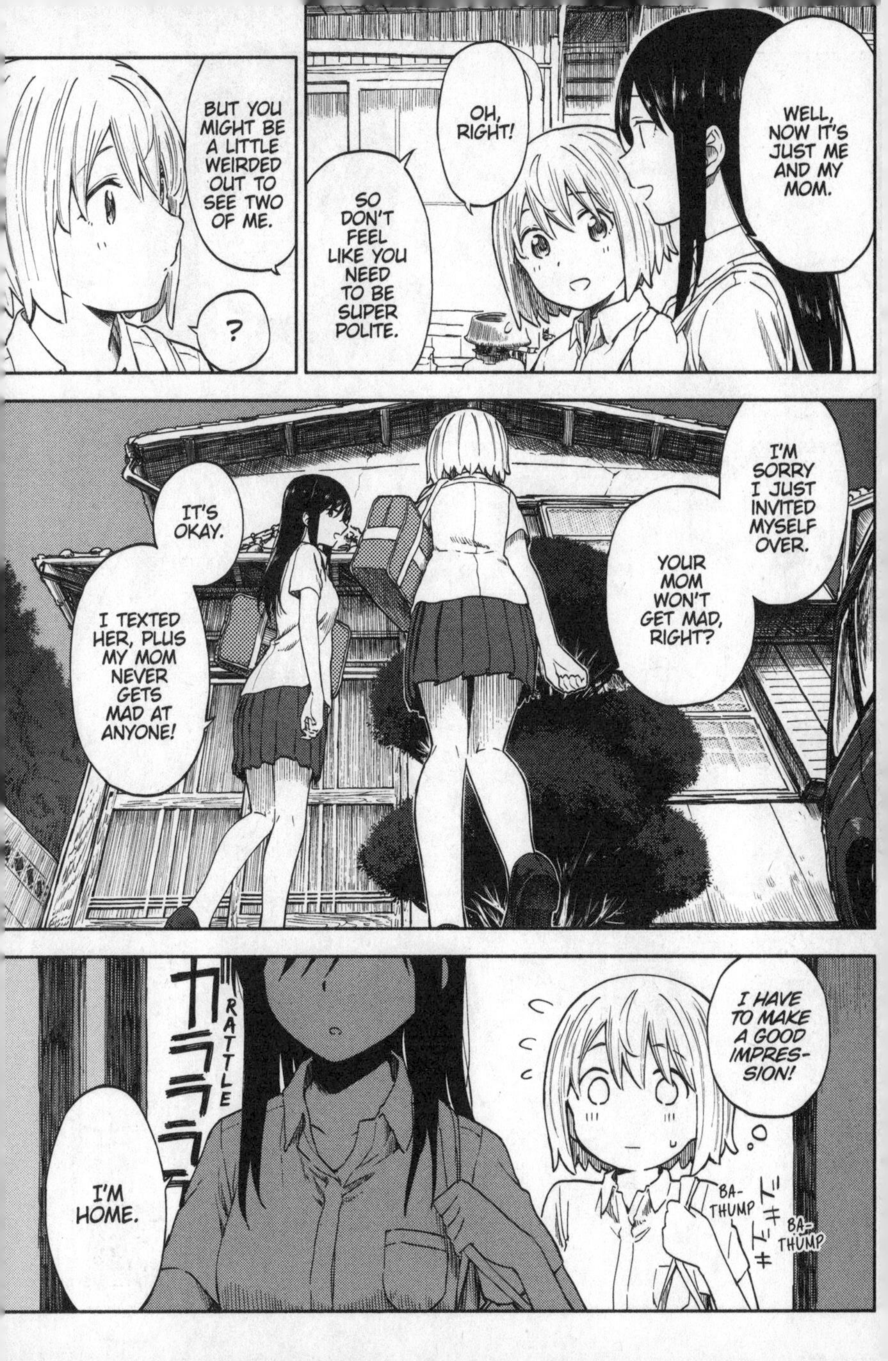
WELL, NOW IT'S JUST ME AND MY MOM.
OH, RIGHT!
SO DON'T FEEL LIKE YOU NEED TO BE SUPER POLITE.
BUT YOU MIGHT BE A LITTLE WEIRDED OUT TO SEE TWO OF ME.
?
I'M SORRY I JUST INVITED MYSELF OVER.
YOUR MOM WON'T GET MAD, RIGHT?
IT'S OKAY.
I TEXTED HER, PLUS MY MOM NEVER GETS MAD AT ANYONE!
I HAVE TO MAKE A GOOD IMPRESSION!
ドキドキ
BA-THUMP
BA-THUMP
ガラララ
RATTLE
I'M HOME.

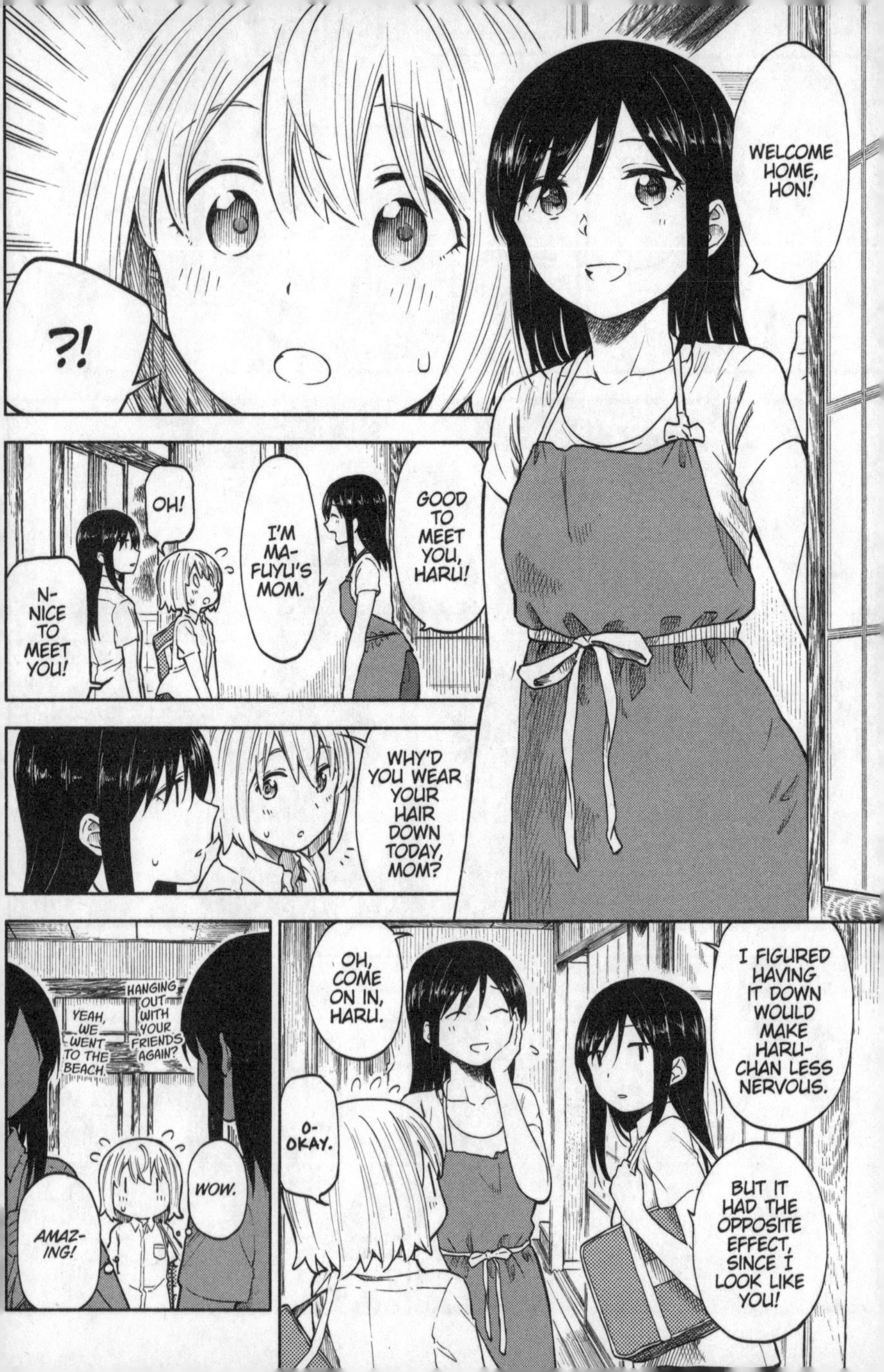
WELCOME HOME, HON!
?!
GOOD TO MEET YOU, HARU!
I'M MA-FUYU'S MOM.
OH!
N-NICE TO MEET YOU!
WHY'D YOU WEAR YOUR HAIR DOWN TODAY, MOM?
I FIGURED HAVING IT DOWN WOULD MAKE HARU-CHAN LESS NERVOUS.
OH, COME ON IN, HARU.
BUT IT HAD THE OPPOSITE EFFECT, SINCE I LOOK LIKE YOU!
O-OKAY.
HANGING OUT WITH YOUR FRIENDS AGAIN?
YEAH, WE WENT TO THE BEACH.
WOW.
AMAZ-ING!

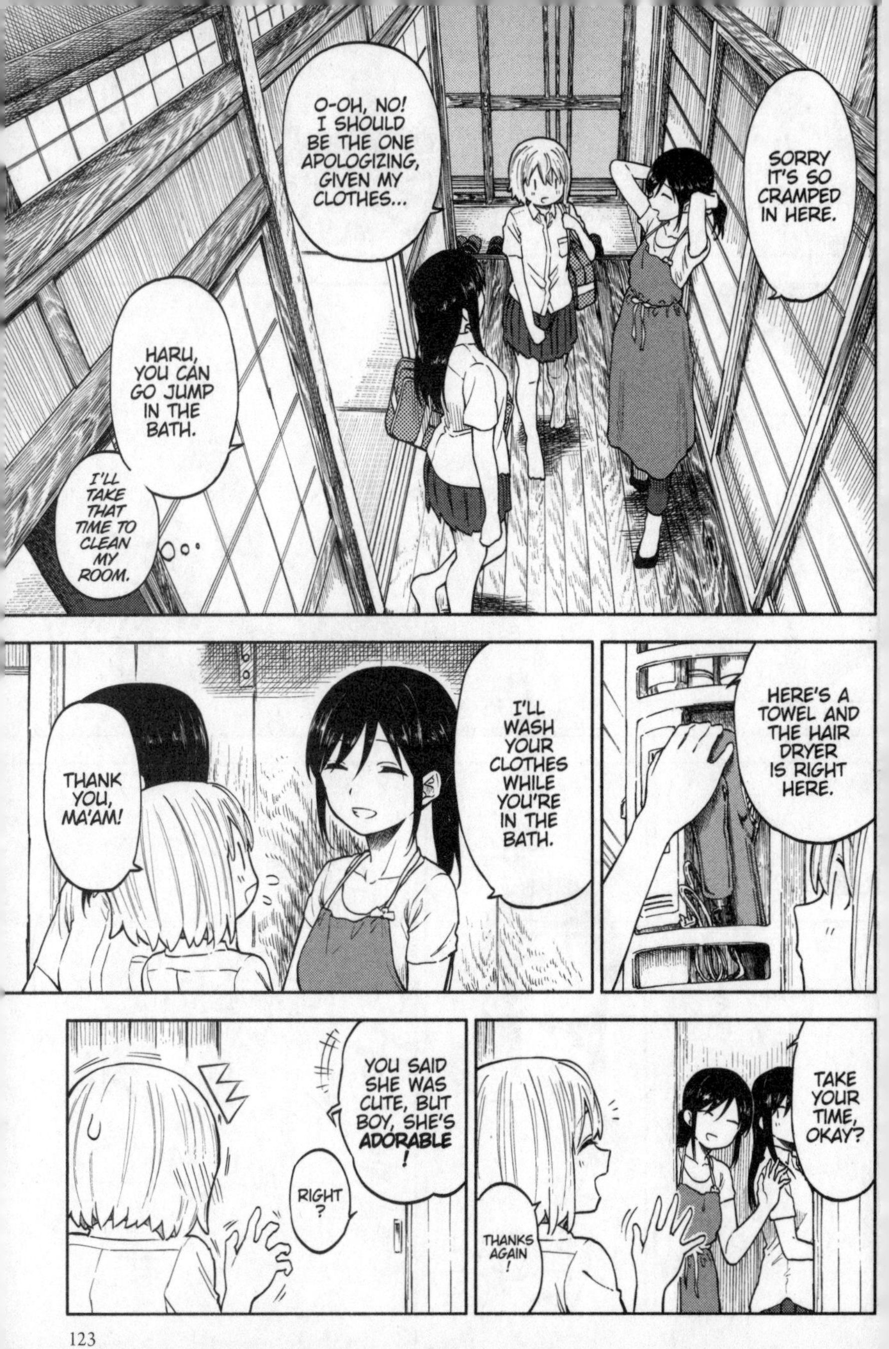
SORRY IT'S SO CRAMPED IN HERE.
O-OH, NO! I SHOULD BE THE ONE APOLOGIZING, GIVEN MY CLOTHES...
HARU, YOU CAN GO JUMP IN THE BATH.
I'LL TAKE THAT TIME TO CLEAN MY ROOM.
HERE'S A TOWEL AND THE HAIR DRYER IS RIGHT HERE.
I'LL WASH YOUR CLOTHES WHILE YOU'RE IN THE BATH.
THANK YOU, MA'AM!
TAKE YOUR TIME, OKAY?
THANKS AGAIN!
YOU SAID SHE WAS CUTE, BUT BOY, SHE'S **ADORABLE**!
RIGHT?

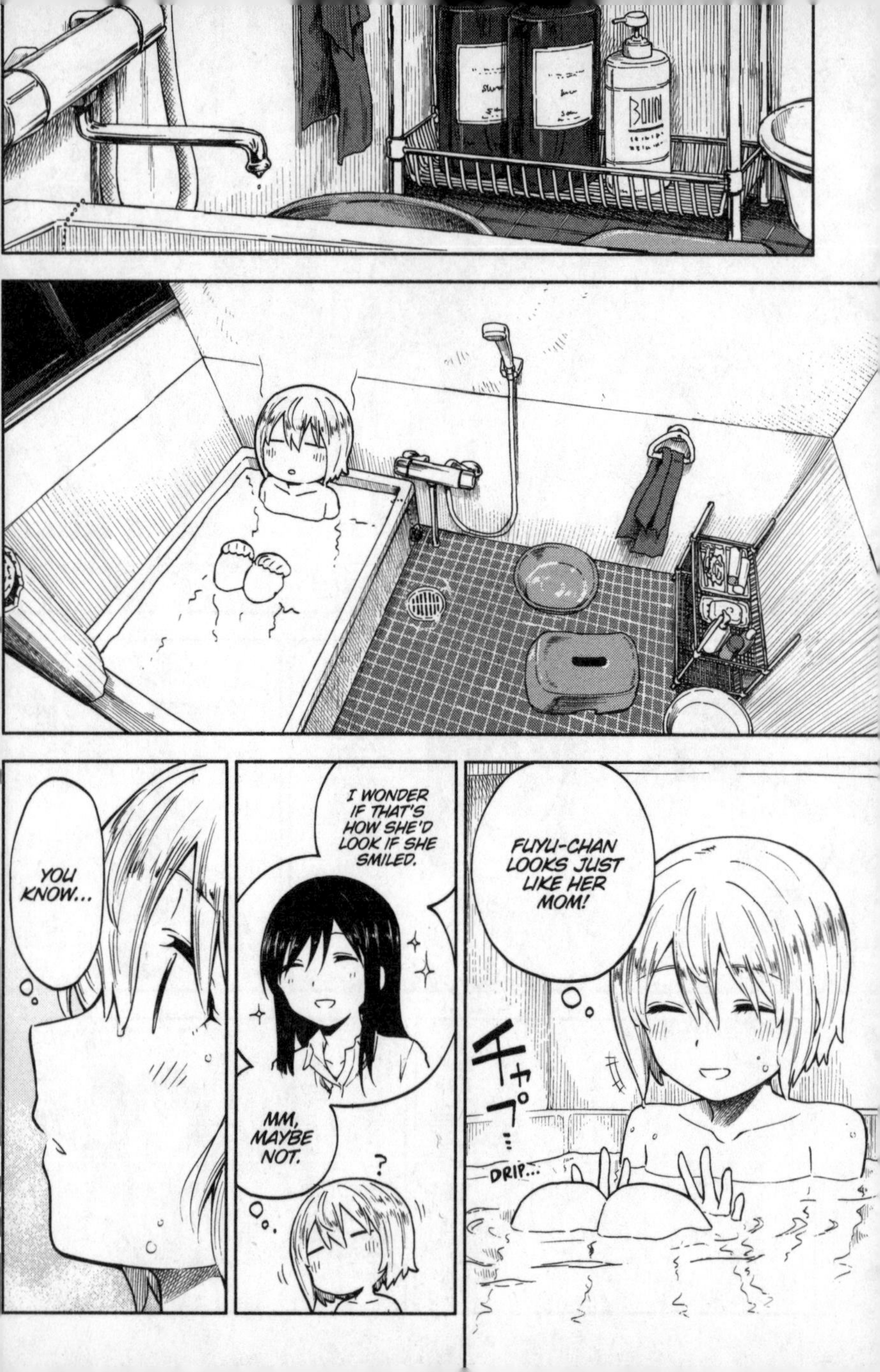
FUYU-CHAN LOOKS JUST LIKE HER MOM!
チャプ
DRIP...
I WONDER IF THAT'S HOW SHE'D LOOK IF SHE SMILED.
MM, MAYBE NOT.
?
YOU KNOW...

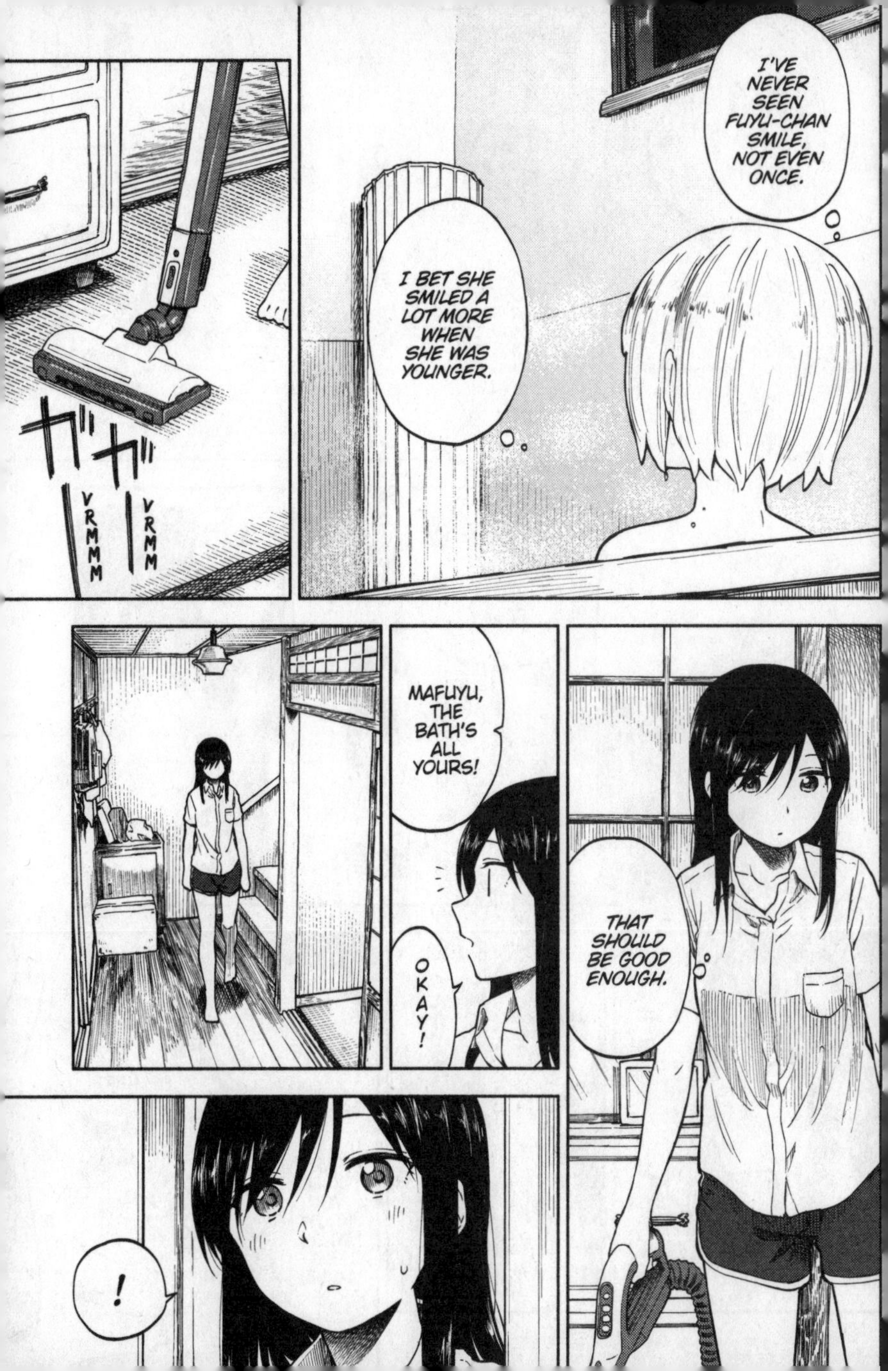
I'VE NEVER SEEN FUYU-CHAN SMILE, NOT EVEN ONCE.
I BET SHE SMILED A LOT MORE WHEN SHE WAS YOUNGER.
VRMM
VRMMM
THAT SHOULD BE GOOD ENOUGH.
MAFUYU, THE BATH'S ALL YOURS!
OKAY!
!

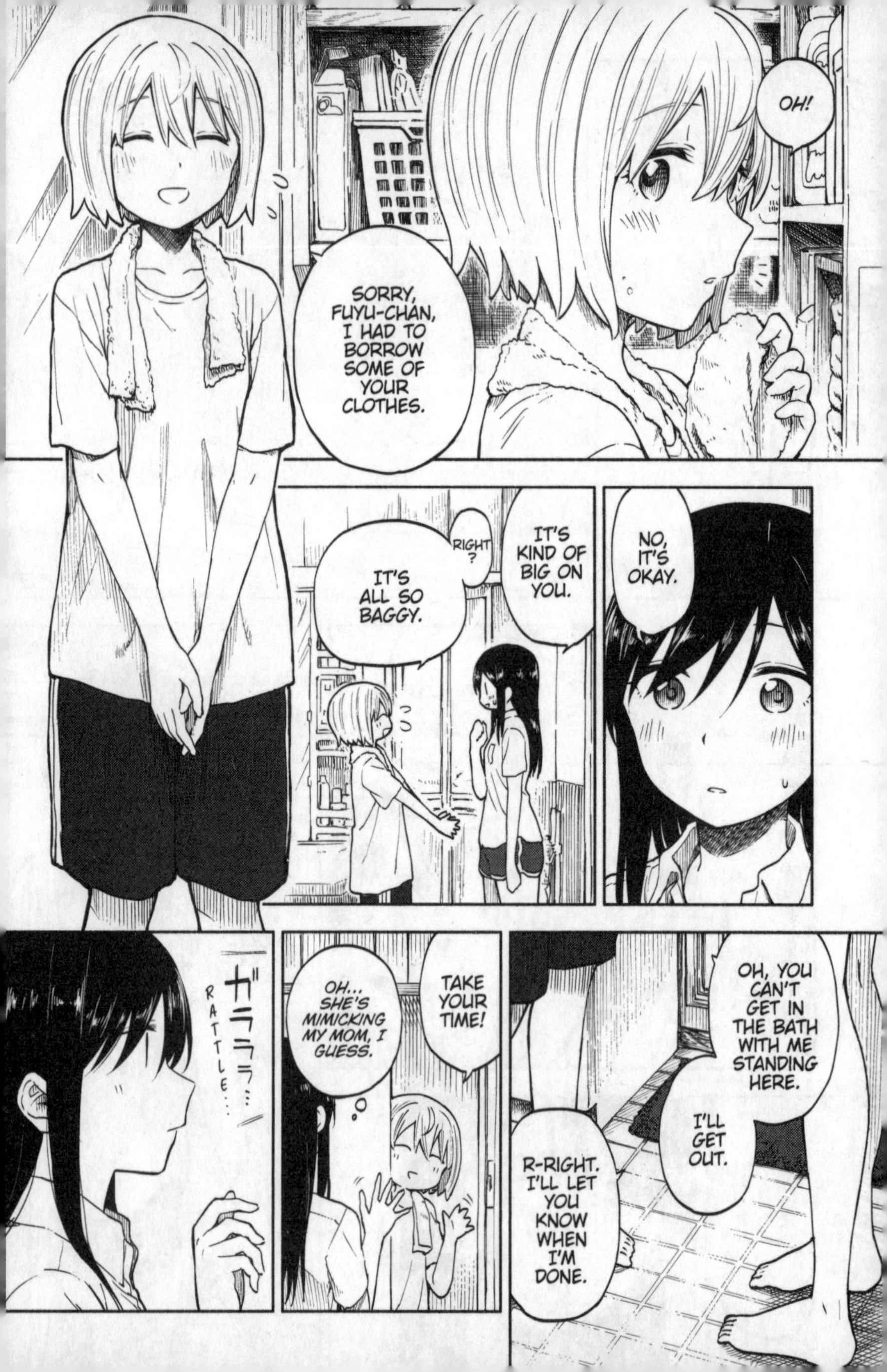
OH!
SORRY, FUYU-CHAN, I HAD TO BORROW SOME OF YOUR CLOTHES.
NO, IT'S OKAY.
IT'S KIND OF BIG ON YOU.
RIGHT?
IT'S ALL SO BAGGY.
OH, YOU CAN'T GET IN THE BATH WITH ME STANDING HERE.
I'LL GET OUT.
R-RIGHT. I'LL LET YOU KNOW WHEN I'M DONE.
TAKE YOUR TIME!
OH... SHE'S MIMICKING MY MOM, I GUESS.
ガラララ…
RATTLE...

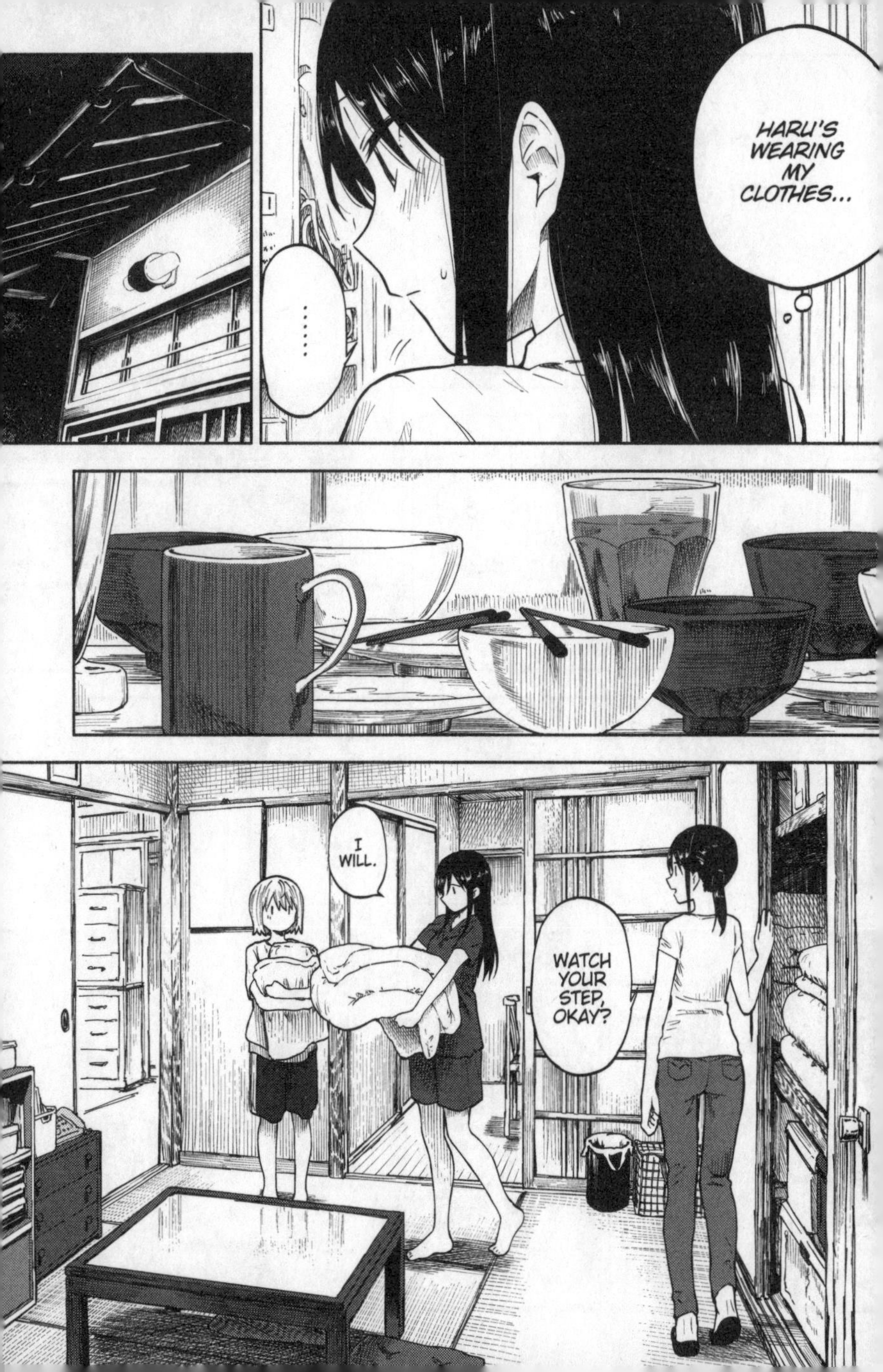
HARU'S WEARING MY CLOTHES...
......
WATCH YOUR STEP, OKAY?
I WILL.

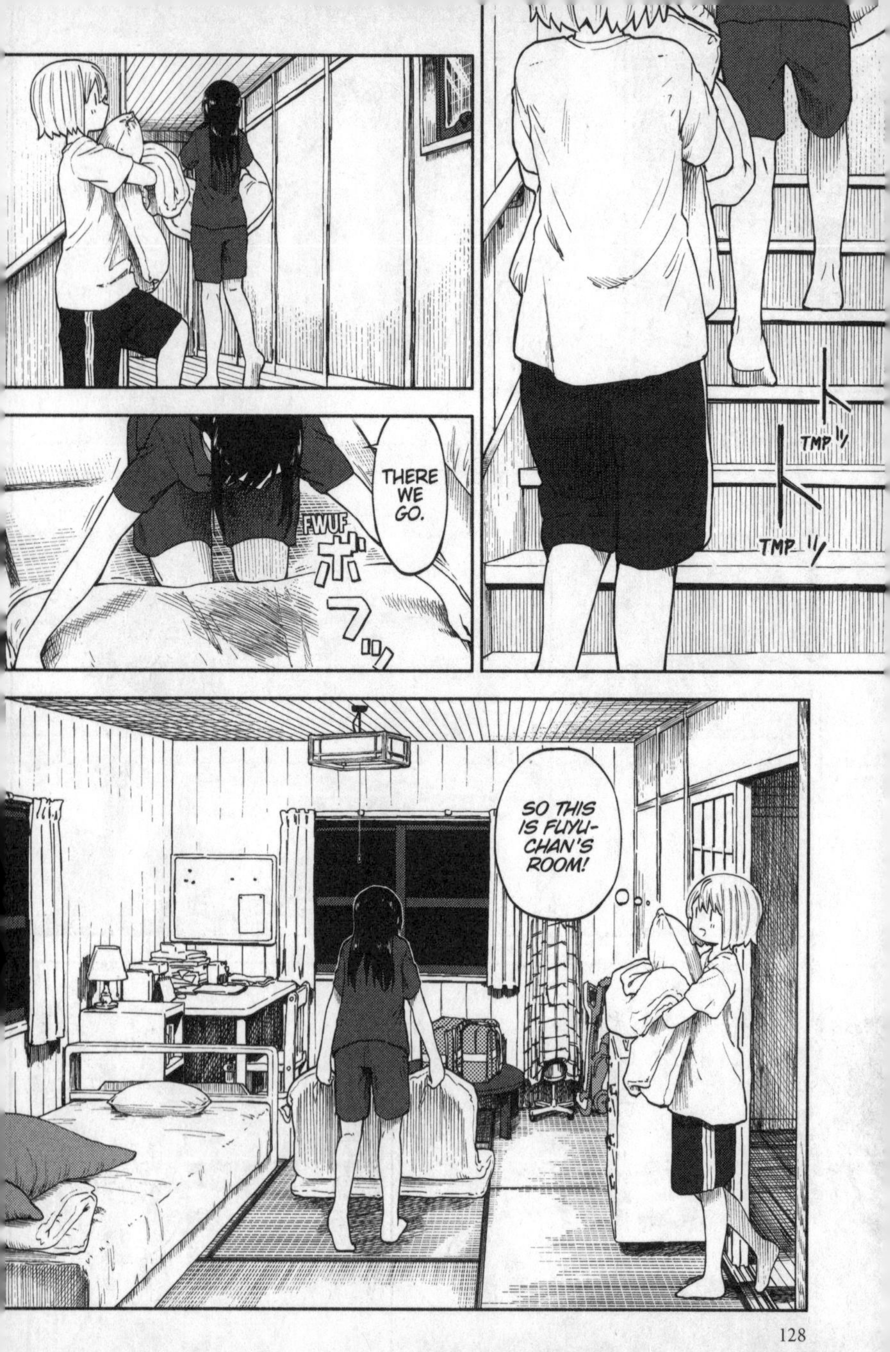
TMP
TMP
THERE WE GO.
FWUF
ボフッ
SO THIS IS FUYU-CHAN'S ROOM!

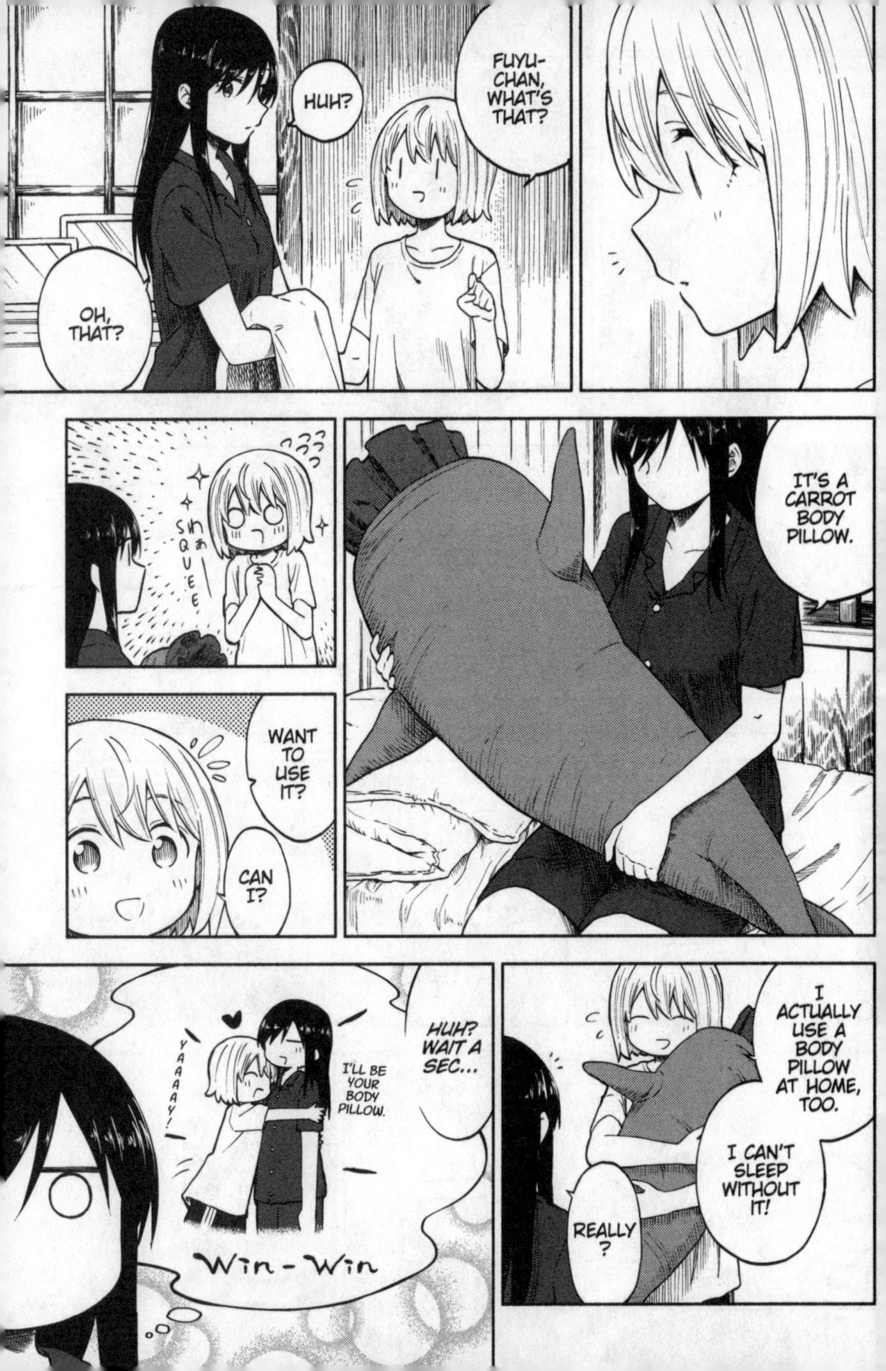
FUYU-CHAN, WHAT'S THAT?
HUH?
OH, THAT?
IT'S A CARROT BODY PILLOW.
SQUEE
WANT TO USE IT?
CAN I?
I ACTUALLY USE A BODY PILLOW AT HOME, TOO.
I CAN'T SLEEP WITHOUT IT!
REALLY?
HUH? WAIT A SEC...
I'LL BE YOUR BODY PILLOW.
YAAAAY!
Win-Win

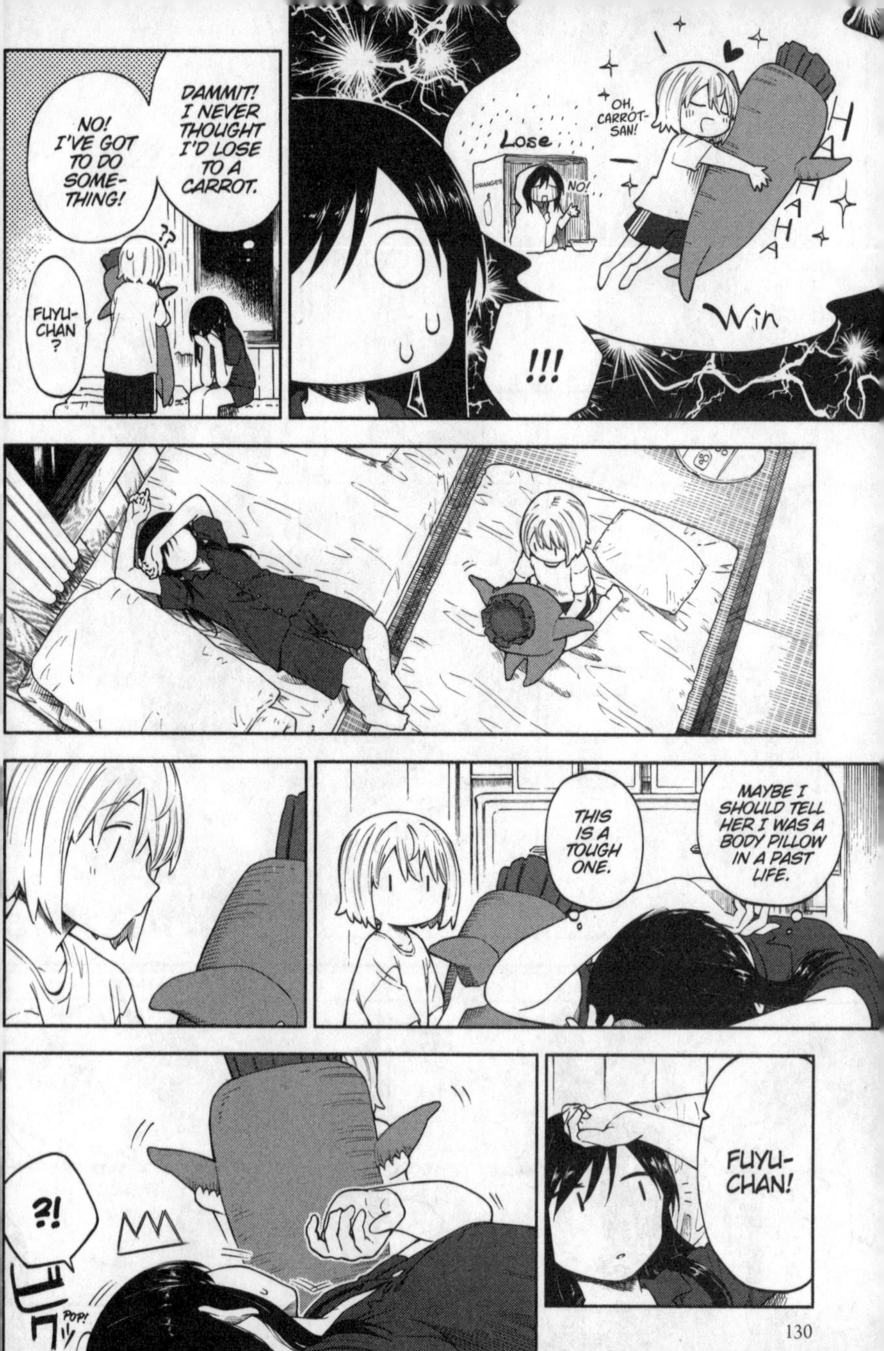
OH, CARROT-SAN!
HAHAHAHA
Lose
ORANGES
NO!
Win
!!!
DAMMIT! I NEVER THOUGHT I'D LOSE TO A CARROT.
NO! I'VE GOT TO DO SOMETHING!
??
FUYU-CHAN?
MAYBE I SHOULD TELL HER I WAS A BODY PILLOW IN A PAST LIFE.
THIS IS A TOUGH ONE.
FUYU-CHAN!
?!
POP!

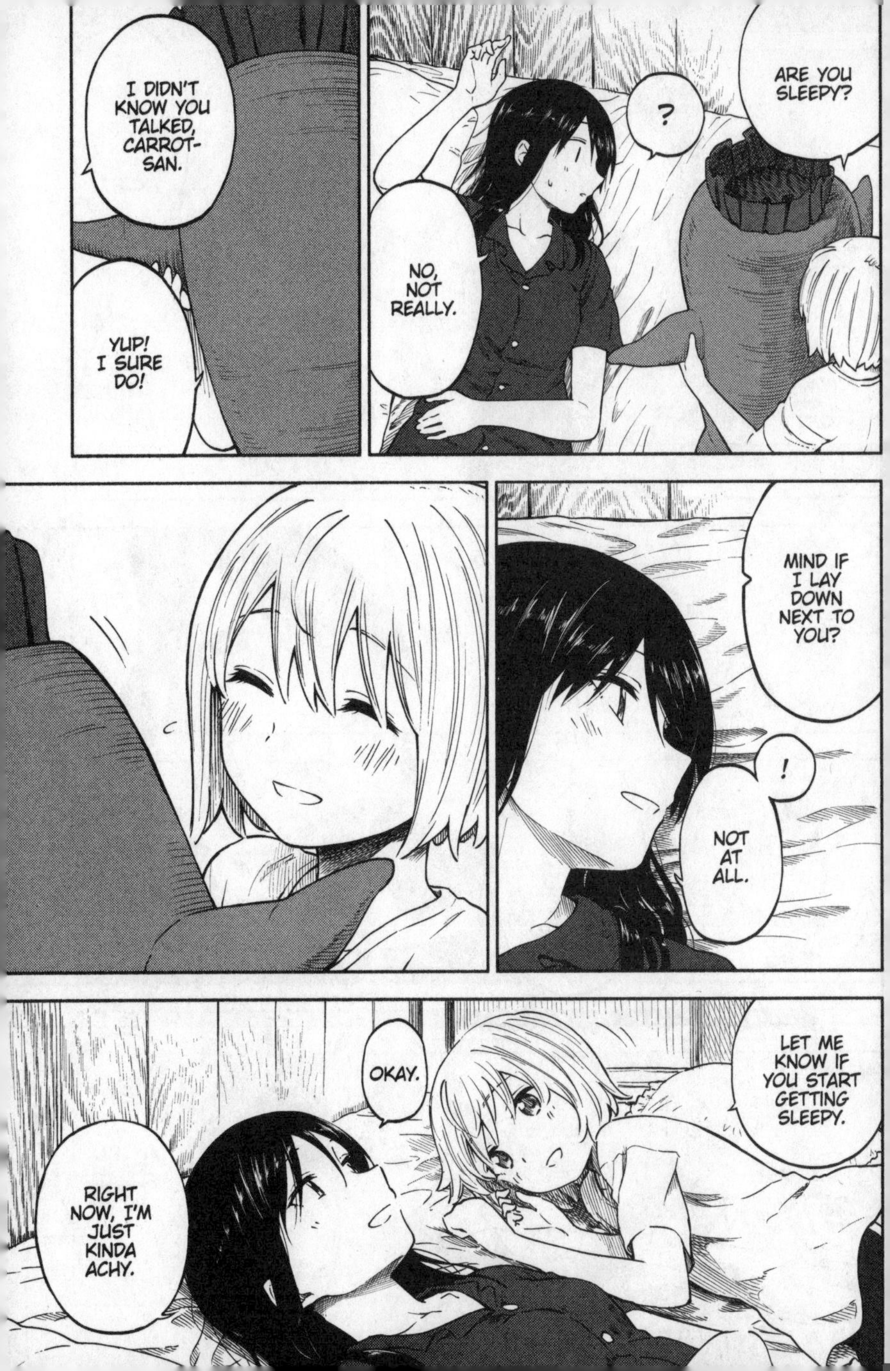
ARE YOU SLEEPY?
?
NO, NOT REALLY.
I DIDN'T KNOW YOU TALKED, CARROT-SAN.
YUP! I SURE DO!
MIND IF I LAY DOWN NEXT TO YOU?
!
NOT AT ALL.
LET ME KNOW IF YOU START GETTING SLEEPY.
OKAY.
RIGHT NOW, I'M JUST KINDA ACHY.

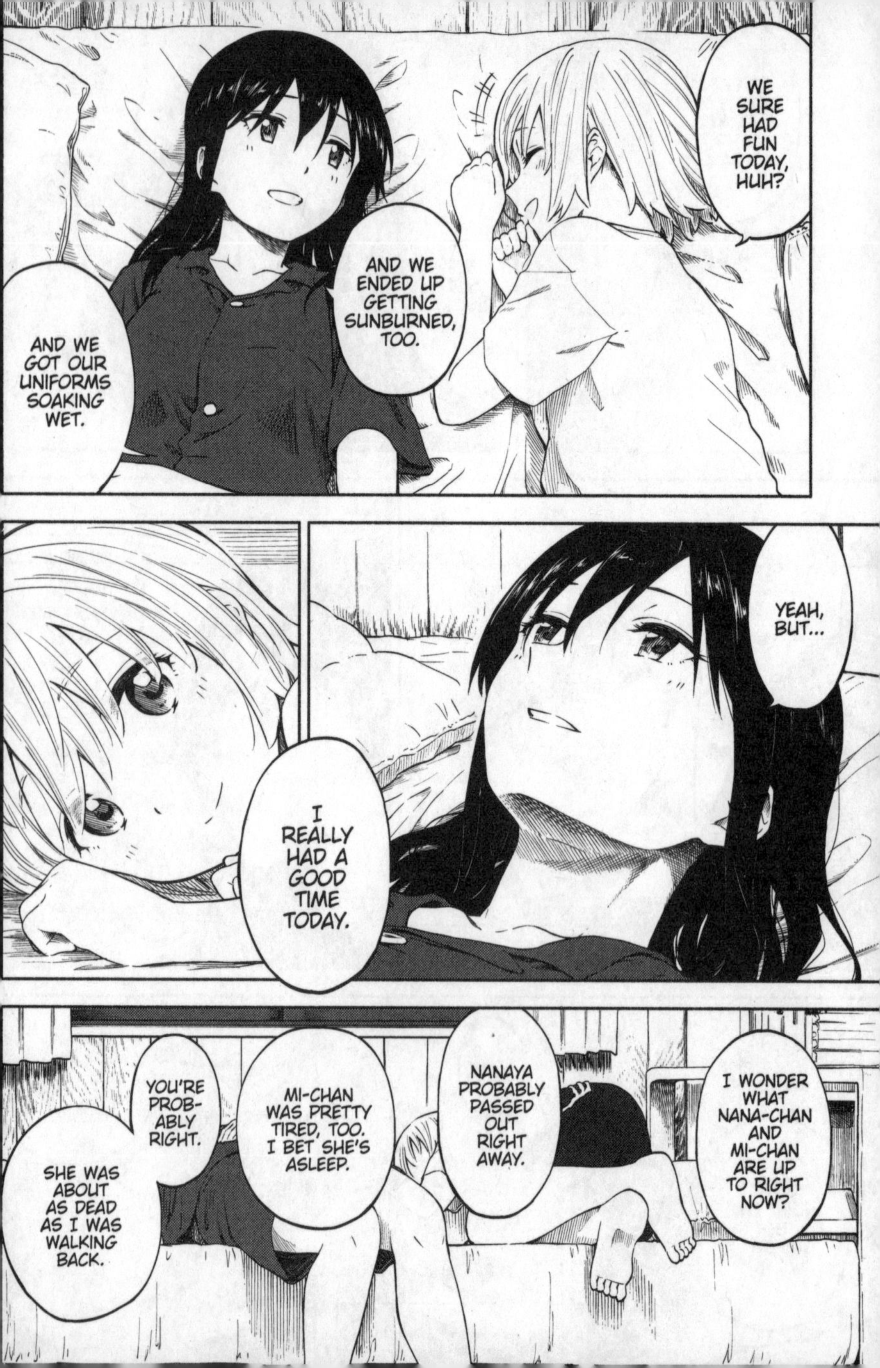
WE SURE HAD FUN TODAY, HUH?
AND WE ENDED UP GETTING SUNBURNED, TOO.
AND WE GOT OUR UNIFORMS SOAKING WET.
YEAH, BUT...
I REALLY HAD A GOOD TIME TODAY.
I WONDER WHAT NANA-CHAN AND MI-CHAN ARE UP TO RIGHT NOW?
NANAYA PROBABLY PASSED OUT RIGHT AWAY.
MI-CHAN WAS PRETTY TIRED, TOO. I BET SHE'S ASLEEP.
YOU'RE PROB-ABLY RIGHT.
SHE WAS ABOUT AS DEAD AS I WAS WALKING BACK.

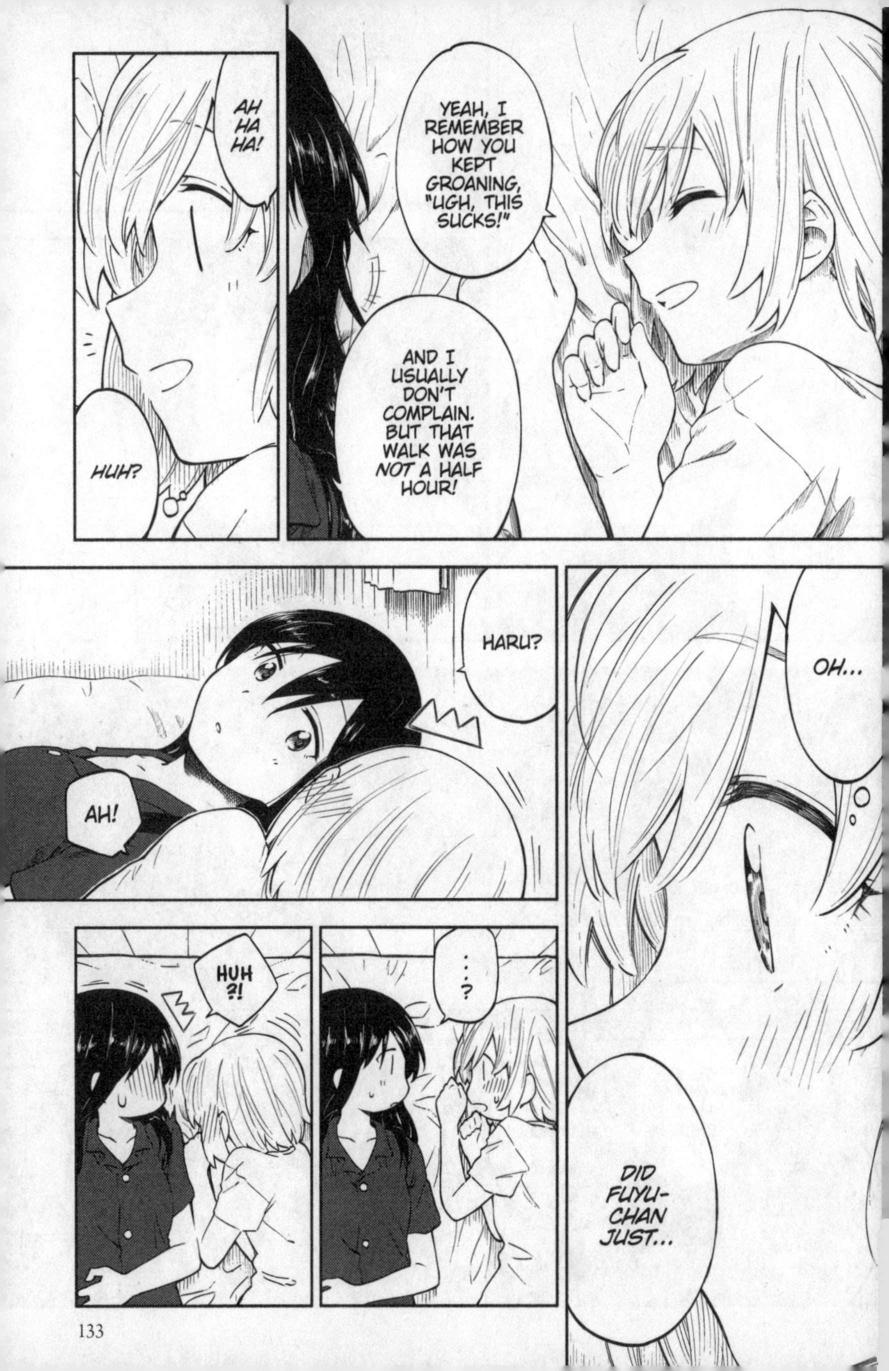
YEAH, I REMEMBER HOW YOU KEPT GROANING, "UGH, THIS SUCKS!"
AND I USUALLY DON'T COMPLAIN. BUT THAT WALK WAS *NOT* A HALF HOUR!
AH HA HA!
HUH?
OH...
DID FUYU-CHAN JUST...
HARU?
AH!
...?
HUH ?!

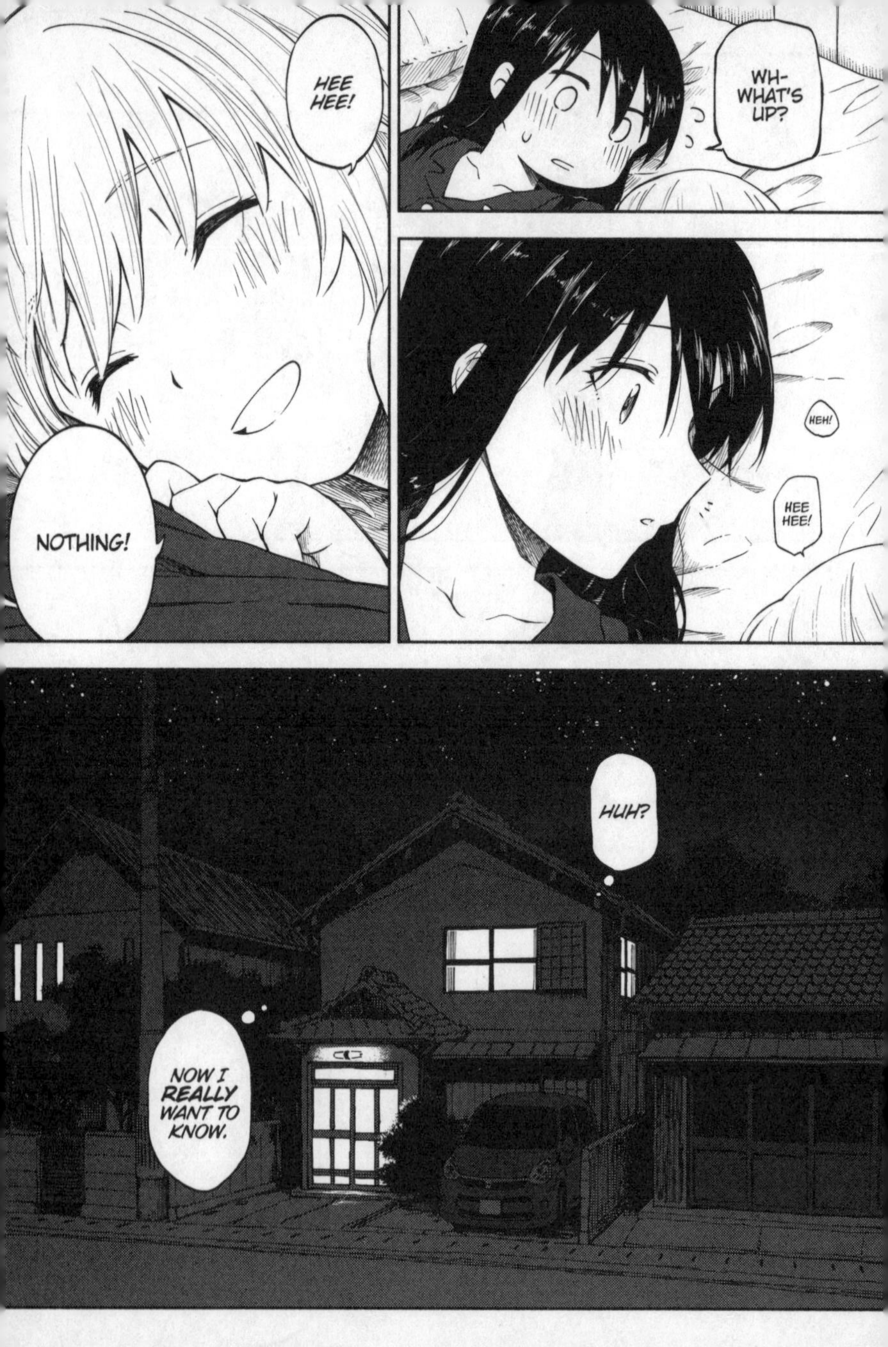
WH-WHAT'S UP?
HEH!
HEE HEE!
HEE HEE!
NOTHING!
HUH?
NOW I REALLY WANT TO KNOW.

Our Wonderful Days

story & art by Kei Hamuro

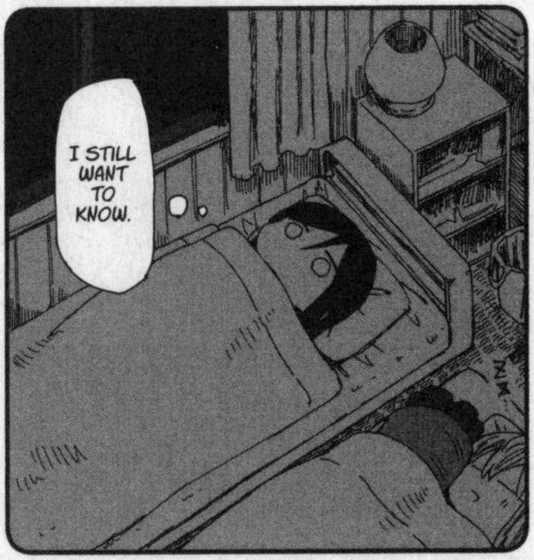
I STILL WANT TO KNOW.

Our Wonderful Days
Tsurezure Biyori

Chapter 13
A Decisive Morning

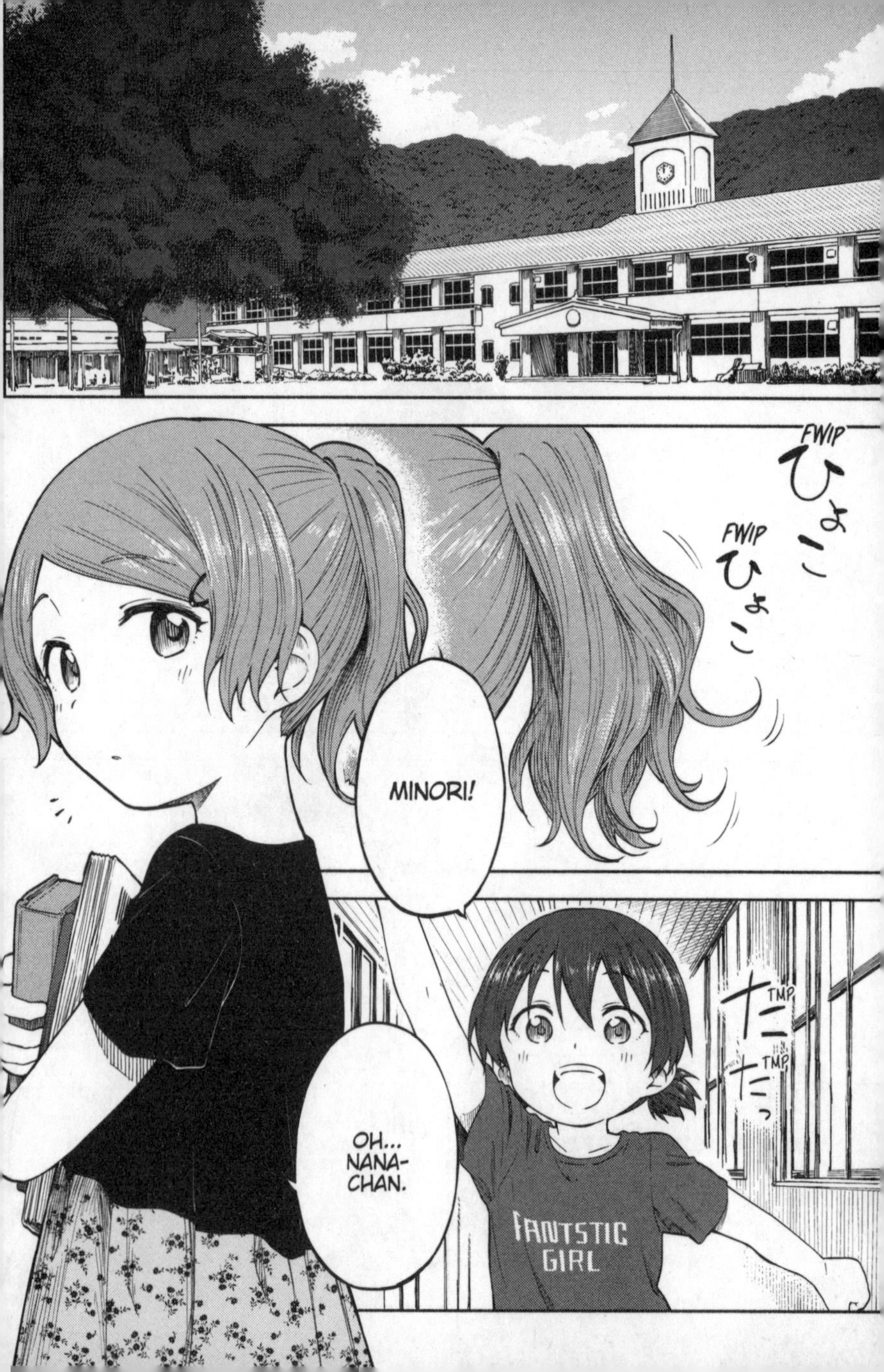
FWIP
ひょこ
FWIP
ひょこ
MINORI!
TMP
たー
TMP
たっ
OH... NANA-CHAN.
FANTSTIC GIRL

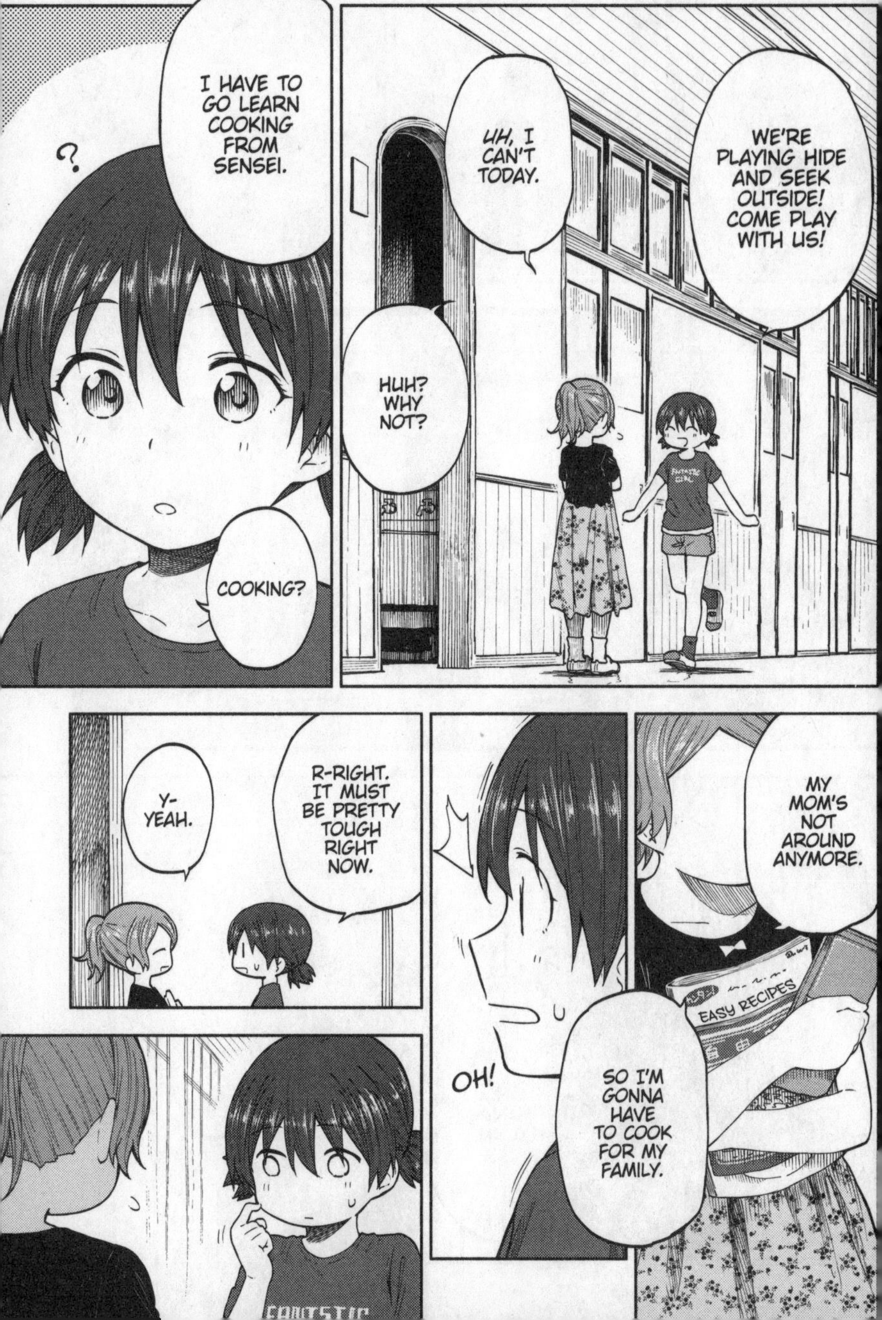
WE'RE PLAYING HIDE AND SEEK OUTSIDE! COME PLAY WITH US!
UH, I CAN'T TODAY.
HUH? WHY NOT?
I HAVE TO GO LEARN COOKING FROM SENSEI.
?
COOKING?
MY MOM'S NOT AROUND ANYMORE.
EASY RECIPES
SO I'M GONNA HAVE TO COOK FOR MY FAMILY.
OH!
R-RIGHT. IT MUST BE PRETTY TOUGH RIGHT NOW.
Y-YEAH.

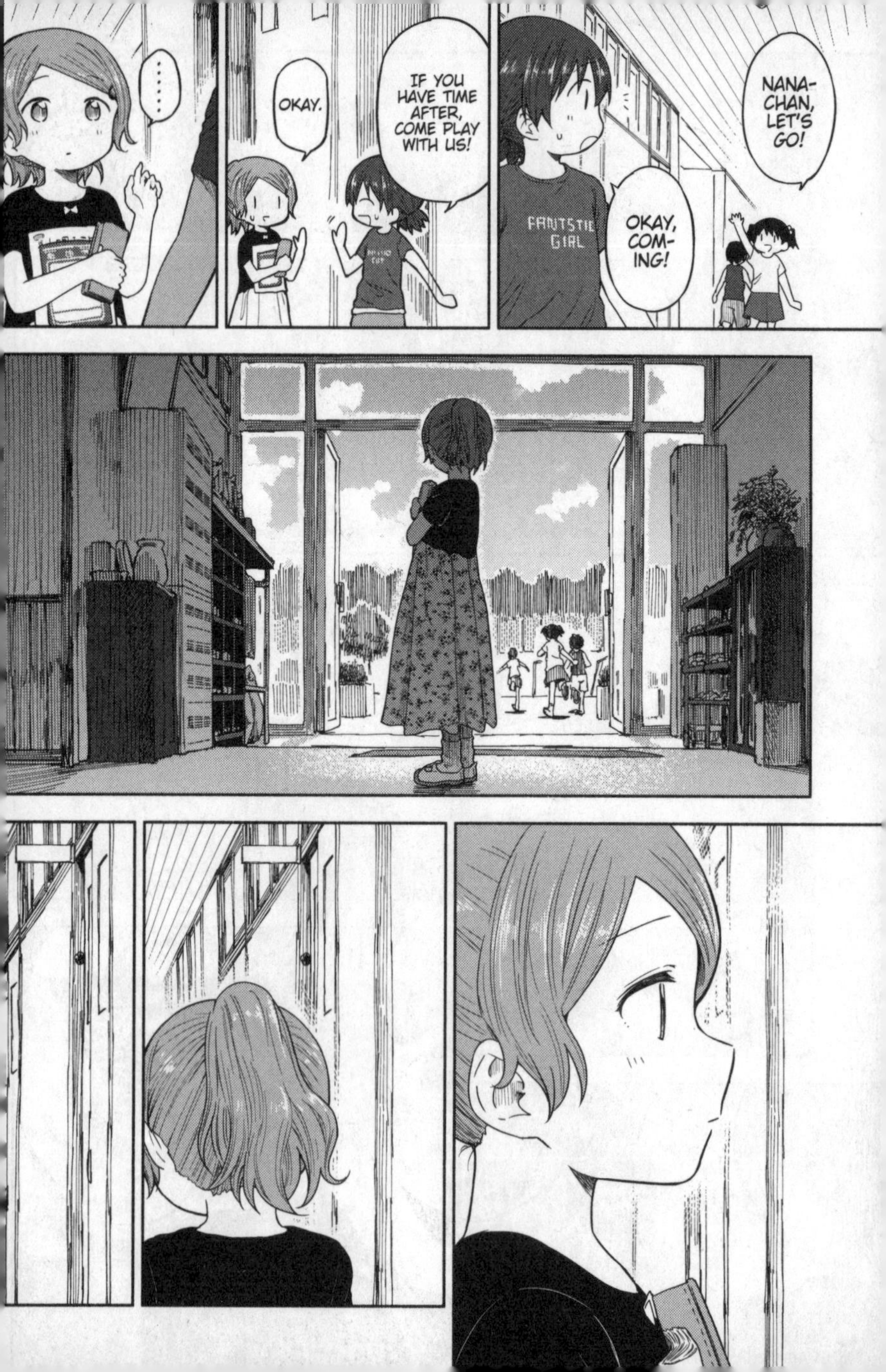
NANA-CHAN, LET'S GO!
OKAY, COM-ING!
FANTSTIC GIRL
IF YOU HAVE TIME AFTER, COME PLAY WITH US!
OKAY.
......

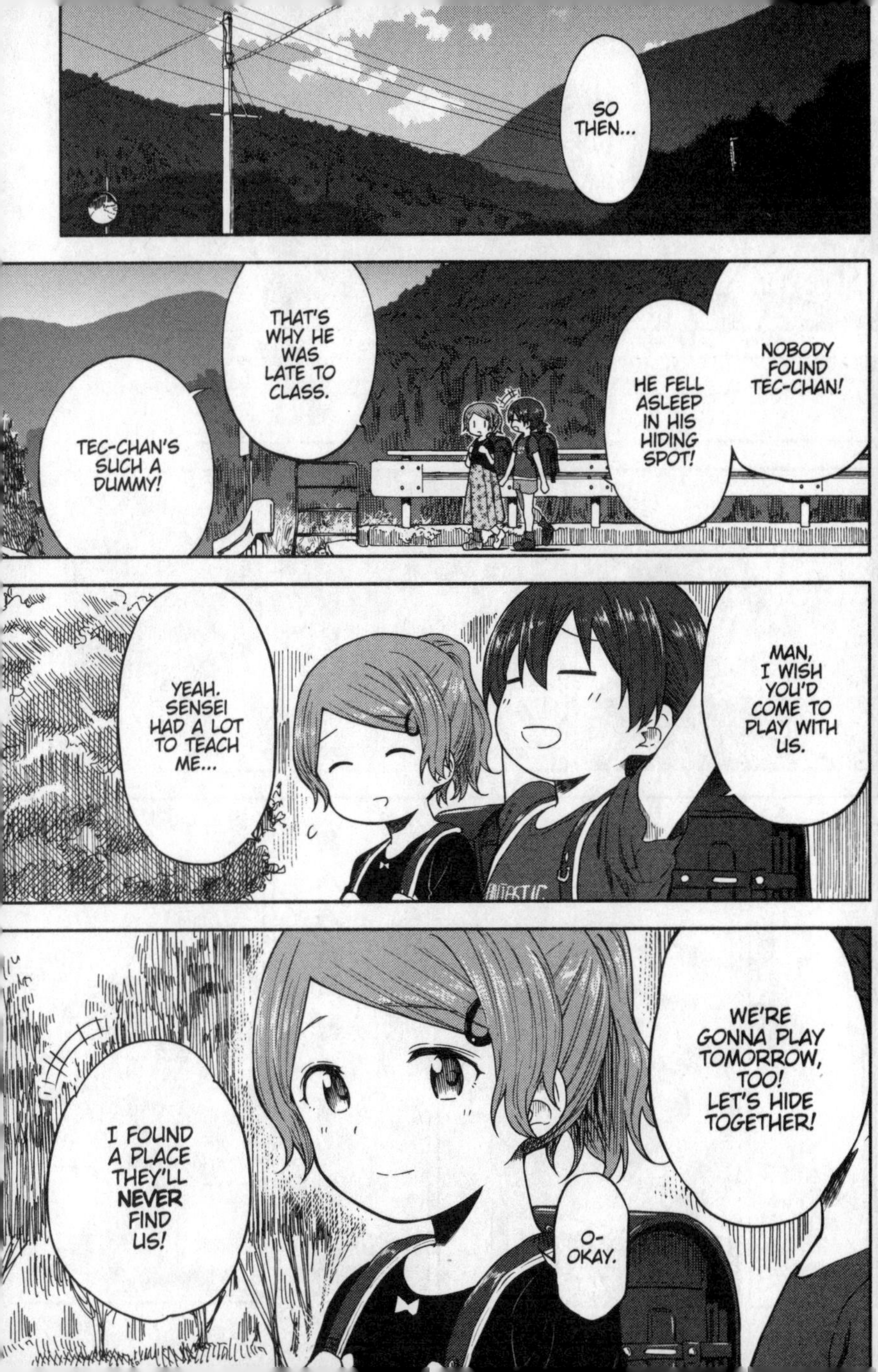
SO THEN...
NOBODY FOUND TEC-CHAN!
HE FELL ASLEEP IN HIS HIDING SPOT!
THAT'S WHY HE WAS LATE TO CLASS.
TEC-CHAN'S SUCH A DUMMY!
MAN, I WISH YOU'D COME TO PLAY WITH US.
YEAH. SENSEI HAD A LOT TO TEACH ME...
WE'RE GONNA PLAY TOMORROW, TOO! LET'S HIDE TOGETHER!
O-OKAY.
I FOUND A PLACE THEY'LL **NEVER** FIND US!

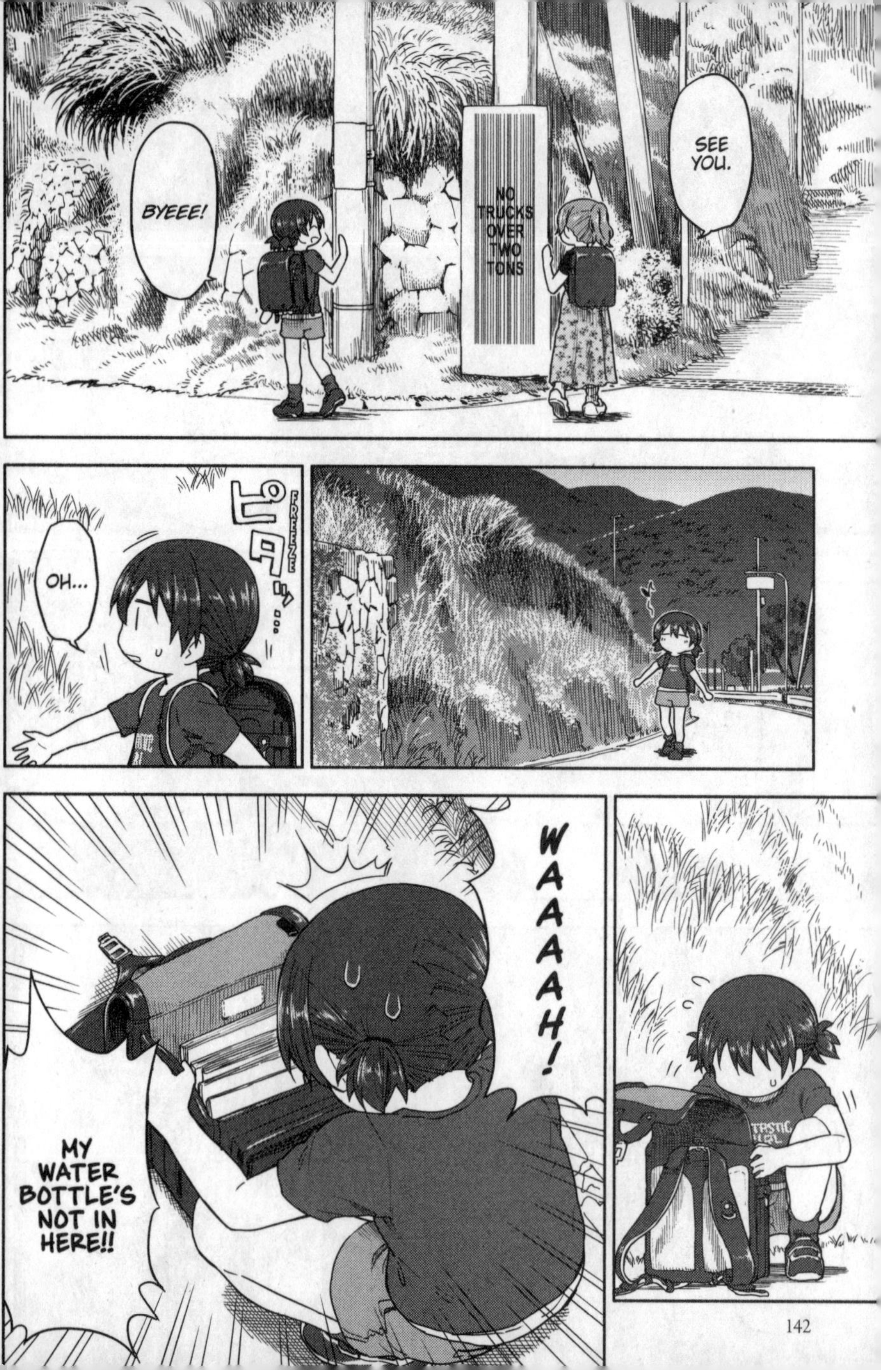

SEE YOU.
NO TRUCKS OVER TWO TONS
BYEEE!
ピタッ...
FREEZE
OH...
WAAAAAH!
MY WATER BOTTLE'S NOT IN HERE!!

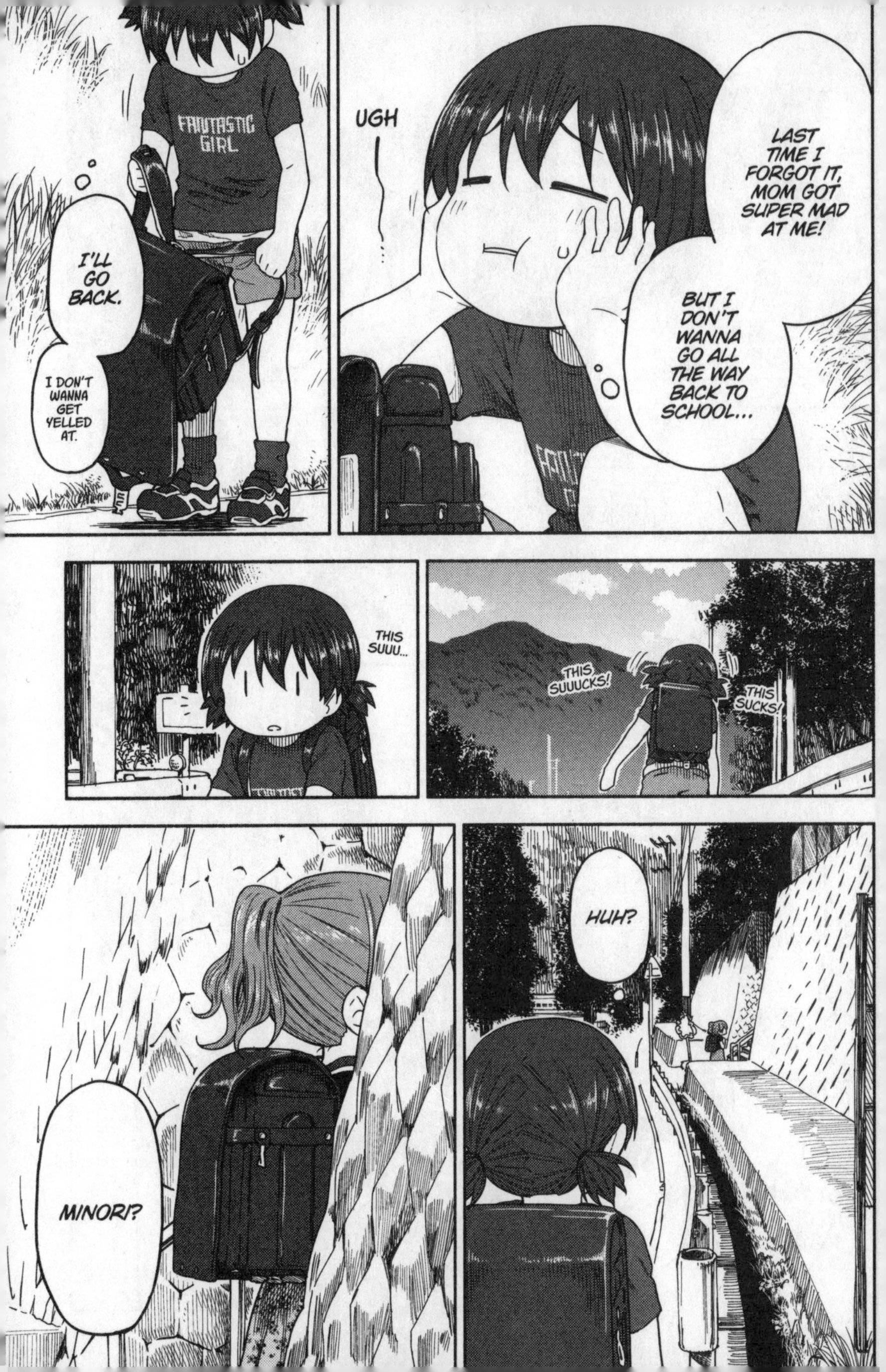
LAST TIME I FORGOT IT, MOM GOT SUPER MAD AT ME!
BUT I DON'T WANNA GO ALL THE WAY BACK TO SCHOOL...
UGH
I'LL GO BACK.
I DON'T WANNA GET YELLED AT.
THIS SUCKS!
THIS SUUUCKS!
THIS SUUU...
HUH?
MINORI?

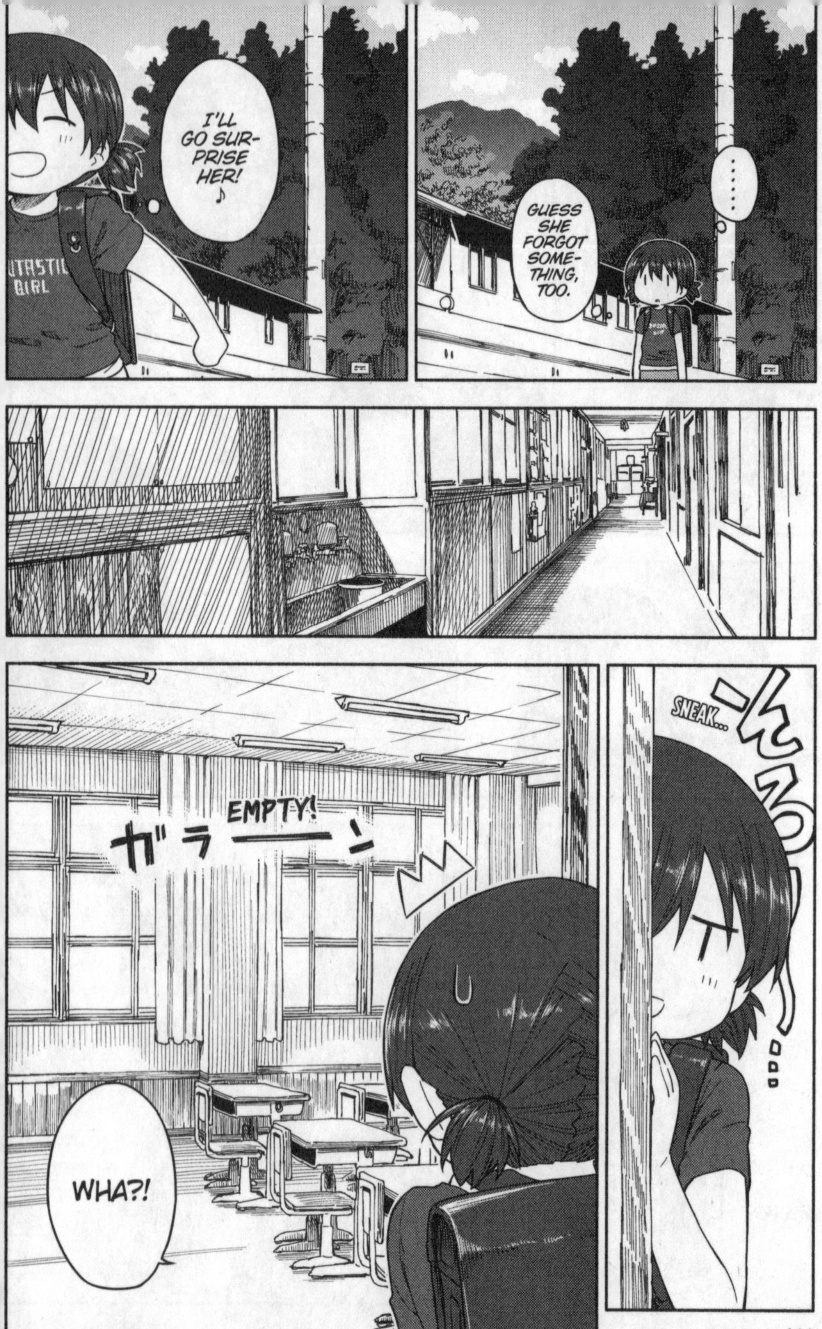
……
GUESS SHE FORGOT SOME-THING, TOO.
I'LL GO SUR-PRISE HER! ♪
SNEAK...
EMPTY!
ガラーーン
WHA?!

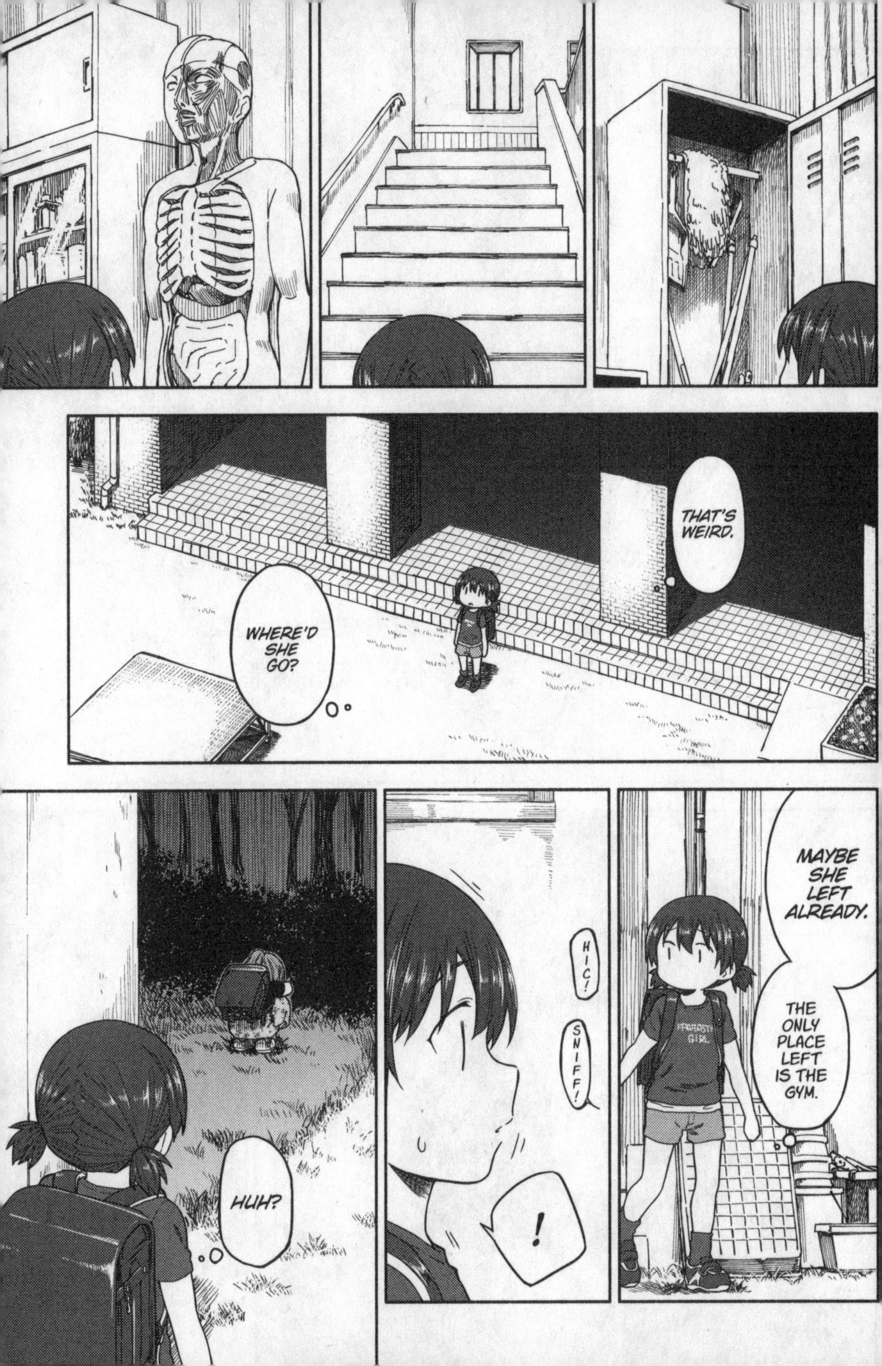
THAT'S WEIRD.
WHERE'D SHE GO?
MAYBE SHE LEFT ALREADY.
THE ONLY PLACE LEFT IS THE GYM.
HIC!
SNIFF!
!
HUH?

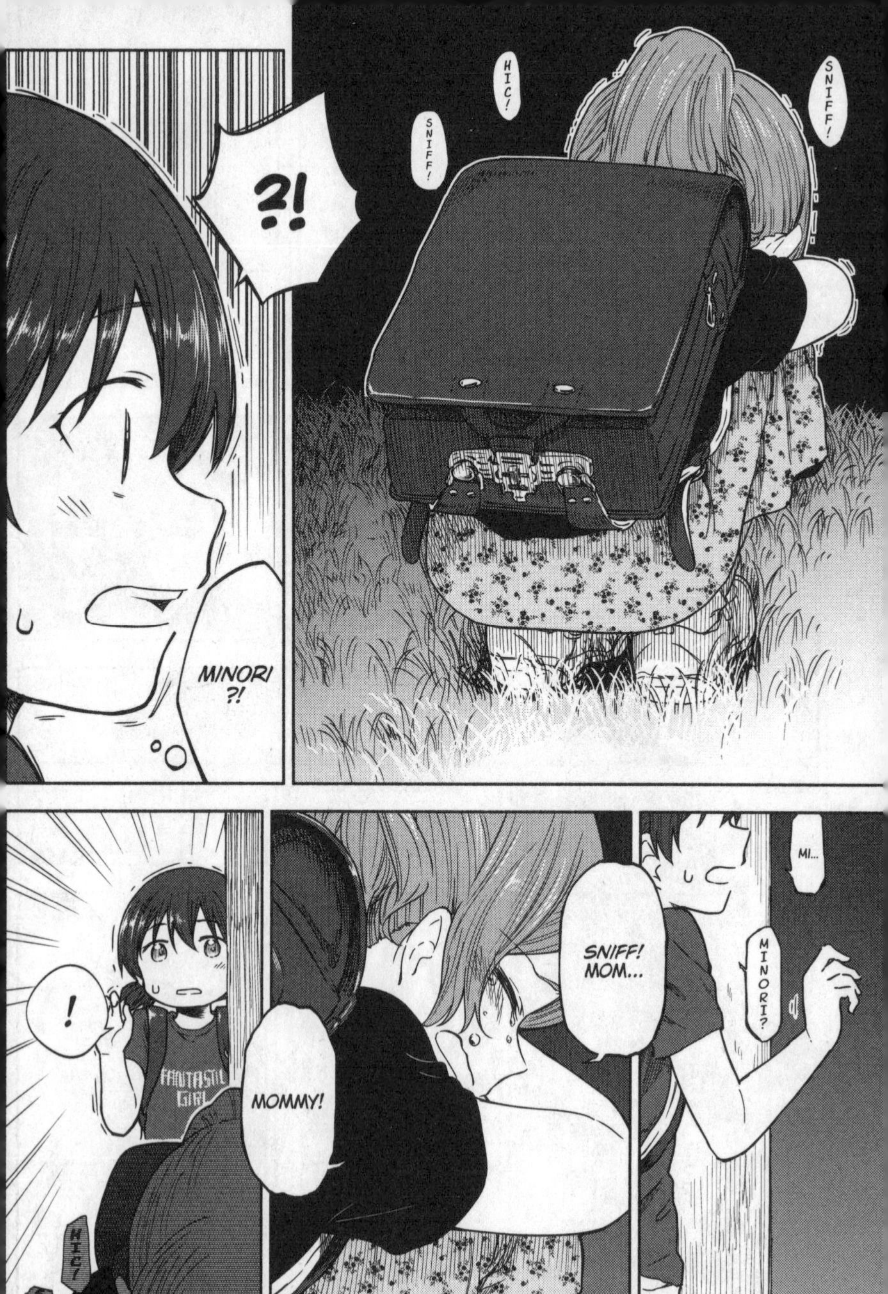
SNIFF!
HIC!
SNIFF!
?!
MINORI ?!
MI...
MINORI?
SNIFF! MOM...
MOMMY!
!
HIC!
SNIFF!

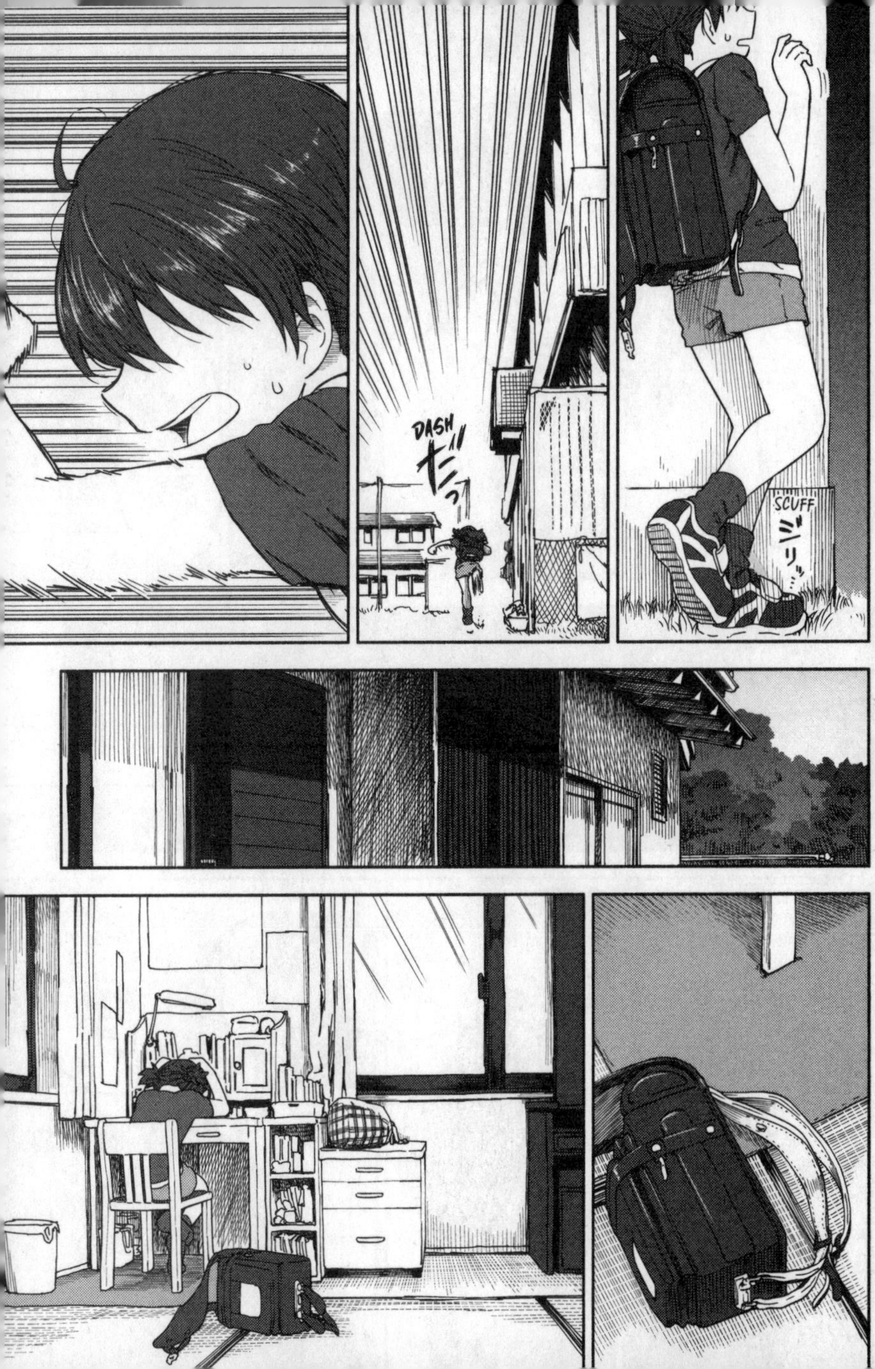
SCUFF
ジリッ…
DASH
だっ

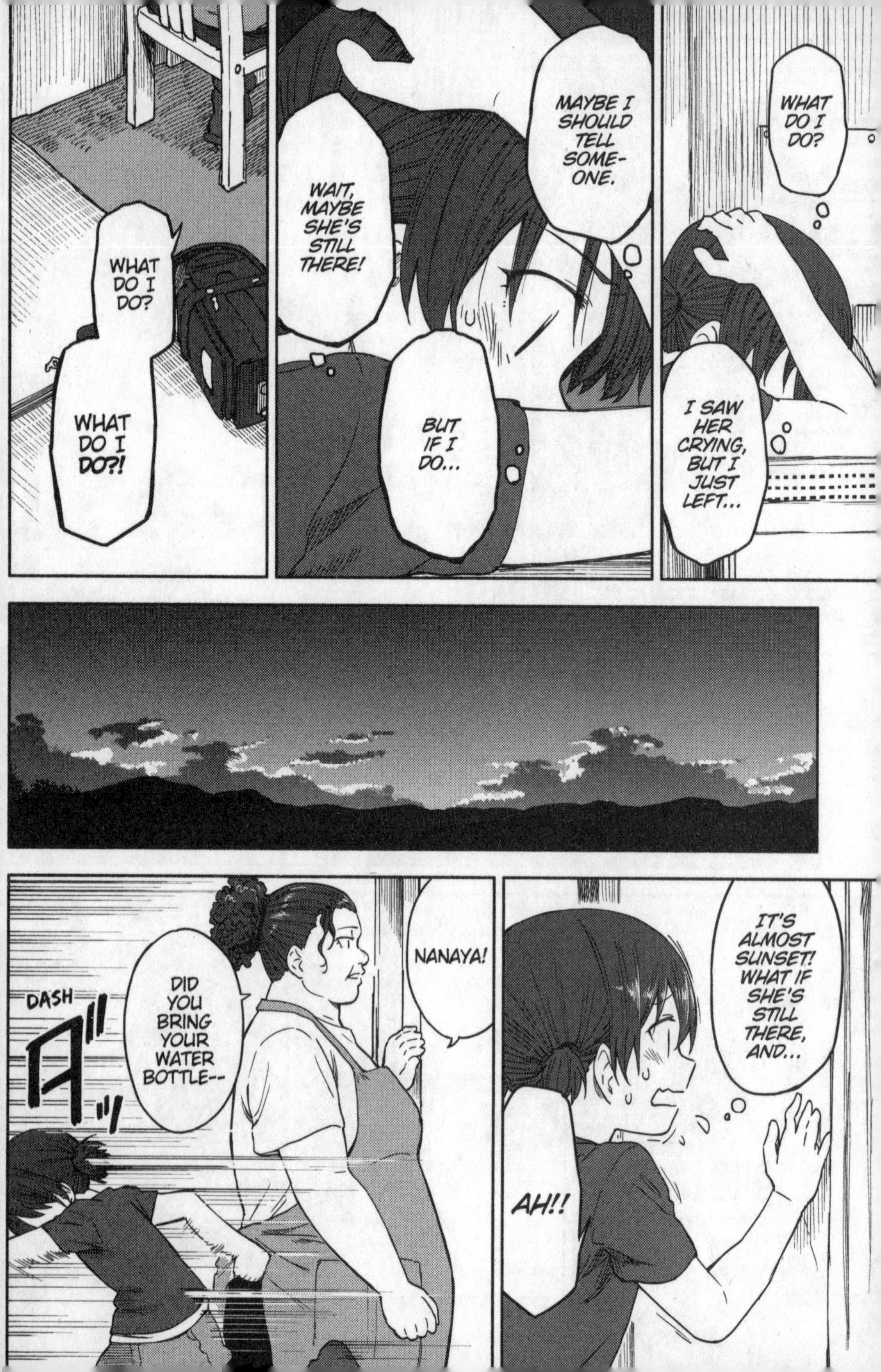
WHAT DO I DO?
I SAW HER CRYING, BUT I JUST LEFT...
MAYBE I SHOULD TELL SOMEONE.
WAIT, MAYBE SHE'S STILL THERE!
BUT IF I DO...
WHAT DO I DO?
WHAT DO I DO?!
IT'S ALMOST SUNSET! WHAT IF SHE'S STILL THERE, AND...
AH!!
NANAYA!
DID YOU BRING YOUR WATER BOTTLE--
DASH

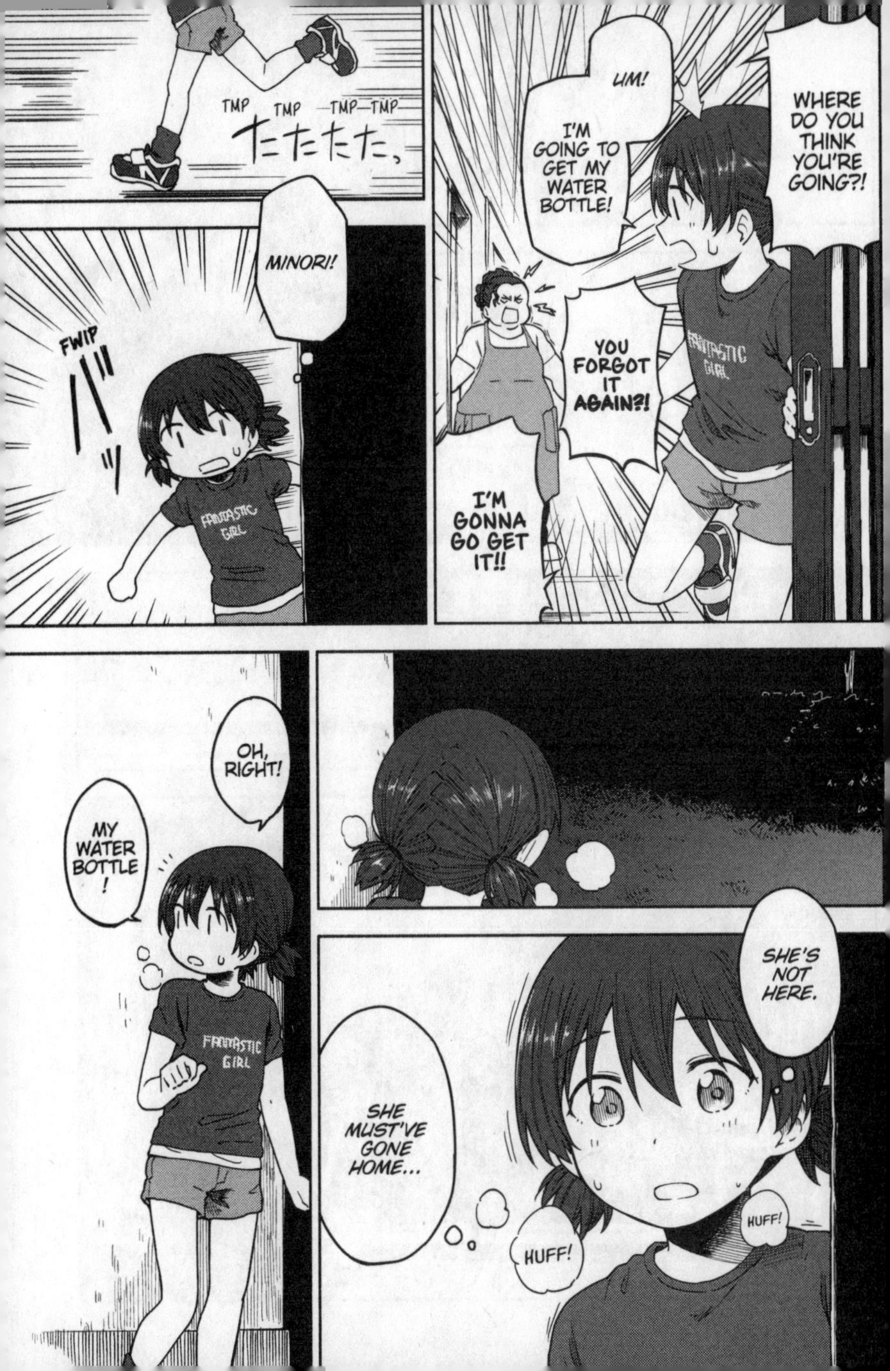
WHERE DO YOU THINK YOU'RE GOING?!
UM!
I'M GOING TO GET MY WATER BOTTLE!
YOU FORGOT IT AGAIN?!
I'M GONNA GO GET IT!!
TMP TMP —TMP—TMP—
たたたた、
MINORI!
FWIP
バッ
SHE'S NOT HERE.
SHE MUST'VE GONE HOME...
HUFF!
HUFF!
OH, RIGHT!
MY WATER BOTTLE!

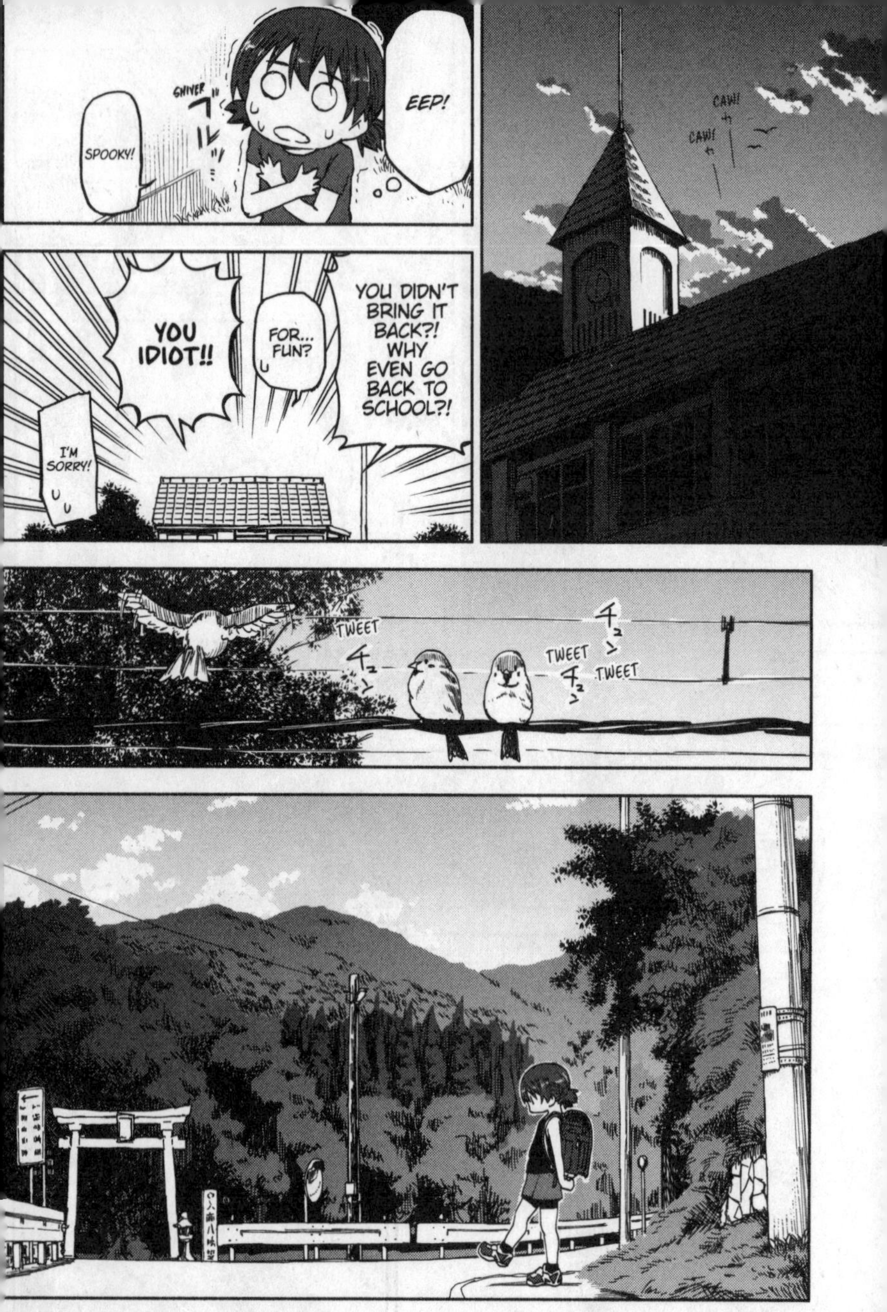
CAW!
CAW!
EEP!
SHIVER
SPOOKY!
YOU DIDN'T BRING IT BACK?! WHY EVEN GO BACK TO SCHOOL?!
FOR... FUN?
YOU IDIOT!!
I'M SORRY!
TWEET
TWEET
TWEET

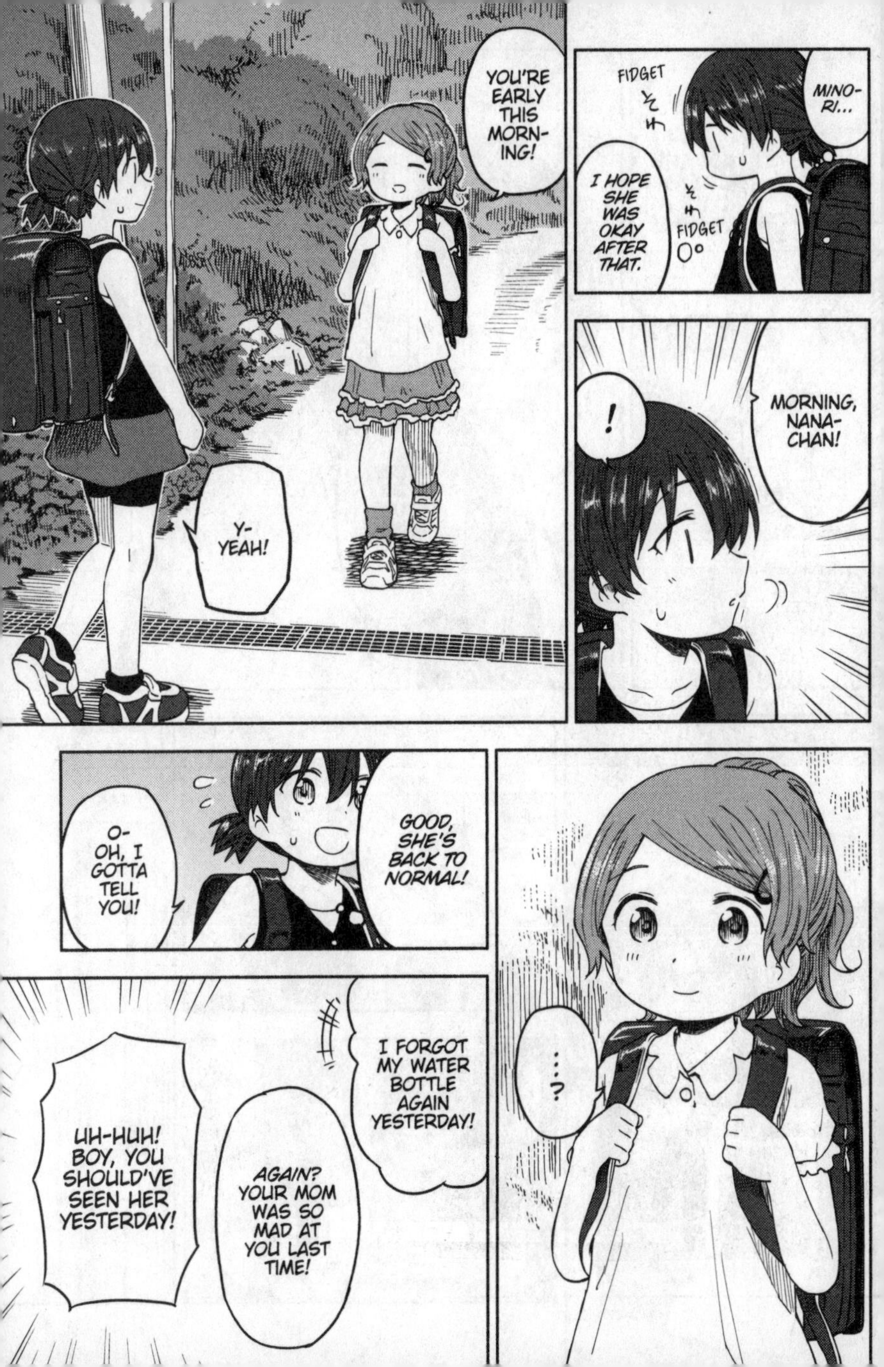
MINO-RI...
FIDGET
I HOPE SHE WAS OKAY AFTER THAT.
FIDGET
!
MORNING, NANA-CHAN!
YOU'RE EARLY THIS MORNING!
Y-YEAH!
...?
GOOD, SHE'S BACK TO NORMAL!
O-OH, I GOTTA TELL YOU!
I FORGOT MY WATER BOTTLE AGAIN YESTERDAY!
AGAIN? YOUR MOM WAS SO MAD AT YOU LAST TIME!
UH-HUH! BOY, YOU SHOULD'VE SEEN HER YESTERDAY!

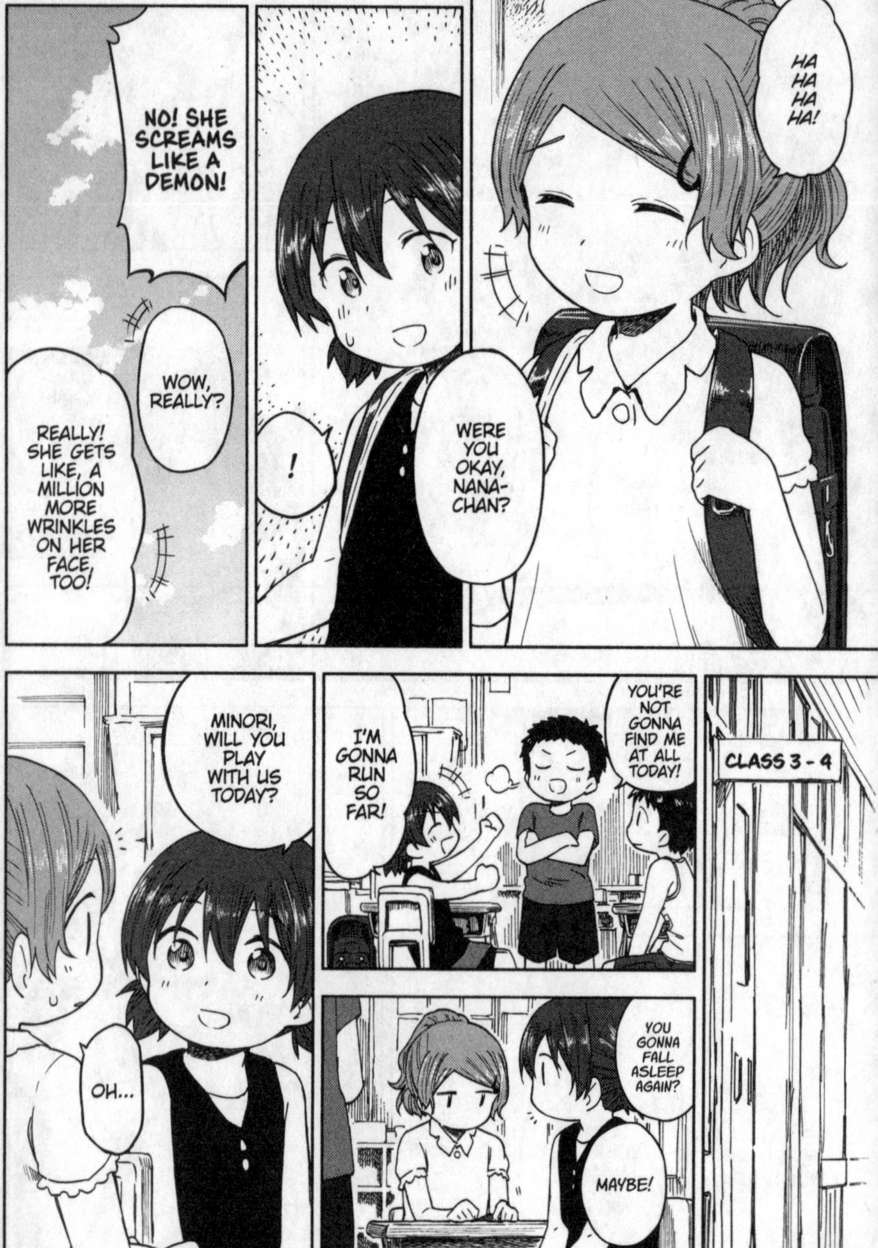
HA HA HA HA!
WERE YOU OKAY, NANA-CHAN?
!
NO! SHE SCREAMS LIKE A DEMON!
WOW, REALLY?
REALLY! SHE GETS LIKE, A MILLION MORE WRINKLES ON HER FACE, TOO!
CLASS 3 - 4
YOU'RE NOT GONNA FIND ME AT ALL TODAY!
I'M GONNA RUN SO FAR!
YOU GONNA FALL ASLEEP AGAIN?
MAYBE!
MINORI, WILL YOU PLAY WITH US TODAY?
OH...

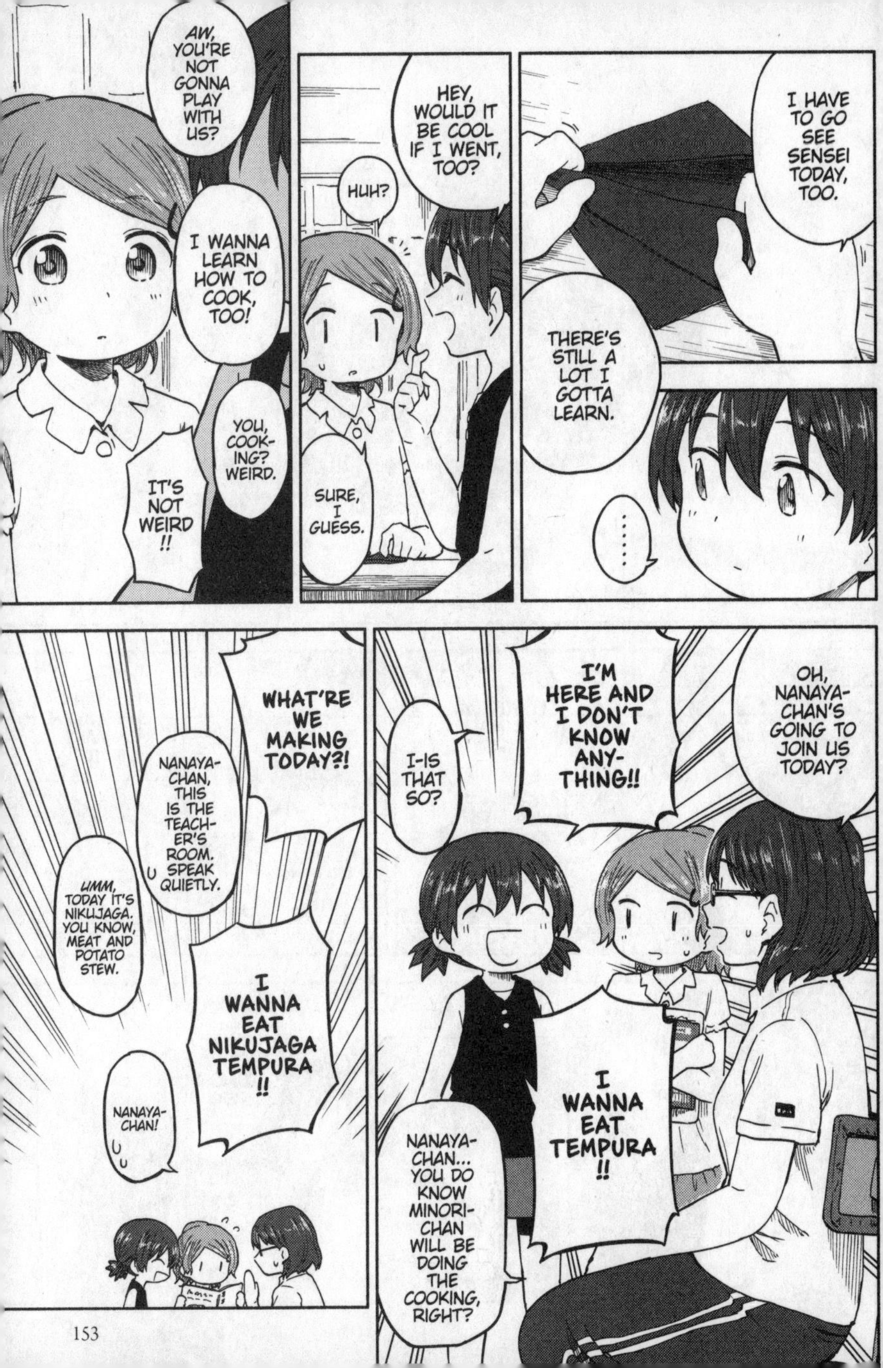

I HAVE TO GO SEE SENSEI TODAY, TOO.
THERE'S STILL A LOT I GOTTA LEARN.
......
HEY, WOULD IT BE COOL IF I WENT, TOO?
HUH?
SURE, I GUESS.
AW, YOU'RE NOT GONNA PLAY WITH US?
I WANNA LEARN HOW TO COOK, TOO!
YOU, COOKING? WEIRD.
IT'S NOT WEIRD!!
OH, NANAYA-CHAN'S GOING TO JOIN US TODAY?
I'M HERE AND I DON'T KNOW ANYTHING!!
I-IS THAT SO?
I WANNA EAT TEMPURA!!
NANAYA-CHAN... YOU DO KNOW MINORI-CHAN WILL BE DOING THE COOKING, RIGHT?
WHAT'RE WE MAKING TODAY?!
NANAYA-CHAN, THIS IS THE TEACHER'S ROOM. SPEAK QUIETLY.
UMM, TODAY IT'S NIKUJAGA. YOU KNOW, MEAT AND POTATO STEW.
I WANNA EAT NIKUJAGA TEMPURA!!
NANAYA-CHAN!

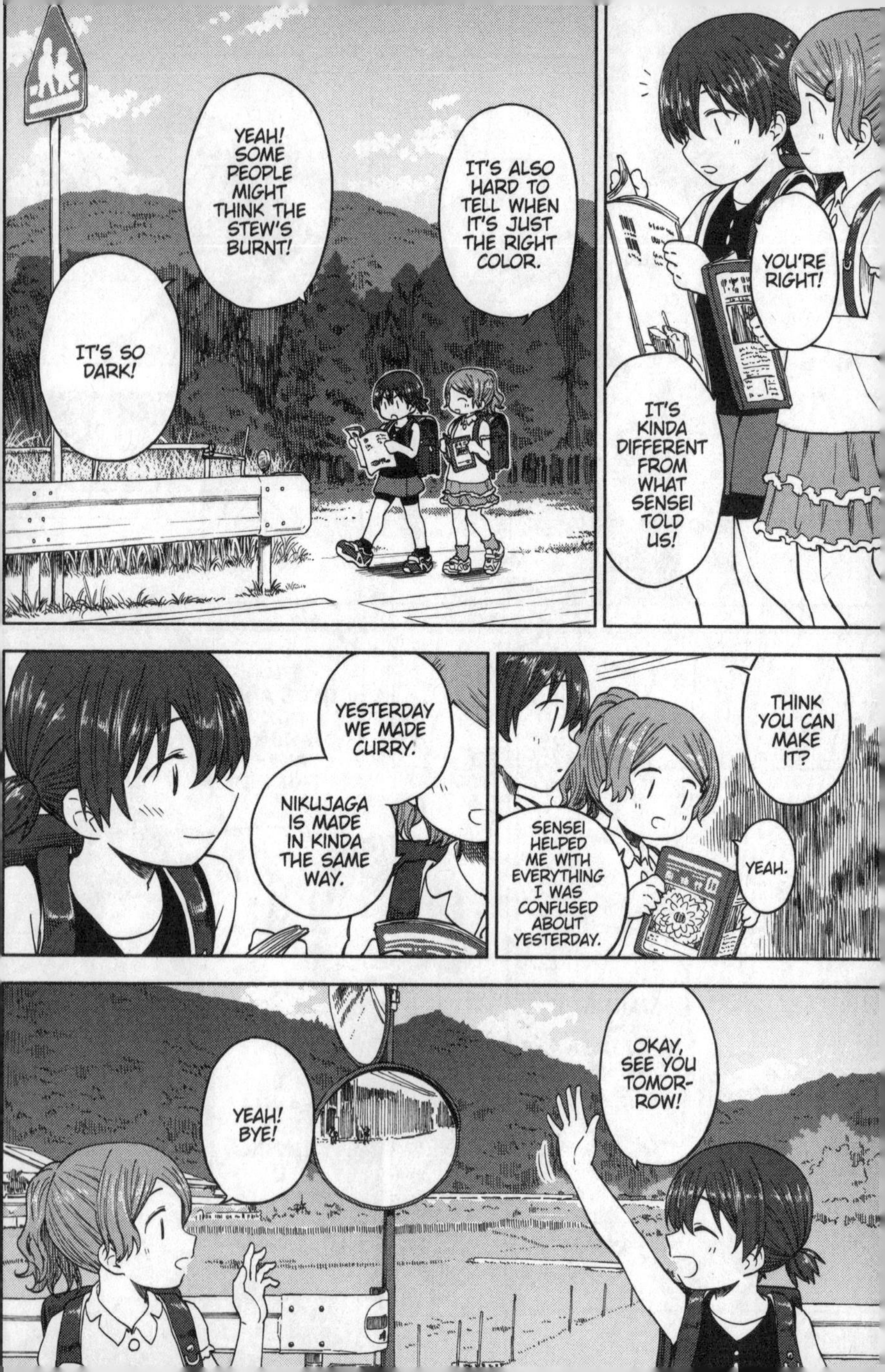
YOU'RE RIGHT!
IT'S KINDA DIFFERENT FROM WHAT SENSEI TOLD US!
IT'S ALSO HARD TO TELL WHEN IT'S JUST THE RIGHT COLOR.
YEAH! SOME PEOPLE MIGHT THINK THE STEW'S BURNT!
IT'S SO DARK!
THINK YOU CAN MAKE IT?
YEAH.
SENSEI HELPED ME WITH EVERYTHING I WAS CONFUSED ABOUT YESTERDAY.
YESTERDAY WE MADE CURRY.
NIKUJAGA IS MADE IN KINDA THE SAME WAY.
OKAY, SEE YOU TOMOR-ROW!
YEAH! BYE!

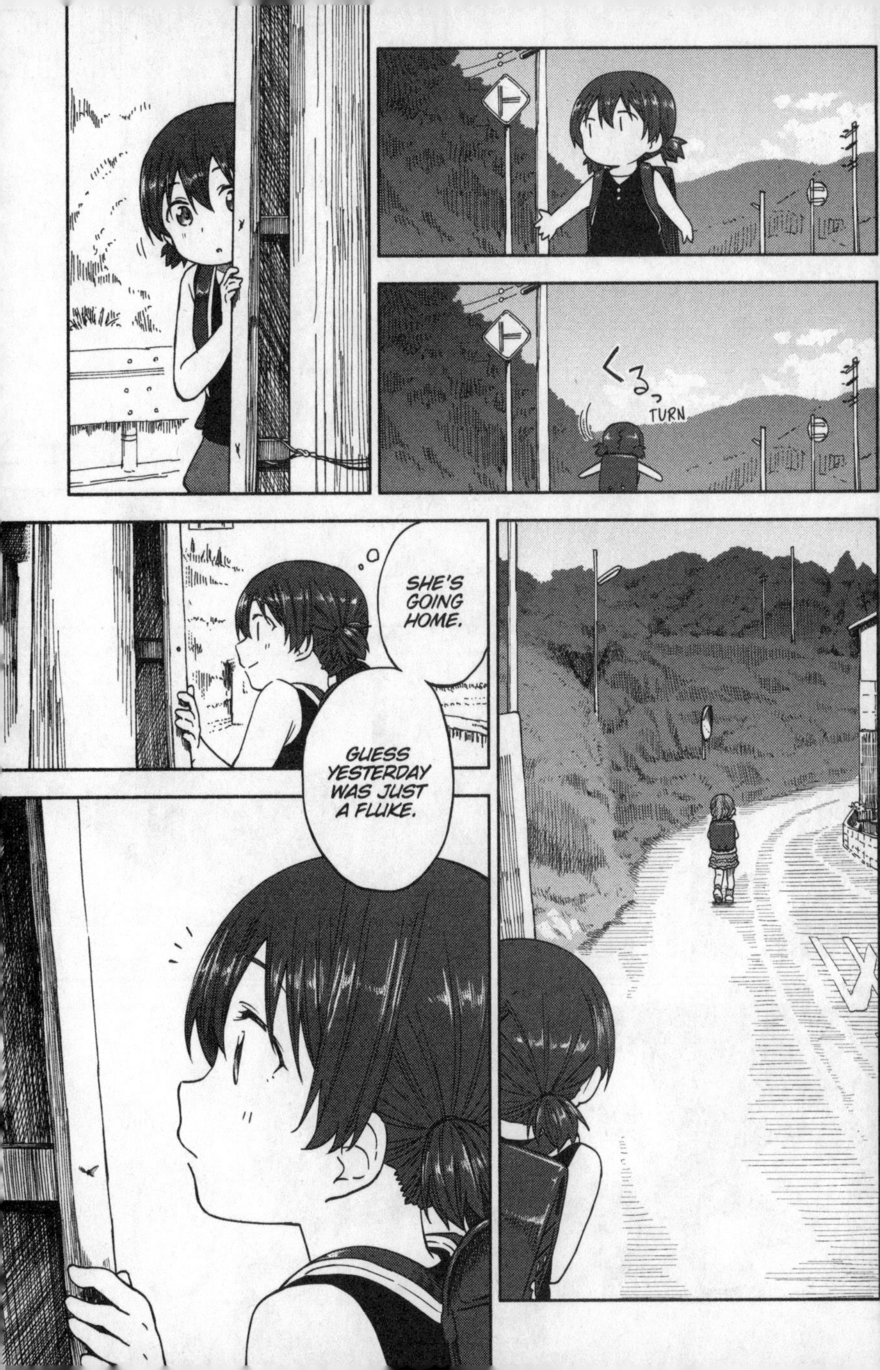
くるっ
TURN
SHE'S GOING HOME.
GUESS YESTERDAY WAS JUST A FLUKE.

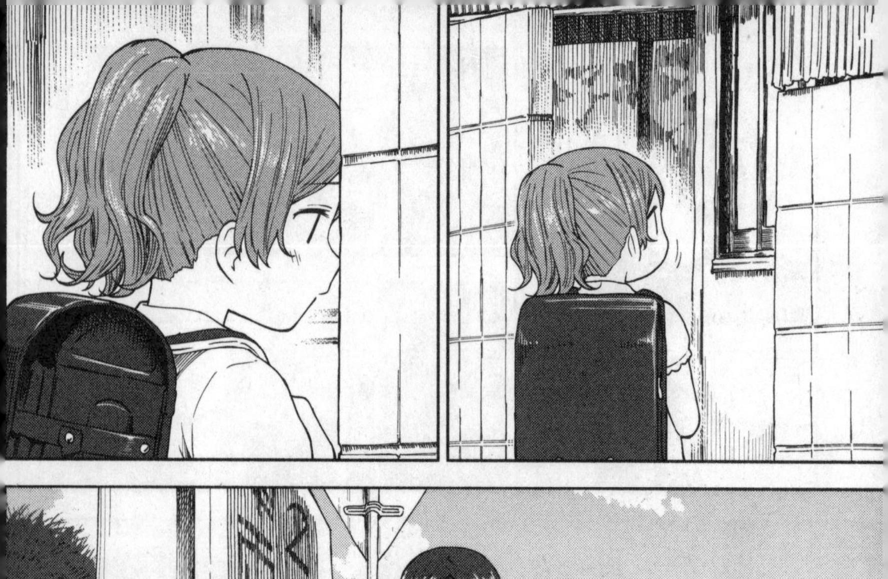

Sign: No Trucks over Two Tons

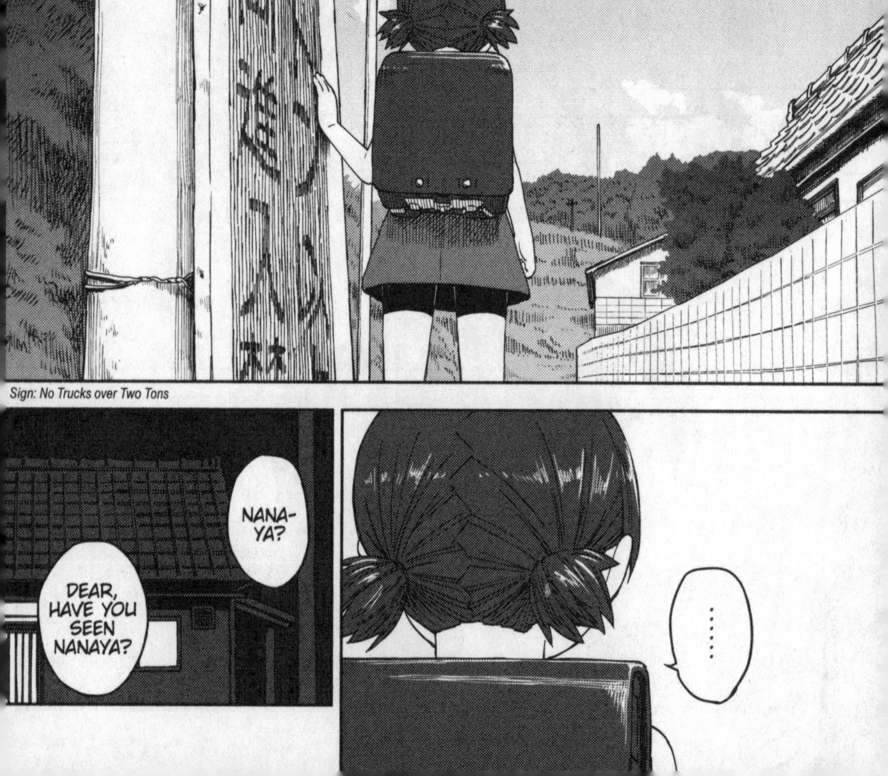
......
NANA-YA?
DEAR, HAVE YOU SEEN NANAYA?

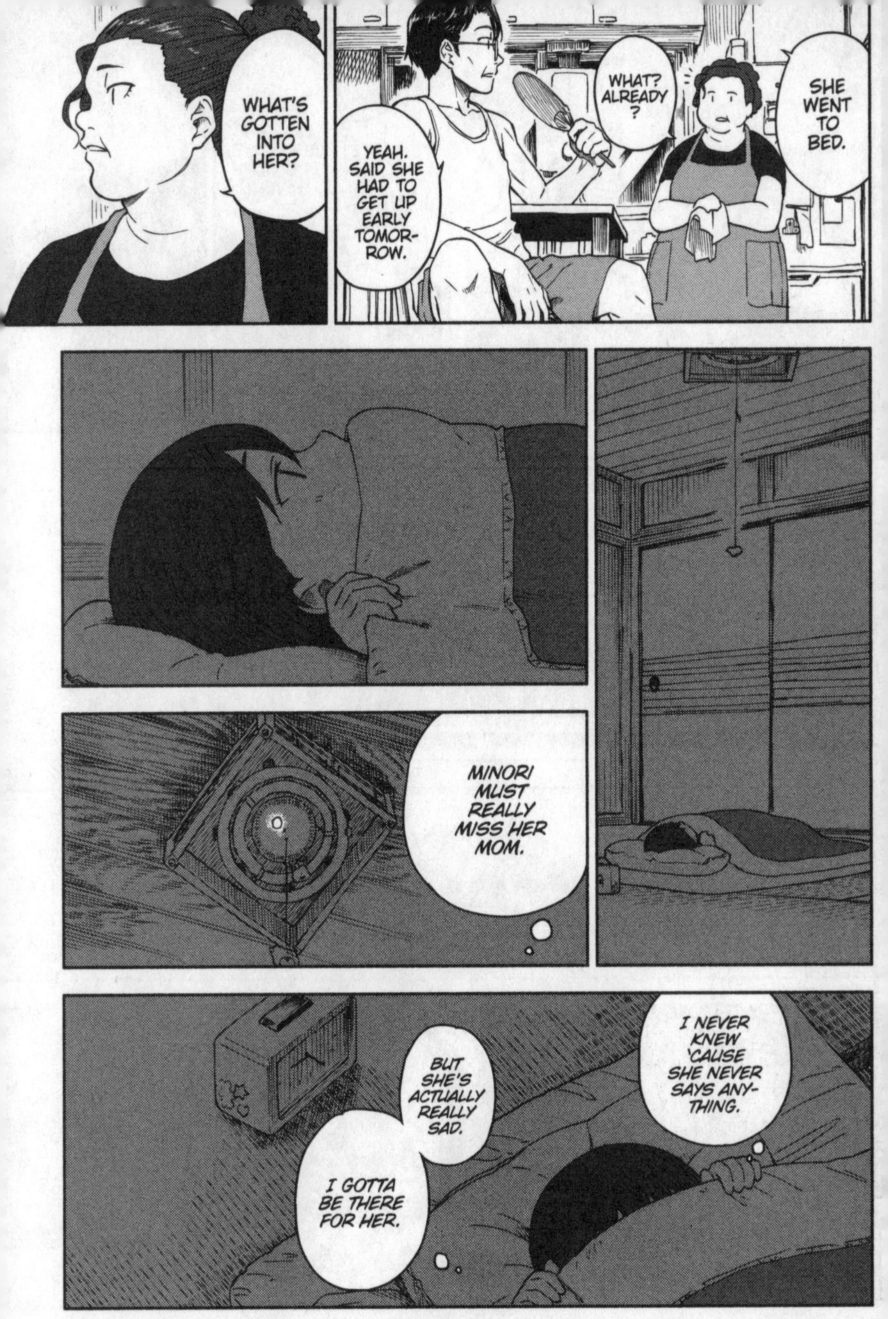
SHE WENT TO BED.
WHAT? ALREADY?
YEAH. SAID SHE HAD TO GET UP EARLY TOMORROW.
WHAT'S GOTTEN INTO HER?
MINORI MUST REALLY MISS HER MOM.
I NEVER KNEW 'CAUSE SHE NEVER SAYS ANYTHING.
BUT SHE'S ACTUALLY REALLY SAD.
I GOTTA BE THERE FOR HER.

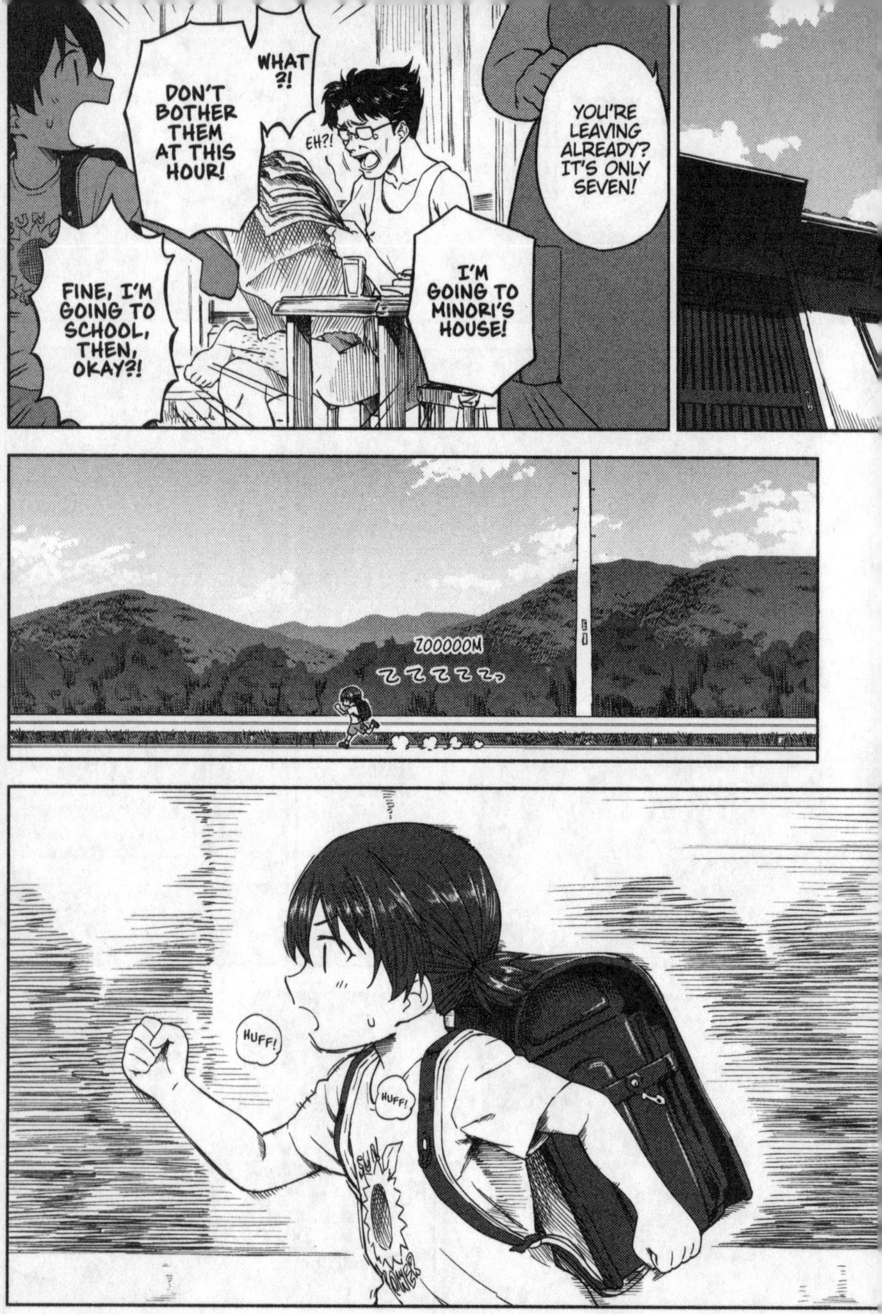
YOU'RE LEAVING ALREADY? IT'S ONLY SEVEN!
I'M GOING TO MINORI'S HOUSE!
WHAT?!
EH?!
DON'T BOTHER THEM AT THIS HOUR!
FINE, I'M GOING TO SCHOOL, THEN, OKAY?!
ZOOOOOM
HUFF!
HUFF!

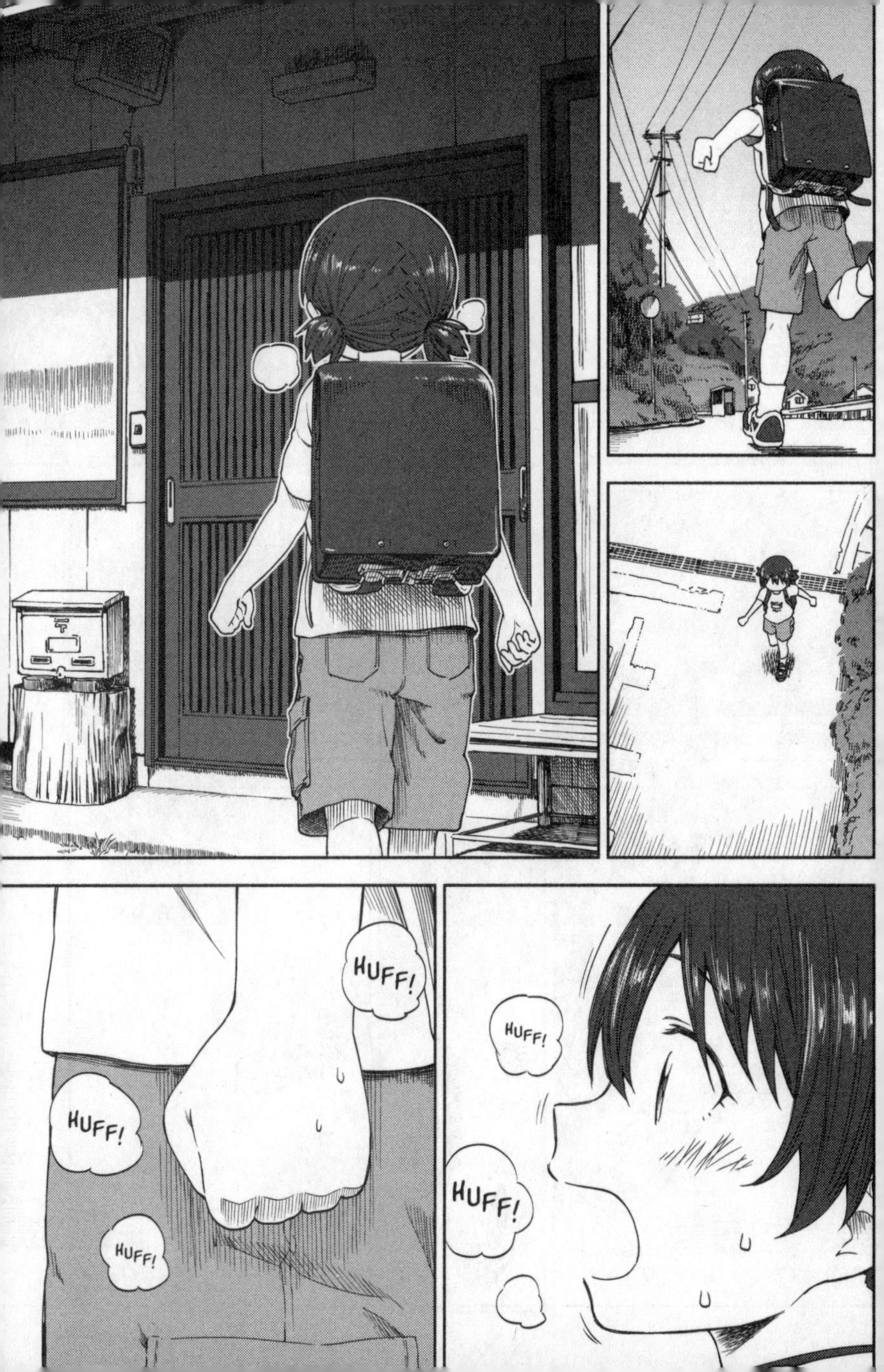
HUFF!
HUFF!
HUFF!
HUFF!
HUFF!

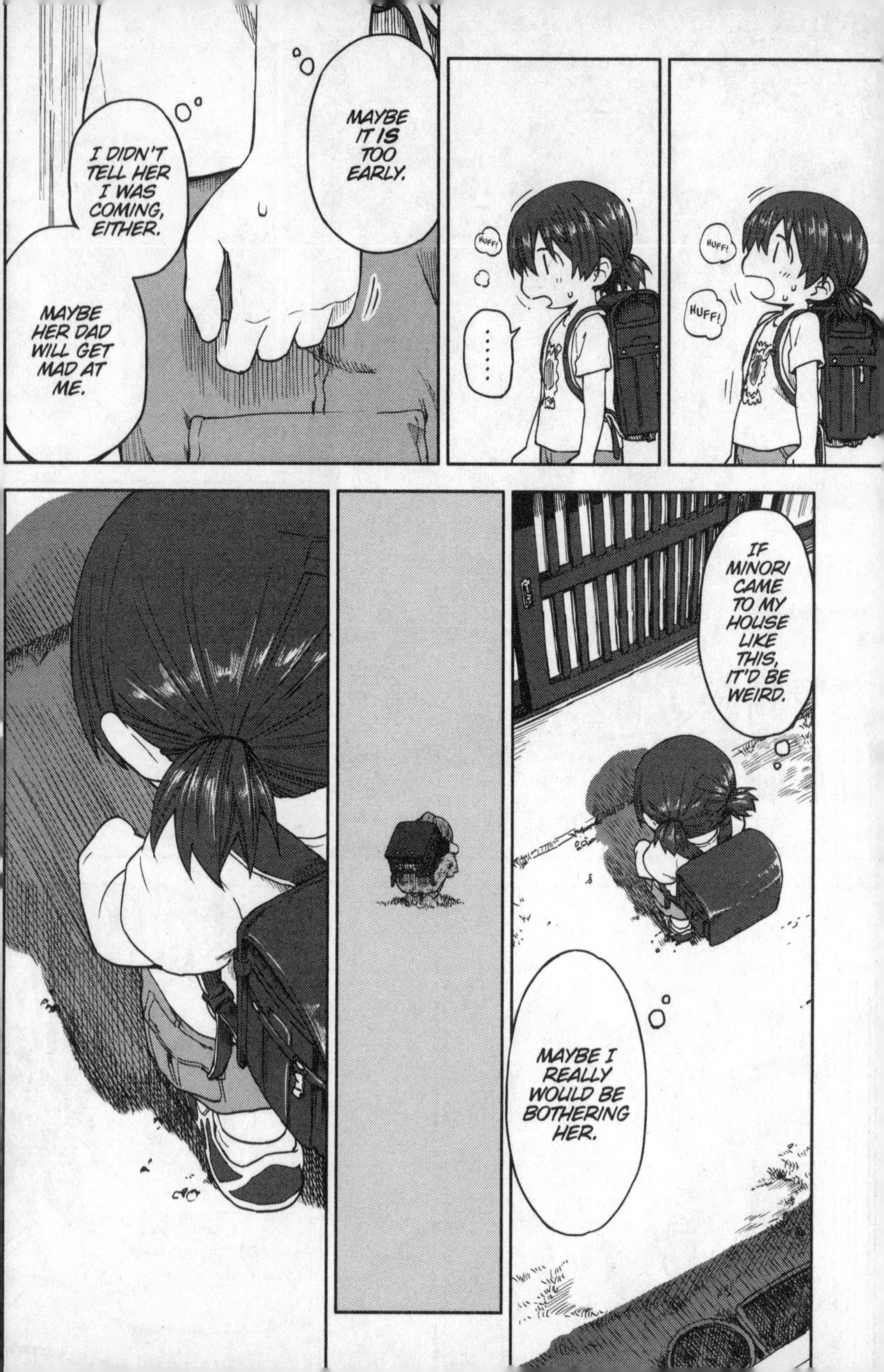
HUFF!
HUFF!
HUFF!
......
MAYBE IT IS TOO EARLY.
I DIDN'T TELL HER I WAS COMING, EITHER.
MAYBE HER DAD WILL GET MAD AT ME.
IF MINORI CAME TO MY HOUSE LIKE THIS, IT'D BE WEIRD.
MAYBE I REALLY WOULD BE BOTHERING HER.

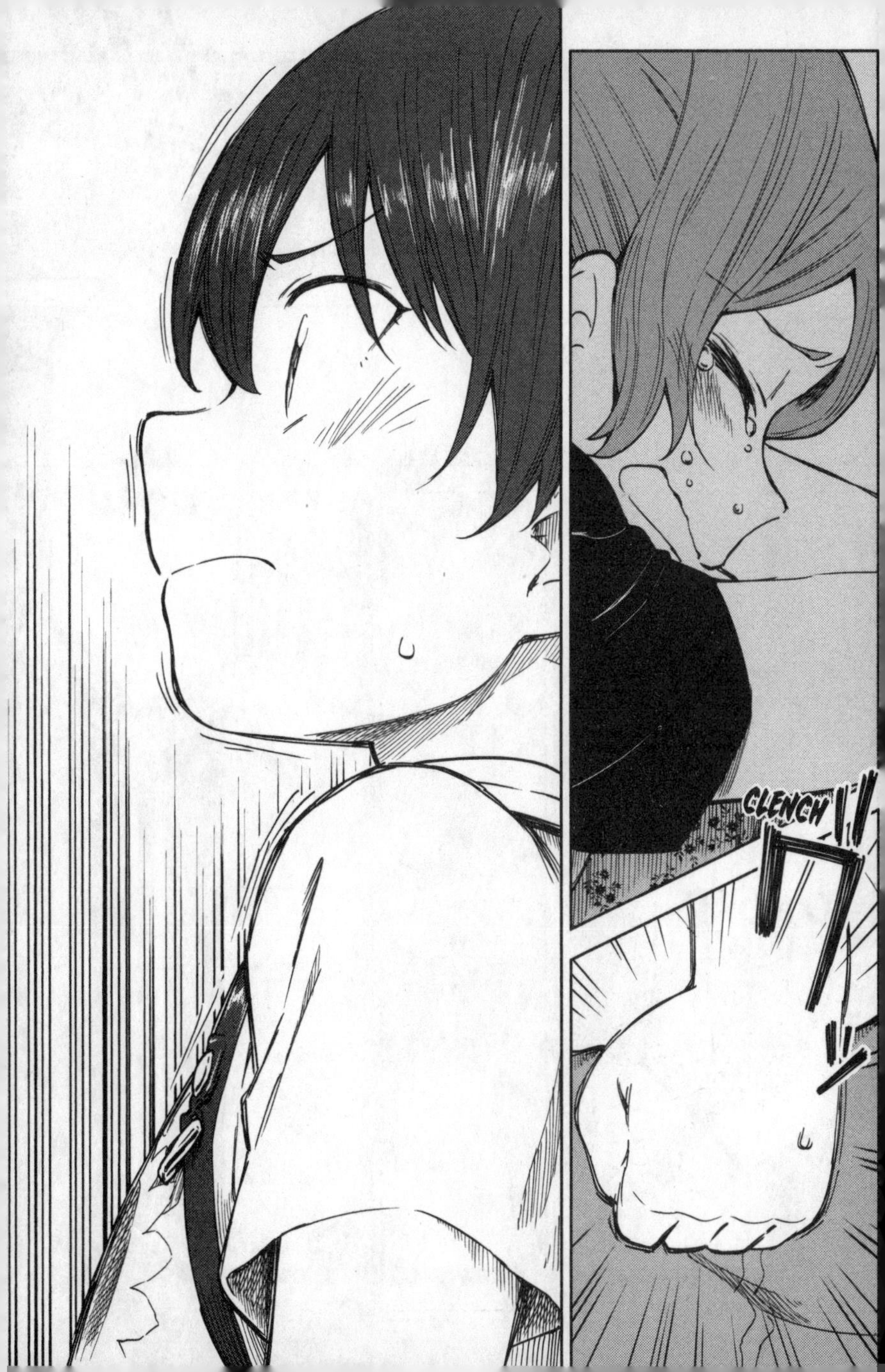
CLENCH

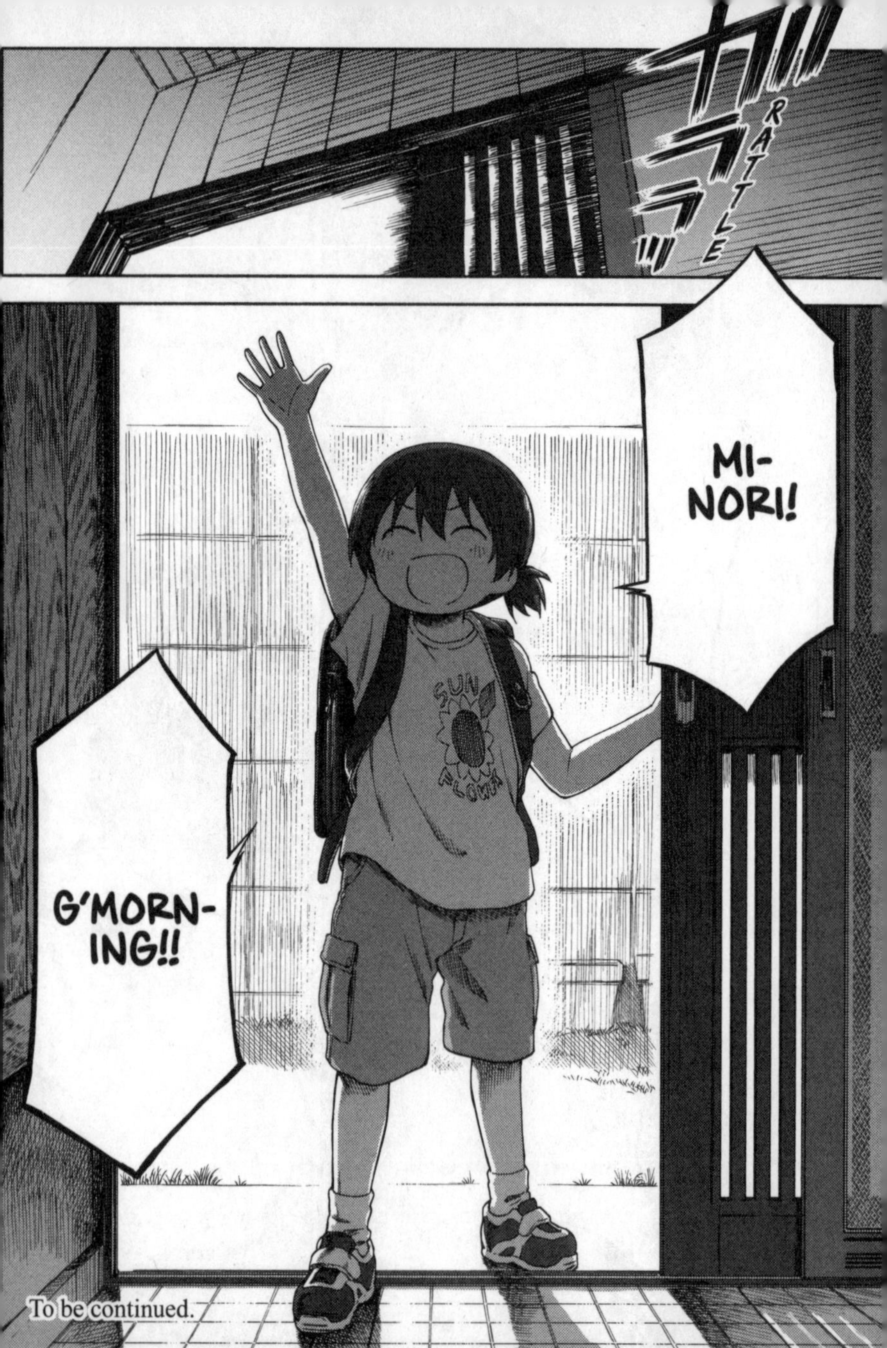
ガラッ
RATTLE
MI-NORI!
G'MORNING!!

To be continued.

SEE YOU IN THE
NEXT VOLUME.

Kei Hamuro

Our Wonderful Days Tsurezure Biyori

BONUS MANGA: COMING HOME FROM THE BEACH

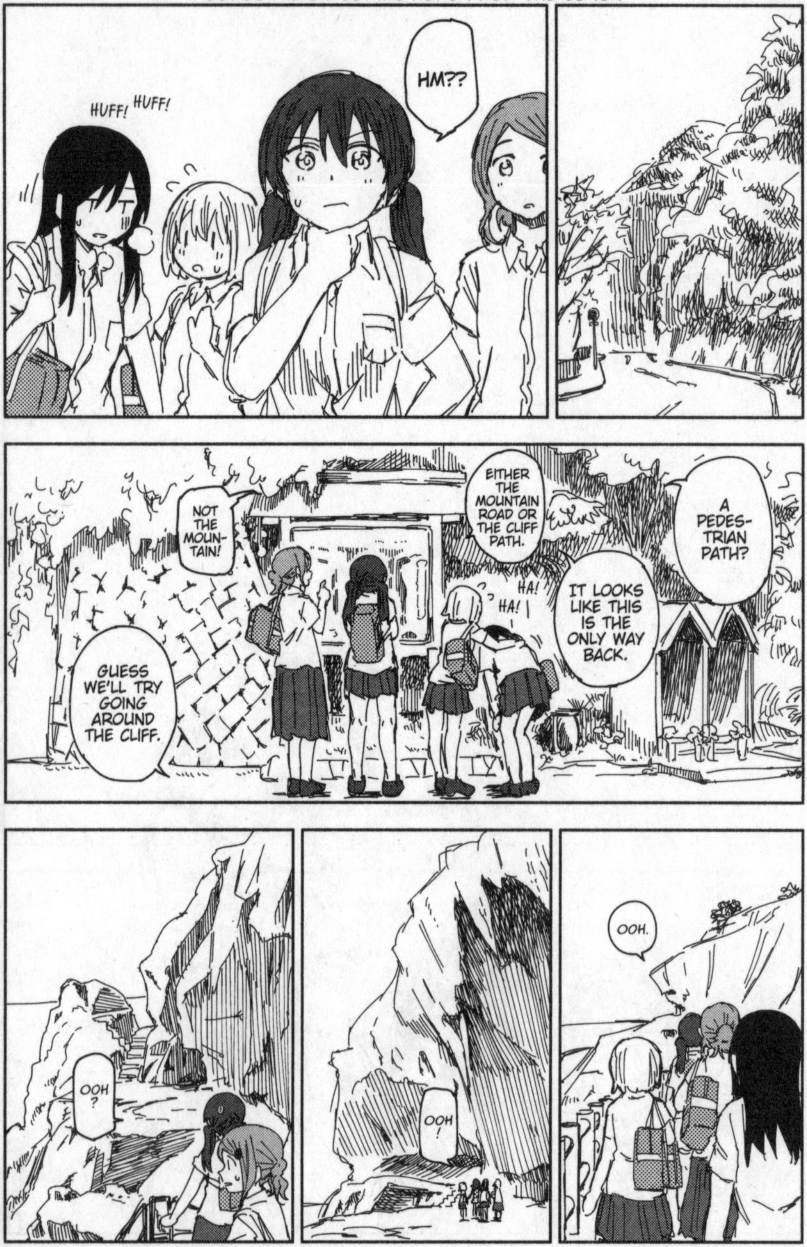
HM??
HUFF! HUFF!
A PEDES-TRIAN PATH?
IT LOOKS LIKE THIS IS THE ONLY WAY BACK.
HA! HA!
EITHER THE MOUNTAIN ROAD OR THE CLIFF PATH.
NOT THE MOUN-TAIN!
GUESS WE'LL TRY GOING AROUND THE CLIFF.
OOH.
OOH!
OOH?

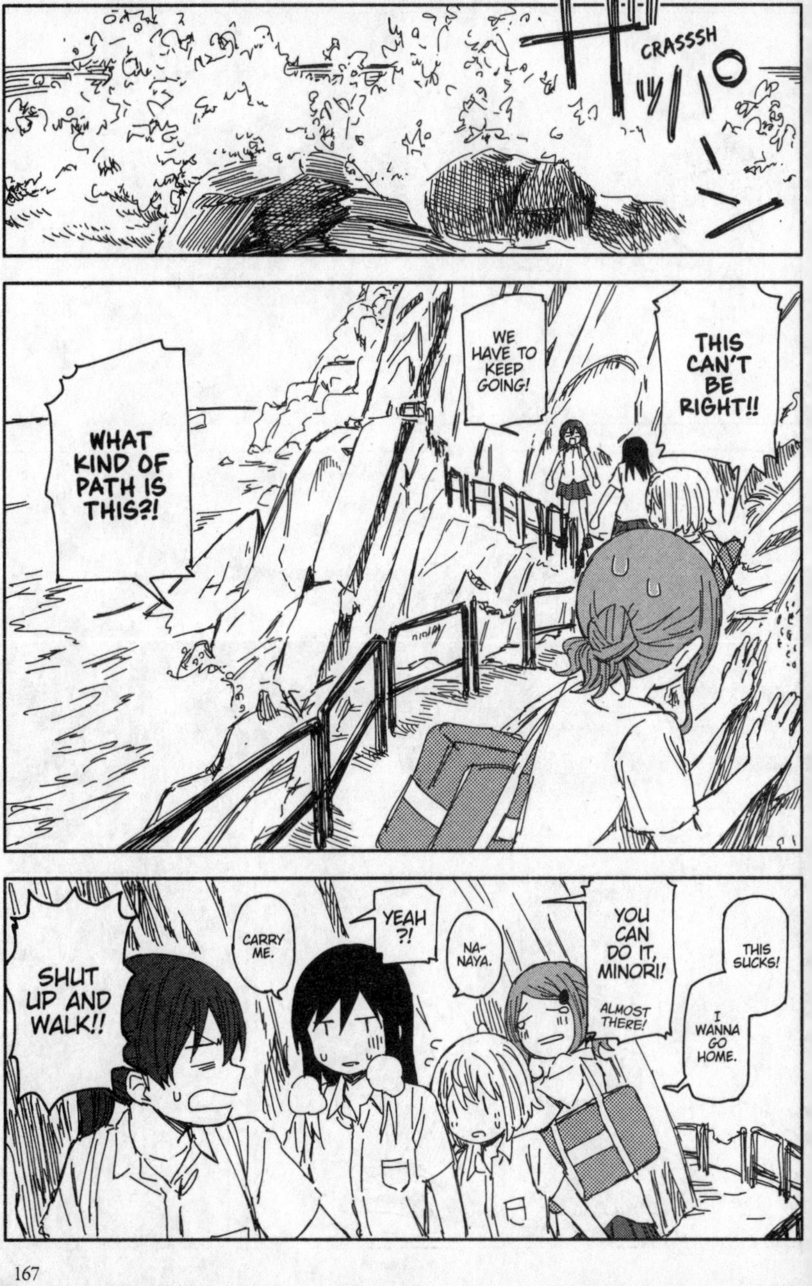
CRASSSH
THIS CAN'T BE RIGHT!!
WE HAVE TO KEEP GOING!
WHAT KIND OF PATH IS THIS?!
THIS SUCKS!
I WANNA GO HOME.
YOU CAN DO IT, MINORI!
ALMOST THERE!
NA-NAYA.
YEAH?!
CARRY ME.
SHUT UP AND WALK!!

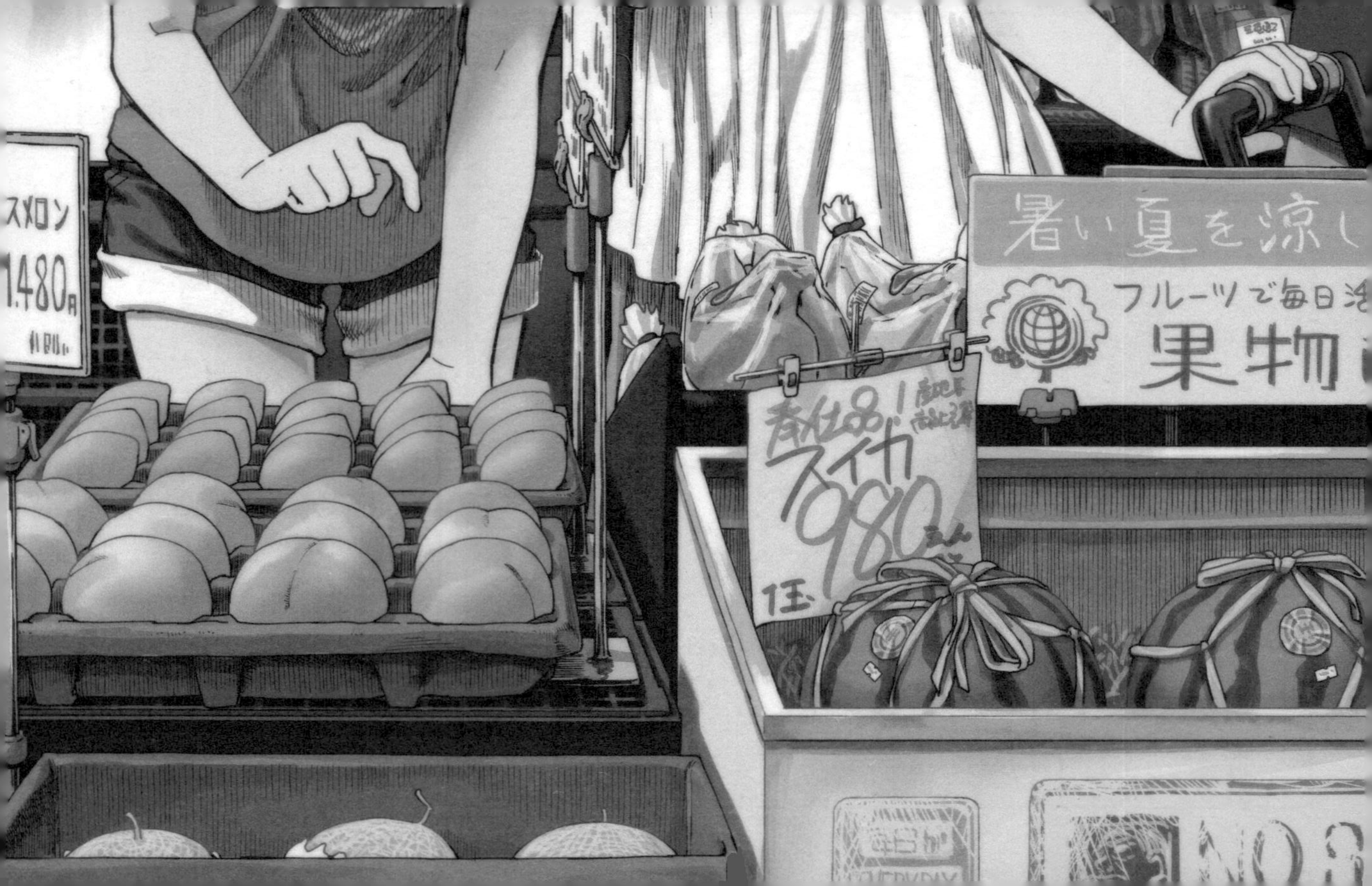
暑い夏を涼し
フルーツで毎日
果物
スイカ
980
スメロン
1.480円

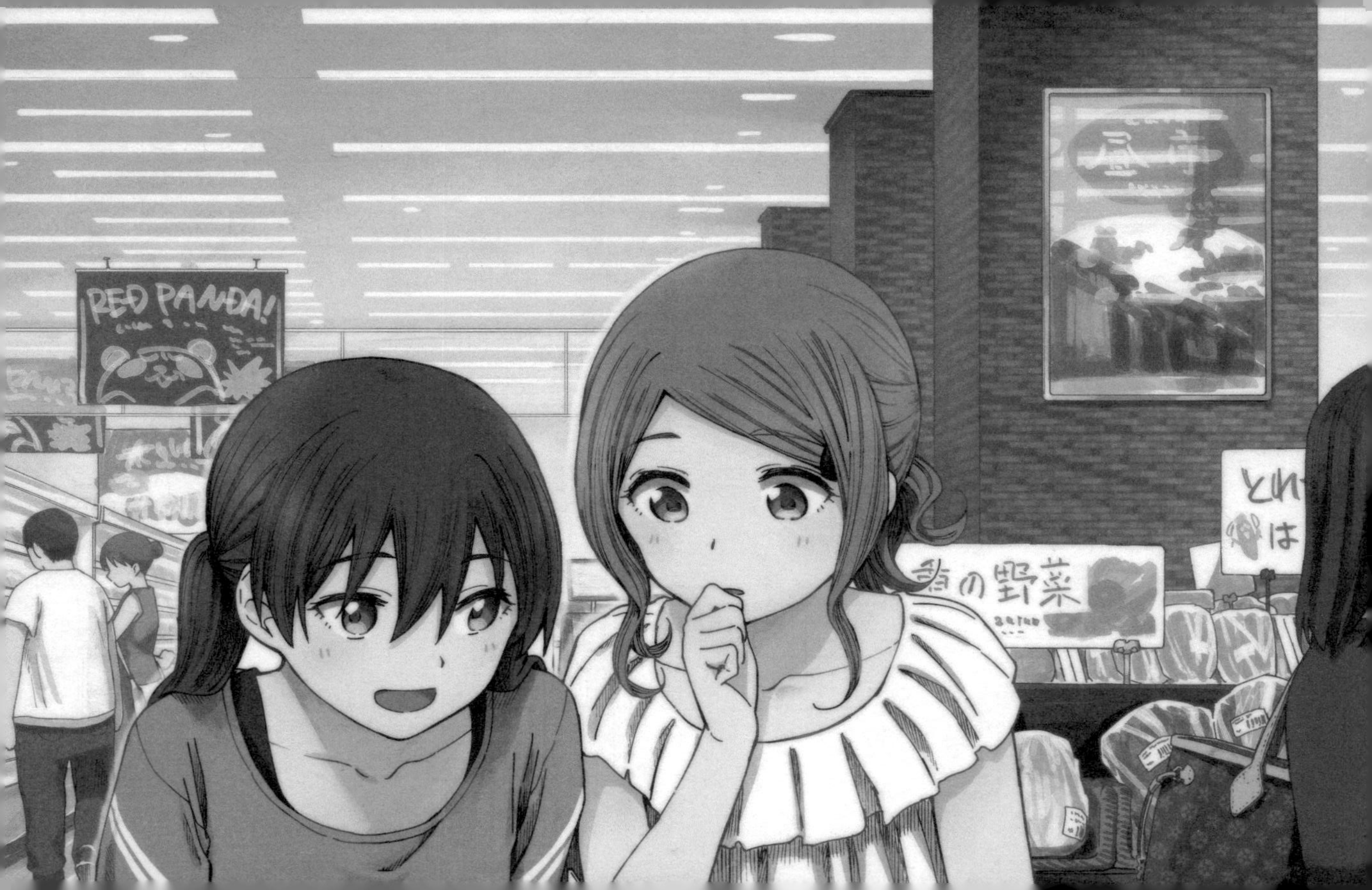
RED PANDA!
旬の野菜

Our Wonderful Days Tsurezure Biyori

SEVEN SEAS ENTERTAINMENT PRESENTS

Our Wonderful Days
Tsurezure Biyori

story and art by KEI HAMURO
VOLUME 2

TRANSLATION
Katrina Leonoudakis

ADAPTATION
Asha Bardon

LETTERING AND RETOUCH
Erika Terriquez

COVER DESIGN
Nicky Lim

PROOFREADER
Stephanie Cohen

EDITOR
Shannon Fay

PREPRESS TECHNICIAN
Rhiannon Rasmussen-Silverstein

PRODUCTION MANAGER
Lissa Pattillo

MANAGING EDITOR
Julie Davis

ASSOCIATE PUBLISHER
Adam Arnold

PUBLISHER
Jason DeAngelis

OUR WONDERFUL DAYS: TSUREZURE BIYORI VOL. 2
© KEI HAMURO 2019
First published in Japan in 2019 by ICHIJINSHA Inc., Tokyo.
English translation rights arranged with KODANSHA.

Seven Seas press and purchase enquiries can be sent to Marketing Manager
Lianne Sentar at press@gomanga.com. Information regarding the distribution
and purchase of digital editions is available from Digital Manager CK Russell
at digital@gomanga.com.

Seven Seas and the Seven Seas logo are trademarks of
Seven Seas Entertainment, LLC. All rights reserved.

ISBN: 978-1-64505-210-4

Printed in Canada

First Printing: February 2020

10 9 8 7 6 5 4 3 2 1

FOLLOW US ONLINE: www.sevenseasentertainment.com

READING DIRECTIONS

This book reads from *right to left*, Japanese style.
If this is your first time reading manga, you start
reading from the top right panel on each page and
take it from there. If you get lost, just follow the
numbered diagram here. It may seem backwards at
first, but you'll get the hang of it! Have fun!!

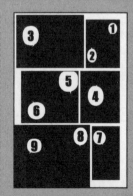